THE EVERY STUDENT
SUCCEEDS ACT

THE EDUCATIONAL INNOVATIONS SERIES

The Educational Innovations series explores a wide range of current school reform efforts. Individual volumes examine entrepreneurial efforts and unorthodox approaches, highlighting reforms that have met with success and strategies that have attracted widespread attention. The series aims to disrupt the status quo and inject new ideas into contemporary education debates.

Series edited by Frederick M. Hess

The Strategic Management of Charter Schools
by Peter Frumkin, Bruno V. Manno, and Nell Edgington

Customized Schooling
Edited by Frederick M. Hess and Bruno V. Manno

Bringing School Reform to Scale
by Heather Zavadsky

What Next?
Edited by Mary Cullinane and Frederick M. Hess

Between Public and Private
Edited by Katrina E. Bulkley, Jeffrey R. Henig, and Henry M. Levin

Stretching the School Dollar
Edited by Frederick M. Hess and Eric Osberg

School Turnarounds: The Essential Role of Districts
by Heather Zavadsky

Stretching the Higher Education Dollar
Edited by Andrew P. Kelly and Kevin Carey

Cage-Busting Leadership
by Frederick M. Hess

Teacher Quality 2.0: Toward a New Era in Education Reform
Edited by Frederick M. Hess and Michael Q. McShane

Reinventing Financial Aid: Charting a New Course to College Affordability
Edited by Andrew P. Kelly and Sara Goldrick-Rab

The Cage-Busting Teacher
by Frederick M. Hess

Failing Our Brightest Kids: The Global Challenge of Educating High-Ability Students
by Chester E. Finn, Jr. and Brandon L. Wright

The New Education Philanthropy: Politics, Policy, and Reform
Edited by Frederick M. Hess and Jeffrey R. Henig

Educational Entrepreneurship Today
Edited by Frederick M. Hess and Michael Q. McShane

Policy Patrons
by Megan E. Tompkins-Stange

The Convergence of K–12 and Higher Education: Polices and Programs in a Changing Era
Edited by Christopher P. Loss and Patrick J. McGuinn

THE EVERY STUDENT SUCCEEDS ACT

What It Means for Schools, Systems, and States

FREDERICK M. HESS
MAX EDEN

Editors

Harvard Education Press
Cambridge, Massachusetts

Paperback ISBN 978-1-68253-012-2
Library Edition ISBN 978-1-68253-013-9

Library of Congress Cataloging-in-Publication Data

Names: Hess, Frederick M., editor. | Eden, Max, editor.
Title: The Every Student Succeeds Act : what it means for schools, systems, and states / Frederick M. Hess, Max Eden, editors.
Other titles: Educational innovations.
Description: Cambridge, Massachusetts : Harvard Education Press, [2017] | Series: Educational innovation series | Includes bibliographical references and index.
Identifiers: LCCN 2016046037 | ISBN 9781682530122 (pbk.) | ISBN 9781682530139 (library edition)
Subjects: LCSH: United States. Every Student Succeeds Act. | Educational law and legislation--United States. | Educational accountability--Law and legislation--United States. | Federal aid to education--United States. | Education--Standards--United States. | Education and state--United States. | School improvement programs--United States.
Classification: LCC LB2806.22 .E95 2017 | DDC 379.1/580973--dc23 LC record available at https://lccn.loc.gov/2016046037

Published by Harvard Education Press,
an imprint of the Harvard Education Publishing Group

Harvard Education Press
8 Story Street
Cambridge, MA 02138

Cover Design: Wilcox Design
Cover Photo: Arthur Tilley/Getty Images
The typefaces used in this book are Minion Pro and Myriad Pro

Contents

Introduction

Frederick M. Hess and Max Eden

When President Barack Obama signed the Every Student Succeeds Act (ESSA) into law on December 10, 2015, he joked that it was "a Christmas miracle." Miracle or not, it was striking to see majorities in both political parties support a major piece of legislation in an era marked by gridlock and government shutdowns. Most experts thought that ESSA was a long shot, even just a few months before it passed.

For our part, we recall walking out of a meeting with Republican Senate Education Committee staffers, convinced that there wasn't a chance. We were both struck by their exasperation with the Obama administration's education agenda. Substance aside, they thought that the administration had played fast and loose with the traditional policy making process. Rather than press Congress to pass a law to replace No Child Left Behind (NCLB), the Obama administration used federal stimulus money to encourage states to accept its policy preferences and waivers from NCLB's penalties to ensure those policies were implemented. This wasn't the way separation of powers was supposed to work. Republicans had little faith that the Obama administration would abandon its strong-arm tactics and let Congress settle these questions by legislation.

Staffers at the Department of Education, however, saw things quite differently. They insisted that they'd love to see Congress replace NCLB, but believed that unprecedented Republican obstructionism made that a distant prospect. So, until then, they had a duty to use the levers they had to try to improve American education.

While this level of polarization has become increasingly common in Washington, DC, until recently education had always been a bipartisan issue, in part because it was traditionally the preserve of the states. But in an effort to rectify long-standing inequalities, federal involvement expanded slowly during the second half of the twentieth century, culminating in 2001 with the bipartisan passage of NCLB.

In the years after NCLB, the center of gravity in education policy shifted from the states to Washington. This made education more of a national political issue, and hence a more polarizing one. The divisions were stark, but they didn't quite hew to traditional partisan lines. An alliance between civil rights groups on the left and the business community on the right pushed for aggressive federal involvement to drive policies designed to aid disadvantaged students. But under the Obama administration, another left-right alliance—between teacher unions and small-government conservatives—became ascendant. The unions argued that high-stakes standardized testing and teacher evaluation were harming teacher morale and undermining the quality of public education; conservatives argued that the administration had far exceeded its authority and was pushing policies without the consent of the governed. The latter alliance held sway in Congress, and the Every Student Succeeds Act was deemed by the *Wall Street Journal* as "the largest devolution of federal control to the states in a quarter century."[1] These political trends had real consequences for schools, teachers, and students, and ESSA was a response to all of that.

So, what exactly is ESSA and what does it do? ESSA is the latest reauthorization of the Elementary and Secondary Education Act (ESEA), passed by Lyndon B. Johnson in 1965. ESSA has ten "Titles" dealing with matters ranging from teacher quality to Native American education. The most important of these is Title I, which is devoted to "improving basic programs operated by state and local education agencies." Today, Title I distributes about $16 billion annually to schools with high concentrations of low-income students. The question at the heart of federal education policy is what the federal government ought to require to ensure that the money is well spent.

In the 2001 reauthorization of ESEA as the No Child Left Behind Act, states were required to test students in grades 3–8 and disaggregate results based on student characteristics to make achievement gaps visible. Schools that failed to make "Adequate Yearly Progress" toward mandated proficiency levels would face a standard set of school interventions. Under the Obama administration, the federal government used carrots and sticks to encourage states to adopt new academic standards and test-based teacher evaluation systems.

ESSA maintained the broad contours of NCLB, but gave states more flexibility within them. It maintained the basic federal testing requirement, but gave states leeway to help address concerns about "overtesting." ESSA removed NCLB's across-the-board school accountability system, allowing states the flexibility to identify and remedy low performing schools. ESSA also gave state leaders significantly more autonomy to set policy on other questions, such as teacher evaluation, diminishing the federal government's influence over state policy.

This sprawling law will have significant (if indirect and often unobserved) effects on the nation's schools and classrooms. This volume explores what those effects will be and what ESSA will mean for American education. Does it effectively address the concerns that bedeviled NCLB? What specifically does and doesn't change under the new law? Does ESSA mark an unfortunate retreat from the insistence that schools adequately serve all students, or might it unlock a new wave of educational innovation, driving meaningful improvements for our nation's students? Or when all is said and done, might there not be so much difference after all?

To be clear, this book does not provide a how-to manual for ESSA implementation. Rather, we've assembled a team of expert scholars and observers to provide a coherent, readable, and in-depth account of where ESSA came from, what it says, what will or won't change, and what it all means for schools. The contributors examine what ESSA means for state policy and for urban education. We hope that it will prove useful for those striving to make sense of the American education landscape.

THE TENSION BETWEEN LOCAL CONTROL AND EQUAL PROTECTION

All the talk about federal versus state power in education strikes a lot of people as beside the point. After all, shouldn't education policy just be about the kids? At best, debates about the federal role can sound like abstruse technical arguments among Washington insiders. At worst, they can sound like politicians using thinly veiled partisan rhetoric to jockey for more power. But the truth is that this debate actually gets to the core of who we are as a nation. An easy shorthand is to think of this debate as the tension between the Tenth and Fourteenth Amendments to the US Constitution.

There is no mention of public schooling in the Constitution. But it's not as though the Founding Fathers didn't think an educated citizenry was essential. In fact, they saw it as a foundational responsibility of any government and determined that it was best left to the states under the Tenth Amendment, which says, "The powers not delegated to the United States by the Constitution, nor prohibited by it to the States, are reserved to the States respectively, or to the people."

The Tenth Amendment intuition is that education cannot be exclusively provided by the government; it must begin with families and spread outward to neighborhoods, religious communities, civic associations, schools, and towns. Adherents of the Tenth Amendment are skeptical that the federal government, so far removed from the fundamental acts of teaching and learning, is well suited to write laws and regulations governing how one hundred thousand schools educate more than fifty million students. More to the point, they worry that well-intentioned policies may, in practice, crowd out and erode the fundamental elements of a quality school.

At the same time, there is the very real concern that, left to their own devices, districts and states might not serve all students equally well. In fact, for generations states did little to rectify palpable, basic inequalities in education. Many people believe that the federal government ought to play a strong role to make good on the promise of the Fourteenth Amendment, that the government shall not "deny to any person within its jurisdiction the equal protection of the laws." Adherents of the Fourteenth Amendment believe that the federal government has a duty to ensure fairness by directing funds to underresourced communities and holding states accountable for the performance of all students.

Though they are often in tension, both intuitions are deeply rooted in the American experience. The balance between liberty and opportunity is at the core of who we are as a nation and comes up in many, if not all, political issues. In education policy, it's been at the forefront of debates for the past half-century.

FROM ESEA TO NCLB

In 1965, nearly one hundred years after the conclusion of the Civil War, Congress passed ESEA in an effort to break the cycle of intergenerational poverty by directing federal funds to schools that served high concentrations of low-income children. President Johnson had high hopes, declaring that "by passing this bill, we bridge the gap between helplessness and hope."

Unfortunately, it wasn't that easy. ESEA faced an extraordinary challenge: attempting to reform a system that had been carefully designed to impede centralized power. The tradition of local governance was deeply rooted, and pumping federal funding into the system was no guarantee that anything would change. Indeed, four years after ESEA was passed, a landmark study found that Title I had often "not reached the eligible [students], and has been little used to meet their needs."[2] Federal policy makers were disappointed that districts often used Title I funds for their own purposes rather than for the betterment of low-income students. However, they had few useful levers to change that.

In response, policy makers attached more strings to Title I money to try to ensure effective implementation. But those rules and regulations came at a cost. They inhibited district and school flexibility and increasingly transformed local school governance into a compliance exercise. The financial and educational costs were difficult to gauge, but stories bubbled up about teachers who were afraid to use Title I staplers on essays by non–Title I students and Title I staff who wouldn't break up playground fights between Title I and non–Title I students due to liability concerns. As Patrick McGuinn will cover in more detail in chapter 1, perhaps the most significant consequence of ESEA in the latter half of the twentieth century was the bureaucratization and centralization of education policy.

Meanwhile, one glaring problem lingered for decades. It was first raised publicly not by a conservative, but by liberal firebrand Robert F. Kennedy, then a Democratic senator from New York: how could we know whether the federal funding was making a difference? By and large, the state-level testing not only failed to report results disaggregated by race and class, but often wasn't even administered to low performing students. State testing reports often resembled dispatches from Garrison Keillor's fabled Lake Wobegon, where all the children are above average.

While it wasn't clear where federal efforts were making significant headway, a handful of states launched initiatives to try to raise achievement and address inequities. In what became known as the "excellence movement," states like Massachusetts, North Carolina, and Virginia took steps to raise and refine academic standards and introduce more reliable standardized testing. One of the most notable "laboratories of democracy" was Texas, where governors on both sides of the aisle pursued a reform agenda, starting in the early 1980s, centered on higher academic standards, standardized testing, school accountability, competition, and choice. One Republican governor, George W. Bush, went on to run for president in 2001 while promising to be an "education president" and take the "Texas model" national. His signature domestic policy initiative would have made LBJ smile, as NCLB extended ESEA and infused it with an even grander ambition.

No Child Left Behind put the federal government firmly in the driver's seat to expand and enforce state education reform. As mentioned previously, it mandated that states test students in grades 3–8 in reading and math and report disaggregated results. It also required that all schools make Adequate Yearly Progress (AYP) to 100 percent proficiency in reading and math by 2014 and prescribed specific interventions for schools that failed to make AYP.

NCLB's aspirations made for good politics, and the law passed by overwhelming bipartisan margins. After all, no one wanted to argue that *some* children should be left behind. But its complex reality proved to be less appealing. The emphasis on reporting disaggregated data and closing racial achievement gaps earned plaudits from the civil rights and business communities, but the school accountability system fostered friction and discontent. Scores on the National Assessment of Educational Progress, the gold standard in measuring educational achievement, inched up slightly through the Bush administration, but NCLB was far from a magic bullet.

In fact, the more parents learned about NCLB, the less they liked it. In 2003, about a third of Americans said that they knew enough to form an opinion of NCLB, and almost two-thirds expressed a favorable opinion. By 2007, three-quarters of Americans said that they knew enough to form an opinion, but only about 40 percent approved of the law.[3] Parents worried that the drive to increase performance on state tests came at the cost of an ever-narrowing curriculum and that the focus on getting the "bubble kids" from slightly below proficient to slightly above proficient came at the cost of teaching kids who were way behind or ahead. By the time Bush left office in January 2009, NCLB had turned from a shining bipartisan achievement to a tarnished bipartisan albatross; Republicans and Democrats were both discontented, but they couldn't agree on how to fix it.

THE PATH TO ESSA

Bush's successor, former Illinois senator Barack Obama, campaigned for president on the promise to be a pragmatic "postpartisan" who would change business as usual and focus on doing "what works." The Obama administration earmarked a portion of money from the American Recovery and Reinvestment Act for an initiative called Race to the Top. States submitted policy plans to the Department of Education, promising to adopt the priorities set by the secretary of education around college- and career-ready standards, test-based teacher evaluation, charter schooling, and more. At first, this approach received bipartisan approbation. David Brooks, a right-leaning columnist at the *New York Times*, wrote, "Obama's activism isn't overbearing. It's catalytic. The administration hasn't defeated the forces of the status quo, but in state after state, you're seeing reformers moving forward."[4]

But the applause eventually gave way to grumbling. The stimulus money ran out and, as 2014 drew closer, more and more schools became subject to federal sanctions for failing to meet NCLB's goal of 100 percent proficiency. So the Obama administration offered states a deal: it would grant states "waiver" relief from NCLB sanctions if they stuck with the program on education policy.

Supporters credited Secretary of Education Arne Duncan with advancing good policies in the face of congressional inaction. But detractors saw NCLB waivers as an executive overreach without any statutory basis. For example, Senator Lamar Alexander (R-TN), chairman of the Senate Education Committee and a former secretary of education himself, decried the transformation of the Department of Education into a "national school board." On the right, the Common Core, or "Obamacore" as it was often called, became a *bête noire* to conservative activists. On the left, teacher unions fretted that the teacher evaluation systems the federal government was pushing weren't ready for primetime and would lead to perverse consequences in the classroom.

As Alyson Klein will explain in chapter 3, this bipartisan backlash created a window of opportunity for major legislation. For all the noble aspirations that fueled the decades-long drive toward greater federal involvement, the friction and frustration created as Fourteenth Amendment hopes crashed into Tenth Amendment realities paved the way for the Every Student Succeeds Act.

Some critics worried that ESSA was an unfortunate retreat from the ideals of equal protection and educational equity. Others fretted that it didn't go far enough in returning authority to states and communities. But ultimately, American education will always be a balancing act between the principles of the Tenth Amendment and the Fourteenth Amendment, and ESSA's supporters argued that it struck a healthy and stable balance. Senator Alexander declared, "We've got a law that will govern the federal role in K–12 education for ten or twenty years" and "unleash a whole flood of innovation and ingenuity, classroom by classroom, state by state, that will benefit children."[5]

WHAT DOES ESSA MEAN FOR SCHOOLS AND STATES?

Does ESSA get the federal role right? It will take years before the dust settles and we can get a handle on its impact, and it's highly unlikely that everyone will be satisfied for long. But, for now, we feel prepared to offer three takeaways to help educators and policy makers navigate the law.

First, you don't have to dive into ESSA's fine print to understand it. The text itself is confusing and sprawling, and people working in schools and systems generally have better things to do than read federal statute. But you should have an understanding of the basics—of what's settled and what's open for input. There will be plenty of enthusiastic policy wonks saying that ESSA means you have to do this or that. If you come to the table with the basics in mind, you'll be prepared to engage in the conversation rather than be overwhelmed by it.

Second, what you as a teacher, administrator, or policy maker bring to that conversation should be of a distinctly different character than what you might be accustomed to. More often than not, in the era of No Child Left Behind and its waivers, education policy became an exercise in compliance. You did what you were told; if you wanted to try something new, you had to ask, "May I?" The theory behind ESSA is that schools and systems can be better governed from the bottom up than from the top down. So the sooner you shift your mentality from asking, "May I?" to asking, "*How* can we?" the sooner you'll stop being shaped by your environment and start actually shaping it.

Third, much is up in the air and nothing is guaranteed. As you read the chapters ahead, you may be struck (as we were) by the mix of cautious optimism and lingering doubt. ESSA has the potential to foster significant improvements in schooling, but only where and when educators and administrators take advantage of it. Some states and schools will leap forward; others will lag behind. Ultimately, it will work only as well as the people in schools, communities, and states manage to make it work.

PLAN OF THE BOOK

Our hope is that this volume will equip you to understand what ESSA means and how to make the most of it. With that in mind, here is a brief roadmap for the chapters ahead. The book is arranged in four parts.

The first section takes the reader on a bit of a whirlwind tour of the fifty years from the passage of ESEA to ESSA. In chapter 1, Drew University political scientist Patrick McGuinn surveys the first thirty-five years of ESEA, explaining how high hopes for federal involvement were repeatedly frustrated by the realities and complexities of our education system, and how federal strategies to foster educational improvement have shifted. In chapter 2, Teachers College–Columbia University professor of political science and education Jeffrey R. Henig, along with colleagues David M. Houston and Melissa Arnold Lyon, shows how politics reasserted itself between NCLB and ESSA and how an issue many hoped would be postpartisan was actually anything but. In chapter 3, Alyson Klein, a veteran reporter and the author of *Education Week*'s popular *Politics K–12* blog, provides you with a front-row seat to the ins and outs and ups and downs of the legislative drama around ESSA.

The second section explains what ESSA actually says and does and offers the case for and against the wisdom of the law. In chapter 4, veteran Capitol Hill staffer and director of Democrats for Education Reform Charles Barone makes plain sense of the law. He explains what's changed and what hasn't, and what the new provisions around preschool, school accountability, and the rest actually say and mean. In chapter 5, Martin West, a professor of education at the Harvard Graduate School of Education who helped draft ESSA during a stint as senior education policy advisor to Senator Alexander, argues that the law strikes the proper balance for our federalist system. In chapter 6, Chad Aldeman, an associate partner at Bellwether Education Partners and a former official in the Obama Department of Education, contends that ESSA asks too little of states, and states are likely to disappoint without pressure from the federal government.

The third section explores what ESSA means for states and districts. In chapter 7, Lawrence University professor of government Arnold F. Shober discusses the administrative challenges states face, asking whether states are technically competent or politically positioned to make the most of the opportunity. In chapter 8, Ashley Jochim, a research analyst at the Center on Reinventing Public Education, discusses how ESSA will shape state policy around assessments, accountability, teacher evaluation, and more. And, in chapter 9, Michael Casserly, the executive director of the Council of Great City Schools, writes about what ESSA means for major urban districts.

The book concludes by taking a step back and offering two peerless policy thinkers an opportunity to put it all in perspective. Cynthia G. Brown, of the Center for American Progress, and Chester E. Finn, Jr., of the Thomas B. Fordham Institute, have spent decades on the front lines of the debates over school reform and federal policy from opposite ends of the political spectrum. They will reflect on how ESSA fits into the decades they've spent working on federal education policy. The exchange will also showcase how intelligent, thoughtful experts can approach the same question and reach differing conclusions.

CONCLUDING THOUGHTS

Before wrapping up the introduction, we'd like to leave you with two parting thoughts.

We began by talking about politics rather than education—and frustrating, gridlocked politics, at that. NCLB was supposed to be reauthorized in 2007, but it took almost another decade for Congress to pass ESSA. It's easy to think that Congress was doing nothing and that partisan posturing and bickering was preventing real policy change, but beneath the surface there was a whole lot more going on. Schools, districts, and states were wrestling with conflicting policies and priorities; the right path forward wasn't always clear. But over time, a bottom-up consensus emerged that federal policy should move toward a more restrained approach, and that approach was eventually enacted into law as ESSA.

What might appear to be a story of Congress "not working" can actually be seen as a story of Congress working exactly as it is supposed to, finding agreement on a major issue in a big, diverse, and complicated nation.

The tension that Congress was trying to navigate was no small issue. It's easy for those who view the federal role as indispensable to protecting disadvantaged students to dismiss the concerns of those who think education should be a local endeavor, and vice versa. But both views have their virtues and drawbacks. The intuition that schools are best governed as close as possible to the students they serve is well grounded. So, too, is the fear that without strong federal oversight, local communities will leave the most vulnerable students behind. Both principles are essential, even if they are often in tension.

The Every Student Succeeds Act is the latest attempt to find a balance between the principles of the Tenth and Fourteenth Amendments. We hope that this book will help relate how these lofty, abstract arguments will play out as this new federal law filters its way down through states and districts to the schoolhouse. And it's our humble hope that by helping to equip educators, school leaders, and students of education policy with a firm understanding of what's possible under ESSA, we might be doing our small part to help make good on its promise.

From ESEA to NCLB

*The Growth of the Federal Role and
the Shift to Accountability*

Patrick McGuinn

The Every Student Succeeds Act of 2015 (ESSA) is the latest reauthorization of the Elementary and Secondary Education Act of 1965 (ESEA). Therefore, to understand ESSA, we must first look backward and place it in the broader historical context of federal education policy.

The United States is unusual. In most countries, policy making is centralized in the hands of a single national leader, but the United States divides policy making between the federal and state levels and across legislative and executive branches. Our decentralized system of policy making is intended to prevent any one political actor from consolidating too much power. America also has a particularly strong historical attachment to local control in the area of education. The word *education* does not appear anywhere in the US Constitution, and there was very little federal (or even state) involvement in schools until the second half of the twentieth century. As a result, schools in America evolved over time from the ground up by a process of local competition and organic growth. So, rather than a single national education system, as is found in most other nations around the world, we have fifty distinct state education systems with widely divergent policies and outcomes.

NATIONAL GOALS FOR LOCAL SYSTEMS

Since the 1950s, however, US policy makers have articulated three major arguments for increased federal involvement in education: racial (fixing the legacy of racial injustice), national security (promoting defense research), and economic (alleviating poverty). Each of these rationales mutated over time but continued to provide a justification for federal expansion. The racial rationale shifted under George W. Bush from integration and racial access to racial achievement. The national security rationale was redoubled with the 1983 report *A Nation at Risk*, which gave Americans the sense that education wasn't merely a tool for national defense, but for a broader national competitiveness in the global marketplace. The economic rationale, meanwhile, seems to have shifted under the Clinton administration, moving from an antipoverty issue to an economic growth imperative.

But the federal government has had to rely on indirect levers of influence to prod states to reform their schools and embrace national goals. The primary tool for federal policy makers has been the grant-in-aid system— or more simply, money. States are always eager to accept federal education funding—which has grown dramatically over time—and generally willing to accept the strings that come with it. America's strong tradition of local control, however, has meant continued resistance to the expansion of federal authority. The result has been an increasingly contentious relationship between the growing ambitions of federal education policy, the willingness of state officials to accept it, and the ability of educators to implement it. This has led to a cyclical dynamic of federal education policy expansion and retrenchment, as will be described in the rest of this chapter.

During the 1950s and 1960s the country underwent a conceptual realignment as it started thinking about education in national terms for the first time. This was followed by a period of expansion and friction (1965–1980) when federal involvement took root and expanded. Local control was curtailed and education bureaucratized, but the feds didn't have enough power to really control reform efforts at the local level. A period of retrenchment (1980–1988) followed, with a backlash against this expansion leading to a period of deregulation. In the background, a state-based "excellence agenda" started to form, which ultimately led to another conceptual realignment (1988–1994) during which the federal government attempted to direct states toward standards-based reform. Another period of expansion and friction began (1994–2000), but few states embraced the federal call for new standards, tests, and accountability measures. Finally, a federal breakthrough occurred in 2001 with the passage of the No Child Left Behind Act (NCLB); the dam constraining federal power was broken, and a new paradigm of test-based accountability was consolidated.[1]

CONCEPTUAL REALIGNMENT (1950–1965)

The federal role began to grow in the 1950s in response to a series of perceived national crises. The first crisis centered on race and segregation. The US Supreme Court's 1954 *Brown v. Board of Education* decision declared segregated schools to be "inherently unequal" and ordered states to integrate. But states, particularly those in the South, were angered and engaged in "massive resistance." All three branches of the federal government had to take concerted action to prod them to integrate. States still made objections on the grounds of states' rights and local control, but these objections were viewed with increasing suspicion by the feds and the civil rights community.

The second national crisis that precipitated an expanded federal role in education came in 1957 when the Soviet Union launched Sputnik, the world's first orbiting satellite, and heightened fears that the United States was losing the space race and the arms race in the Cold War. The National Defense Education Act (NDEA) of 1958 was enacted to help states expand their offerings in math, science, and foreign language. While the investment was small in absolute terms (less than $1 billion), the political precedent and psychological breakthrough were profound.

The third national crisis occurred in the 1960s when President Lyndon Johnson declared a "war on poverty" in his effort to create a "great society." LBJ believed that improved educational opportunity was the best path out of poverty. He declared that "very often, a lack of jobs and money is not the cause of poverty, but the symptom. The cause may lie deeper—in our failure to give our fellow citizens a fair chance to develop their own capacities in a lack of education and training."[2] If education was the key to social mobility, however, it was clear that too many schools lacked the resources to provide the necessary skills to students from disadvantaged backgrounds. This economic rationale, together with the racial and national defense arguments, pushed Congress to enact the most expansive and expensive federal education law in American history, the Elementary and Secondary Education Act of 1965.

EARLY ESEA: EXPANSION AND FRICTION (1965–1980)

Upon signing ESEA, President Johnson declared, "I believe deeply no law I have signed or will ever sign means more to the future of America."[3] The bill was supported by large majorities in both chambers, passing by a vote of 263–153 in the House and 73–18 in the Senate.[4] It put a powerful equity rationale at the heart of federal education policy and created a plan to provide supplemental resources and programs to increase opportunity for disadvantaged children. The centerpiece of this effort and of the legislation itself was the Title I program, which received $1.06 billion of the initial $1.3 billion appropriated for ESEA.[5] The text of Title I stated that "the Congress hereby declares it to be the policy of the United States to provide financial assistance . . . to expand and improve . . . educational programs by various means . . . which contribute particularly to meeting the special educational needs of educationally deprived children."[6] Title I was designed to assist communities with a high concentration of low-income families by raising per-pupil expenditures. The original law contained five additional titles directed toward helping districts and states implement reforms.[7]

Many observers at the time recognized that an important threshold had been crossed. Both supporters and opponents of federal aid to education acknowledged that the federal role in education was likely to expand after ESEA. Congressman John Williams (R-DE), for example, remarked after the act's passage, "Make no mistake about it, this bill . . . is merely the beginning. It contains within it the seeds of the first federal education system, which will be nurtured by its supporters in the years to come long after the current excuse of aiding the poverty stricken is forgotten . . . The needy are being used as a wedge to open the floodgates, and you may be absolutely certain that the flood of federal control is ready to sweep the land."[8] Together, NDEA and ESEA were to dramatically increase federal education funding.

But while the money flowed, grew substantially over time, and created a cadre of committed stakeholders, the federal "control" that Williams feared didn't quite follow. The redistributive edge of ESEA got rubbed off as money was spread around in exchange for political support. In the end, the funding formula was designed to maximize the number of school districts (and thus congressional districts) that would be eligible, and the restrictions on how the money would be spent were loosened considerably. Ninety-four percent of American school districts ultimately received Title I funds that could be used for a variety of purposes, including hiring additional staff, purchasing classroom equipment, or augmenting classroom instruction.[9] Federal spending for education—particularly when it was dispersed widely and came with few strings attached—was very popular among politicians, educators, and parents. And once the federal role in education policy had been institutionalized, it became more difficult for opponents of that role to substantially reduce or change it.

The role that was institutionalized, however, was not particularly well targeted toward the original rationale, and didn't have strong mechanisms to deliver on its original promise. The policy paradigm undergirding this equity regime was that the majority of schools were doing fine, that federal education reform efforts should target schools with high concentrations of poor and minority students, and that the primary problem facing these schools was a lack of integration and/or adequate funding. As historian Hugh Davis Graham notes, "by the end of the Johnson administration, the very proliferation of Great Society programs . . . reinforced the growing triangular networks with a vested interest in maximizing their benefits by pressing willing congressional authorizing committees to exceed by large margins the president's budget requests, especially in education."[10]

ESEA incorporated multiple goals and methods and gave federal administrators few tools to enforce compliance. Even if such tools had been available, the agency charged with implementing the law, the US Office of Education (USOE), lacked the capacity and political will to rigorously administer it. The politics and implementation of ESEA were also greatly complicated by the addition of new purposes and programs and increasingly contentious racial politics following 1965.

The consequence of ESEA's initial flexibility was that federal funds were used in a wide variety of ways for a wide variety of purposes, and local districts often diverted funds away from redistributive programs.[11] The large amount of discretion accorded to states and districts ensured that compliance with federal goals was spotty at best. Initially, the USOE merely relied on the assurances of state officials.[12] Over time, however, federal legislative enactments, bureaucratic regulations, and court mandates became increasingly numerous and prescriptive, and federal influence grew significantly.

ESEA quickly developed formidable political constituencies that successfully pushed for incremental expansions in its size and scope. Continuing opposition to federal micromanagement in education and the lack of consensus on how to measure the effectiveness of school reform efforts, however, led federal administrators to focus on districts' spending patterns and administrative compliance. The result was that large numbers of bureaucratic regulations were created during the 1970s without any concomitant focus on student or school results—everything was judged by procedure and process. In the 1980s, John Chubb would note that "in federal programs that are not explicitly regulatory, as well as those that are, policy has come to be carried out by increasingly detailed, prescriptive, legalistic, and authoritative means."[13] Between 1964 and 1976 the number of pages of federal legislation affecting education increased from 80 to 360, while the number of federal regulations increased from 92 in 1965 to nearly 1,000 in 1977.[14]

Thus, one of ESEA's most significant consequences was the bureaucratization and centralization of education policy making from the local level to the state and federal levels. Eligibility for federal education funds was often conditioned on the provision of state matching funds, the creation of central offices, and the collection of a variety of statistical information, all of which necessitated that state education agencies expand. Meanwhile, the number of independent school districts dropped from approximately 150,000 in 1900 to 15,000 in 1993. This administrative centralization at the state level ultimately made education more susceptible to federal regulation.[15] Centralization also meant that local school leaders had less and less flexibility. As Diane Ravitch observed, "During the decade after 1965, political pressures converged on schools . . . in ways that undermined their authority to direct their own affairs . . . Congress, the courts, federal agencies, and state legislatures devised burdensome and costly new mandates. In elementary and secondary schools, almost no area of administrative discretion was left uncontested."[16]

Despite local frustration, ESEA expansion remained a winning political proposition for congressmen. As opponents of federal control had feared, ESEA had given a crucial beachhead to those who sought to further increase the federal role in education policy. It was expanded in 1968, 1974, and 1978, and over one hundred new programs were added, covering everything from migrant children to children with handicaps. Democratic President Jimmy Carter continued the institutionalization of the federal role in education when he created a cabinet-level Department of Education (DOE) in 1979.[17] The new department quickly became a powerful symbol to both proponents and opponents of federal involvement.

By 1980 federal spending had expanded dramatically and ESEA had facilitated the centralization, bureaucratization, and judicialization of education policy making. The logic behind ESEA—that the federal government needed to defend the most vulnerable children from local majorities—had led to increasing federal involvement but also increasingly inflexible and copious regulations and increasingly intrusive court intervention. By 1980 the Department of Education administered approximately five hundred different federal education programs.[18] Ironically, however, ESEA reduced the autonomy of schools and districts without really giving the federal government any *control* over schools—it just fostered an increasingly stifling compliance culture.

RETRENCHMENT (1980–1988)

The federal focus remained on access and equity rather than on improving schools' or students' academic performance; there was little effort to measure the educational progress of students who received federal funds. This fueled the growing perception in the 1970s that federal education policy—like many other Great Society policies—had become more about providing entitlements and protecting rights than about enhancing opportunity. This led to growing discontent among Republicans, states' rights advocates, and even some Democrats about the nature and effectiveness of federal aid.

As ESEA continued to expand and to cover more disadvantaged groups despite its apparent failure to deliver on its promise, support for a fundamental reconsideration of the federal role in education gained momentum. Its implementation also quickly became enmeshed in the highly charged struggles over integration and busing fought across the country during the 1960s and 1970s. States that failed to comply with court integration decrees would lose their share of federal funding. By the 1980s the contentious politics of desegregation and growing skepticism about the efficacy of federal involvement led to a backlash against ESEA and fueled a reform movement that promoted administrative flexibility, parental choice, and outcome standards.

In the 1980 presidential election, Ronald Reagan, a champion of conservative Republicans, seized on growing public opposition to the federal role in education to defeat Democratic incumbent Jimmy Carter. The 1980 Republican platform called for "deregulation by the federal government of public education and . . . the elimination of the federal Department of Education." The platform fretted that "parents are losing control of their children's schooling" and that Democratic education policy had produced "huge new bureaucracies to misspend our taxes."[19]

As part of his "New Federalism" program, Reagan passed the Education Consolidation and Improvement Act (ECIA) of 1981, dramatically reforming many provisions of ESEA. The changes reduced the amount of federal funding for education by almost 20 percent and increased flexibility for states. One scholar estimated that the number of regulatory mandates was reduced by 85 percent during the Reagan administration.[20] Reagan hoped to either eliminate the federal role in schools or to redefine the nature of the federal policy by making privatization, choice, and competition—rather than equity—its guiding principles.[21]

In the end, however, Reagan's efforts to convert federal education spending into vouchers or block grants and to dismantle the Department of Education failed after meeting significant resistance from Congress, interest groups, and the public. Though Reagan's effort to disband the DOE was unsuccessful, he succeeded in substantially reducing its staffing, budget, and regulatory authority. The DOE's budget was cut by 11 percent between fiscal year 1981 and fiscal year 1988 (in real dollars) and the National Institute of Education (the federal educational research and development body) lost 70 percent of its funding.[22] In many important ways, however, the trend toward greater federal control and the nationalization of education politics continued during the 1980s despite Reagan's concerted efforts. A large and diverse array of entrenched interest groups united in the Committee for Education Funding (founded in 1969) fought to defend and expand federal spending.

Republican efforts to roll back federal influence also ran smack into fresh evidence and a flurry of media attention to the fact that American schools were in very poor shape. The 1983 report of the National Commission on Excellence in Education, entitled *A Nation at Risk: The Imperative for Educational Reform*, painted a dire portrait of the country's public schools and highlighted how far American students lagged behind their foreign counterparts. The report's title also emphasized its authors' conclusion—that although education had long been primarily a *state* issue, it had become a *national* problem. This point was also cast—as it had been in the years following Sputnik—as a matter of national security in our Cold War struggle with the Soviet Union and in our competition in the global economy. The report declared: "Our once unchallenged preeminence in commerce, industry, science, and technological innovation is being overtaken by competitors throughout the world . . . the educational foundations of our society are presently being eroded by a rising tide of mediocrity that threatens our very future as a Nation and a people . . . If an unfriendly foreign power had attempted to impose on America the mediocre educational performance that exists today, we might well have viewed it as an act of war."[23]

The federal rationale shifted—now it was not about the United States versus the Soviet Union, but rather about the United States versus the world.

The federal government, the report declared, has "the primary responsibility to identify the national interest in education. It should also help fund and support efforts to protect and promote that interest . . . and provide the national leadership." The report's striking tone and conclusions ignited a frenzy of media attention. The Reagan administration highlighted the report's findings as evidence that the growth in federal involvement had been ineffective, and Education Secretary Terrell Bell began a very visible (and controversial) effort to prod state reform by providing public rankings of the states according to the quality of their public education systems.

Perhaps the most important consequence of *A Nation at Risk* was that states began to play a much more active role in education reform. In what became known as the "excellence movement," many states increased spending on schools and established new curricular and achievement standards in the 1980s to guide local school districts. Thomas Toch has written that "the national debate on public education produced scores of reforms . . . Through 1984, 1985, 1986, and beyond, education was a dominant issue in state capitols nationwide . . . In all, there were an estimated 3,000 separate school-reform measures enacted in the states during the mid-1980s."[24] The decade thus saw the building of a public and elite consensus around standards-based education reform.[25] The 1988 reauthorization of ESEA—which required school districts to assess the effectiveness of Chapter 1 programs and develop improvement plans for underperforming schools—represented the first step in shifting federal education policy away from the equity approach and toward a focus on outcome accountability.

REALIGNMENT: GEORGE H. W. BUSH AND BILL CLINTON (1988–1994)

Reagan's Republican successor, George H. W. Bush, campaigned on a pledge to be an "education president." In office he convened a national education summit in Charlottesville, Virginia, in 1989, bringing the nation's governors together to discuss school reform under presidential leadership for the first time. The meeting produced a series of national education goals that Bush attempted (but failed) to codify with his "America 2000" proposal to Congress in 1991. It called for the development of more detailed voluntary national standards in the core academic subjects as well as for the creation of "a system of voluntary examinations" called "American Achievement Tests" for all fourth, eighth, and twelfth graders, which would be made available to governors for adoption.[26] It also proposed the creation of a "New American Schools Development Corporation" to design model schools, publish report cards (for schools, districts, and states), encourage merit pay and alternative certification for teachers and principals, and establish a number of private school choice demonstration projects.

Bill Clinton had joined with Bush during the 1989 Charlottesville summit and by the 1992 campaign a centrist consensus had developed around these ideas. President Clinton's "Goals 2000" proposal (enacted in 1994) created a blueprint for the subsequent ESEA reauthorization and called for the creation of voluntary national standards and assessments based on the six national education goals outlined in America 2000. However, Goals 2000 greatly circumscribed the federal role in creating standards and assessments or in holding states accountable. The final legislation stated that national standards must be "sufficiently general" that they "will not restrict state and local control over curriculum and instruction methods . . . [and that states] can modify them to suit their own circumstances." It also emphasized that the standards were voluntary and that "states and communities can develop their own standards or modify and adopt those developed under national consensus." Federal funds were to flow to states and communities to "help them develop their own rigorous standards and implement their own programs of school reform." The law clearly indicates that "no state is required to have its standards or assessments certified or participate in Goals 2000 systemic improvement programs as a condition of participating in any federal education program."[27]

Clinton's Education Secretary Richard Riley declared that education is "a local function, a state responsibility, and a national priority," and Goals 2000 reflected this complicated division of authority. Despite its flexibility and the lack of new mandates, however, Goals 2000 was widely recognized as a watershed moment. Riley noted that "for the first time in the nation's history, a statutory framework defines the federal role as one of supporting and facilitation to improve all schools for all children."[28] Previous federal programs had been categorical and addressed narrow purposes or populations, but Goals 2000 comprehensively addressed the nation's entire K–12 education system. Goals 2000 marked a fundamental break with the historical focus on promoting equity for disadvantaged groups and initiated a new era in emphasizing academic improvement for all students. Reformers hailed the focus on standards and school performance as an important step, but recognized that its voluntary nature and the restrictions on federal leadership limited its potential impact.

EXPANSION AND FRICTION: IMPROVING AMERICA'S SCHOOLS ACT (1994–2000)

Goals 2000 signified an important new direction, but participation in the program was voluntary, and the only incentive for states to take part was to claim a share of the small pot of money. ESEA, on the other hand, was enormous in size and scope, housing the majority of federal education programs and allocating over $10 billion annually. The original ESEA created a large number of targeted, categorical federal education programs to provide assistance to specifically identified groups and purposes. Subsequent ESEA reauthorizations added further groups and programs, which only exacerbated the disjointed nature of the original law. Federal programs continued to embody federal purposes, operating separately from state and local programs, and focusing on compliance rather than student achievement.

But by the 1990s there was a growing sentiment among Democrats and Republicans alike that ESEA was in dire need of reform. As Clinton's Education Undersecretary Mike Smith noted, "As the 1994 reauthorization of ESEA drew near, it became increasingly clear that the federal programs were out of step with the growing reform movement in the states. They were focused on low-level skills, fragmented, and even on their own terms, they often were ineffective."[29] The Clinton administration's 1994 reauthorization proposal (entitled the Improving America's Schools Act, or IASA) called for tying federal aid for disadvantaged students (Title I), bilingual education, and many other programs to the standards developed under Goals 2000. Clinton's linking of education to economic growth established a strong rationale for broader federal involvement. His emphasis on the need for increased reform, as opposed to merely increased spending, was also very important. However, continuing opposition to a more rigorous federal role in promoting school reform would limit the ability of the Clinton administration to actively implement even the weak enforcement provisions of the new laws.

Even so, the new federal concern about *every* child was remarkable given the historic focus on only *disadvantaged* children. In a major shift, Clinton argued that disadvantaged students in Title I schools should now be expected to make progress toward the challenging content and performance standards and assessments that were applied to all of the other children in the state. The changes to ESEA required states to develop school improvement plans and challenging content standards in core academic subjects in order to receive federal funds. States were also required to develop assessments and set benchmarks for the Adequate Yearly Progress (AYP) that a district's Title I students would have to make. Schools would publish disaggregated test results, and those that failed to meet state targets for two consecutive school years would be identified as needing improvement. States and districts were encouraged to take "corrective action" with failing schools, such as withholding funds, reconstituting staff, instituting new governance, or transferring students.[30]

Much had been made during the congressional debate over Goals 2000 about the voluntary nature of the national standards and federal programs, but this changed with IASA. As Mike Smith noted, the combination of "Goals 2000 and the 1994 ESEA changes imposed on the states a particular kind of reform—to play ball, states had to go along with standards-based reform."[31] Many conservatives in Congress worried the new law would federalize education policy. Despite the support of some Republican moderates, IASA was the most partisan ESEA reauthorization in history. During the 1960s, 1970s, and 1980s the periodic reauthorizations of ESEA enjoyed broad bipartisan support, with between 72 percent and 99 percent of House and Senate Republicans voting in favor. In 1994, however, only 19 percent of House Republicans and 53 percent of Senate Republicans voted for the final ESEA bill.[32] This growing politicization of education in Washington occurred even as a consensus was building across the country among education reformers, governors, business leaders, and the public behind national standards and assessments. While IASA forced states to "play ball" on standards-based reform, it allowed them to write their own rules for how the game would be played, and states were given the freedom to design their own standards, assessments, and accountability systems.

Many ideas that would later form the core of the 2001 No Child Left Behind Act—such as standards, assessments, Adequate Yearly Progress, school report cards, and corrective action—were first expressed in IASA. But in the early 1990s the lingering conservative opposition to a strong federal role in education and the continuing liberal reservations about testing and accountability meant that Goals 2000 and the ESEA reauthorization contained few truly mandatory reforms. In addition, the federal expansion came under determined attack by a Republican-controlled and conservative-led

Congress between 1995 and 1999. Republicans advanced proposals to elimi-nate the Department of Education, cut federal education spending, and con-vert what funds remained into private school vouchers and block grants. These proposals made progress in the House but were defeated by a coali-tion of Democrats and Republican moderates in the Senate. The steadfast support of the business community and the National Governors Association for federal leadership was an important influence during this period.

Though unsuccessful in fundamentally redirecting federal education pol-icy, conservatives were successful in significantly undermining federal influ-ence over state reform efforts. The 1994 reforms gave states great flexibility and discretion in designing and implementing their school reform plans. By 2000, however, it was clear that this approach had failed to bring about major policy change at the state level or to improve student achievement. Whereas the original ESEA had a limited scope of action yet achieved broad penetration in the form of bureaucratic compliance, IASA had a broader ambition of policy alignment, but received shallow buy-in from the states.

GEORGE W. BUSH, NCLB, AND THE FEDERAL BREAKTHROUGH

Compliance with IASA's requirements was poor—as of spring 2002, only six-teen states had fully met the requirements of the 1994 law. President George W. Bush made education reform and accountability a central theme of his 2000 election campaign and of his pledge to govern as a "compassionate conservative." Seizing the mantle of the civil rights movement, he called for a focus on exposing and closing racial achievement gaps and battling the "soft bigotry of low expectations." By the beginning of the twentieth century, then, each of the three original rationales for expanded federal involvement in education (racial, national defense, and economic) had shifted to take on a broader, more ambitious character.

Bush made a grand bargain with congressional Democrats. In exchange for meeting new federal demands and greater federal accountability, No Child Left Behind provided a significant increase in federal spending on education and new flexibility in how states could spend it. In 2002, the year after NCLB was enacted, federal education appropriations increased by 34 percent, going from $42.1 billion in 2001 to $56.2 billion the following year. That was a jump of $14.1 billion. The increase in education funding from 2000 to 2010 was 64 percent, as the department saw $24.6 billion added to its budget.[33] The vote to approve the conference report of NCLB was overwhelming and bipartisan in the House (381–41) and Senate (87–10).

The most important requirements were that states had to adopt academic standards to guide their curricula and adopt a testing and accountability system aligned with those standards.[34] States had to test all students in grades 3–8 every year (as well as once in high school) in math and reading beginning in the 2005–2006 school year. Beginning in 2002–2003, states were required to annually test the English proficiency of students for whom English is not their first language, and by the 2007–2008 school year, states also had to test all students in science at certain grade levels. States were free to develop and use their own standards and tests, but every school, school district, and state had to make student test results publicly available and disaggregated for certain groups of students, including major racial and ethnic groups, major income groups, students with a disability, students with limited English proficiency, and migrant students.

NCLB mandated that every state and school district issue report cards detailing student test scores and identifying schools failing to meet proficiency targets. NCLB explicitly requires that states use this information to track their efforts to close the achievement gaps on reading and math between different racial, ethnic, and income groups. States were required to establish a timeline for making Adequate Yearly Progress toward eliminating these gaps and moving all students to state proficiency levels within twelve years (by 2014). The law's accountability provisions required states to take a number of escalating actions with schools that did not reach their performance objectives.[35]

NCLB represented the most significant overhaul and expansion of the federal role in education since ESEA was created in 1965. Like IASA before it, NCLB was centered on standards, testing, and school accountability. But NCLB was much more prescriptive—a response to the perceived failure of IASA to generate sufficient state reform and increasing pressure on national leaders to bring about better school results. While forty-eight states had standards and tests in place in 2000, for example, only thirteen states were testing students every year in reading and math between the third and eighth grades as NCLB required, and even fewer had strong accountability systems of the sort mandated by the law.

Thus, prior to NCLB, even in states that had adopted standards and testing reforms, there were few consequences for schools that failed to perform well. NCLB's significance was in mandating that *all* states adopt a standards and testing regime, and that they conform to a federal timetable for achieving student proficiency. Under the new federal law, all states also had to collect and disseminate a tremendous amount of school performance data. In stark contrast to the implementation of previous federal education legislation, the Bush Department of Education also developed tough, detailed regulations in support of NCLB and threatened to withhold federal funds from states that did not comply with its mandates.[36]

CONCLUSION

Beginning in the 1950s, US policy makers articulated three primary rationales for expanded federal involvement in education: racial (ending segregation and discrimination), national security (promoting defense research), and economic (alleviating poverty). Each of these rationales evolved over time but continued to provide a justification for an increased federal role. Equal access to schooling has now been joined with a focus on closing racial and socioeconomic achievement gaps. The emphasis on education to bolster national security has been supplemented with an emphasis on global economic competition. And the view of education as an antipoverty strategy has now been augmented with a desire to use it to spur economic growth. These shifting national rationales have led to shifting federal policies and cycles of expanded federal involvement followed by the reassertion of states' rights.

ESEA remains the centerpiece of federal K–12 education policy. The passage of NCLB in 2001 fundamentally changed the ends and means of federal policy, creating a new policy regime. The old regime created in 1965 saw the central purpose of school reform as promoting equity and access for disadvantaged students. Growing concern about the performance of American students and schools in the years following *A Nation at Risk*, however, challenged the assumptions at the heart of the old policy paradigm in education and weakened the position of those who had long defended the status quo. The policy paradigm at the heart of the NCLB regime was centered on the much broader goal of improving education for all students and sought to do so by significantly increasing federal accountability for school performance.[37] The adoption of rigid new federal timetables and prescriptive accountability measures in NCLB was seen as essential to force states to finally comply with the standards, testing, and accountability reforms introduced with IASA in 1994.

For much of American history, deference to local control exerted a powerful restraining influence on the size and character of the federal role in education, but that changed with the passage of ESEA in 1965 and—even more radically—with NCLB. The law created a new educational federalism in the United States, with the US Department of Education functioning as a national schoolmarm, hovering over state school reform efforts and whacking those states that failed to record satisfactory and timely progress toward federal education goals. As you will see in chapter 2, however, states struggled mightily to implement NCLB and meet its performance targets, and chafed at the unprecedented level of prescriptiveness of federal mandates. This set the stage for a political backlash against the law and against federal authority in education more broadly, ultimately leading to another retrenchment with the passage of ESSA and a return of significant control over school reform to states.[38]

2

From NCLB to ESSA

Lessons Learned or Politics Reaffirmed?

Jeffrey R. Henig, David M. Houston, and Melissa Arnold Lyon

The line from the No Child Left Behind Act to the Every Student Succeeds Act is not a straight one, although at first glance it may seem to be.

The enactment of NCLB appeared at the time to reflect a new bipartisan consensus on education, marked by a prominent role on the national government agenda, emphasis on outcomes rather than inputs, accountability exercised via standardized tests, and the injection of market principles and private organizations in the delivery of public education. This new consensus appeared to be built upon and protected by a new set of political alignments, featuring a newly expanded role for some interests, including governors, so-called new Democrats and compassionate conservatives, and interested segments of the for-profit and nonprofit education world. It also allowed for a substantially less prominent role for teacher unions and education professionals. Based on these developments, Drew University political science professor Patrick McGuinn characterized NCLB as marking the emergence of a "new regime."[1] Because national politics have recently been defined by partisan and ideological polarization and often stalemate, the emergence of this new regime seemed to set education as somehow buffered and apart.

Barack Obama campaigned for the presidency on the promise of a sharp break from the Bush presidency, but on education he called for strikingly little substantive change. On important components, like school choice and test-based accountability, the new Democratic administration represented by Obama and Secretary of Education Arne Duncan not only maintained the momentum, but doubled down with even greater emphasis and intentionality.

In December 2015, on the eve of the new presidential election year, Congress once again renewed the Elementary and Secondary Education Act and, as in 2001, did so by a wide margin and with broad bipartisan support. President Obama and Republicans in control of Congress both welcomed this, describing ESSA as an improved version that was tweaked and reshaped based on lessons learned, but consistent with NCLB's emphasis on equity, outcomes, innovation, and accountability.

The notion that education policy is and could remain buffered from the ideological and partisan conflicts that mark other important issues, however, proved naïve in important respects. As we relate in this chapter, twists and turns in the fourteen-year journey from NCLB to ESSA suggest that the seeming confluence of ideas is more fraught and the apparent convergence of political support more fragile than might appear at first glance. The coalition of "strange bedfellows" that formed to pass NCLB began to fray at the edges almost before the ink was dry. Implementation challenges, faulty assumptions, and unanticipated consequences scrambled the political landscape. The surface appearance of consensus and broad support represented in the congressional vote tally and public statements welcoming the new bill masked continuing disagreements and political cleavages.

THE BUSH ADMINISTRATION: CAN AN EXPANDED CENTER HOLD?

Less than one year after his inauguration, George W. Bush signed the NCLB legislation, marking his delivery on what had been a major promise in his campaign. As chronicled by McGuinn in this volume and elsewhere, the new legislation represented both a dramatic departure and long-term continuity.[2]

In its enacted form, NCLB required states to test every student in grades 3–8 in math and reading, disaggregate testing data by subgroup (including nonwhite, low-income, and special education students), ensure progressively higher rates of academic proficiency across all subgroups with a goal of 100 percent proficiency by 2014, place highly qualified teachers in every classroom, and force schools to face cascading consequences for failing to make sufficient academic progress. Students in schools that could not generate adequate student achievement for two consecutive years were allowed to transfer elsewhere in the district. After three consecutive years of unsatisfactory results, schools needed to provide supplemental educational services from public or private vendors. After four years, schools were required to replace their staff and/or curriculum. Lastly, after five years, schools were required to close and reopen as charter schools or hand over control to the state.[3] By forcing states to comply with these requirements, NCLB unequivocally increased federal authority over schooling.

NCLB, in McGuinn's words, represented "a transformative shift in federal education policy—not merely a new policy but a new policy regime as it embodies a different set of ideas, interests, and institutions for federal education policy."[4] Powerful factions in both political parties saw something to like in the theory of NCLB, but no one could project how it would all look in practice. Business leaders on the Republican side and a subset of the civil rights movement on the Democratic side found common cause in the pursuit of higher academic standards and robust accountability mechanisms, guided by the federal government.[5] Both factions viewed these educational goals as the necessary tonic for lackluster student achievement in general and among historically disadvantaged groups in particular. On the right, business leaders diverged from traditional conservative skepticism of federal authority, while on the left civil rights leaders challenged traditional liberal resistance to test-based accountability.

NCLB passed by wide margins: 381–41 in the House and 87–10 in the Senate. Much of this apparent consensus reflects the Bush administration's active pursuit of bipartisan support. Although Republicans nominally had unified control of the federal government, they did not have enough votes in the Senate to block a Democratic filibuster. Moreover, pursuing a strictly party-line initiative immediately after a razor-thin election victory may have soured any chances for future bipartisanship. Perhaps most importantly, the terrorist attacks of September 11th occurred just months before NCLB went up for a vote. In response to the crisis, leaders in both parties agreed that a display of bipartisan unity was essential to assure Americans and the world that the US government could continue to conduct its everyday business and function effectively.[6] So, in order to secure votes on the left, Bush put up little defense of the provisions in earlier versions of the bill that converted portions of ESEA into block grants and permitted the use of private school vouchers. Moreover, to accompany the new school accountability rules, NCLB included a 20 percent increase in spending on Title I.[7] On the right, conservatives were reluctant to withhold their support from the popular president of their own party. Similarly, the support for NCLB among civil rights leaders granted wide cover for liberals to also get on board.[8]

The breadth of support depended in part on timing and in part on a vague and conflicting understanding about how the provisions of the law would actually play out. This moment of national cooperation would not last forever. Some of the tailwind behind the new regime faded quickly, and strong headwinds developed as the law's intentionally staged consequences took hold.

Diminishing Support and Challenges of Implementation

The seemingly broad foundation of support for NCLB began to crumble almost immediately after the law's passage. Senator Ted Kennedy had rallied liberal Democrats to support the law in exchange for what he believed were assurances of greater funding to help struggling schools meet standards. In February 2002, however, only a month after NCLB was signed into law, the Bush administration released a budget that proposed drastically smaller appropriations to the US Department of Education than congressional liberals expected. Bush ultimately allocated an additional $7.1 billion to the programs that made up NCLB. But it was reported that Kennedy hoped for an additional $56 billion and was shocked and outraged that Bush requested so much less.[9]

Conservative Republicans were unhappy that Bush sacrificed vouchers, but hoped that provisions for public school choice and privately provided supplemental services for students in failing schools would demonstrate the advantages of market-oriented strategies. But for various reasons, relatively few families exercised NCLB-required choice; in 2003–2004, 2.75 million students were eligible for NCLB choice, but only 32,000 participated nationwide (1.2 percent).[10] After an initial flurry of action, the private supplemental educational services industry found the market less attractive than had been anticipated. A 2015 analysis declares, "[A]lmost all major providers have since gone out of business or retooled their strategies for today's market. A once-thriving market of billions of dollars is now a faint shadow of what it once was."[11]

It's not surprising that Democrats and Republicans who had reluctantly supported NCLB would grumble. But the more important shift was in the comfort level of the larger number of voters and elected officials who had been casual supporters in large part because they assumed that the costs and sanctions would fall on others. Americans have long had a bifurcated view of the condition of public education; they are critical of the state of the nation's schools while they give their own a high grade.[12] Suburbanites paid little attention at first, assuming that NCLB sanctions would fall on a limited number of schools, primarily in large urban districts, whose struggles had dominated public discourse. But indifference turned to discomfort as it became clearer that even schools with relatively high average test scores could fail to make Adequate Yearly Progress (AYP) because of the lagging performance of just a single subgroup, as gradually tightening proficiency targets raised the bar and an increasing number of schools began climbing through the staged levels of sanctions.

By 2004, none of the fifty states were on track to meet NCLB's stipulation that all classrooms should be staffed by a highly qualified teacher, and only nineteen states were ready to release annual report cards on school performance.[13] Moreover, the strict demands of AYP surpassed many schools' capacity. By the 2007–2008 school year, about 35 percent of all schools failed AYP, and this rose to 48 percent in 2011.[14] These included not only high-poverty, high-minority, urban schools (as many of the framers of the law expected), but also a nontrivial number of affluent, mostly white, suburban schools. Paradoxically—and adding to a growing mistrust of the basic approach—because states were able to set their own proficiency cutoffs, states recognized as having strong schools (based on NAEP tests) often had many more schools labeled as AYP failures than those with generally weak systems. For example, in 2011, 82 percent of schools in Massachusetts were failing to make AYP, compared to only 16 percent in Kansas.[15]

Active resistance to the law began to surface. The National Education Association (NEA), the country's largest teacher union, filed a lawsuit against the secretary of education, arguing that the law was an unfunded mandate. Some members of the civil rights community, including the NAACP, worried aloud that the accountability mechanisms in the law, while shining a spotlight on the plight of disadvantaged students, cultivated a narrower, more regimented curriculum and caused educators to teach exclusively to the state tests. The conservative House Republican Study Committee warned Bush that he would face a greater challenge in the future if he attempted to expand the federal government again. States themselves also bristled against the law. By 2004, over half of the states considered laws and resolutions challenging the legitimacy of NCLB. Five states—Colorado, Illinois, Maine, Utah, and Virginia—successfully passed laws allowing state and local education agencies to ignore provisions of NCLB that contradicted state law.[16]

Public support of NCLB grew increasingly tepid over the course of its implementation. Initial polls showed slight majorities in favor of the law a few years after its passage. However, as time progressed, this support began to erode. Figure 2.1 displays two trends from the annual PDK/Gallup Poll, a nationally representative survey of public attitudes toward educational issues. The first line indicates the percentage of respondents who held a favorable opinion of the law (among those that answered the question). The second tracks the percentage of respondents who felt that they knew enough about NCLB to form an opinion. As more Americans felt that they knew something about the law, a smaller proportion expressed support for it.

Inconsistent Results and a Growing Political Divide

The Bush administration initially approached the implementation of the law with a firm stance toward states. On the day after the law was passed, Secretary of Education Roderick Paige met with thirty state education chiefs to instruct them, in no uncertain terms, that they would be held to the letter of the law and that those who had grown accustomed to waivers from ESEA provisions from previous administrations would not receive similar treatment from Bush's Department of Education.[17] But this position ultimately proved unworkable. After his reelection in 2004, Bush replaced Paige with

FIGURE 2.1   Tracking public attitudes toward the No Child Left Behind Act

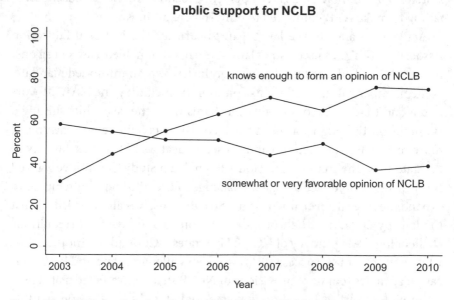

Source: "The PDK/Gallup Poll of the Public's Attitudes Toward Public Schools," http://pdkpoll. pdkintl.org/october/.

Margaret Spellings, who in an early speech announced that the department would be more flexible as long as states met her four "bright lines": annual testing, disaggregating scores by subgroups, improving teacher quality, and distributing school information to parents.[18] The increased flexibility on behalf of the federal government and the underlying infrastructure of education policy in the United States—which grants considerable discretion to states in terms of policy implementation—resulted in extensive variation from state to state even within the confines of NCLB's requirements. Although all states ultimately produced standards, tests, and accountability policies, they differed greatly in their academic rigor.[19]

The authors of NCLB scheduled it to be reauthorized in 2007, which presumably could have been an opportunity to adjust provisions of the law that had proven difficult to implement or had lost political support. However, by then the conditions that generated such broad bipartisan support in 2001 had dissipated. In March 2007, more than fifty Republicans, including some who had supported NCLB, introduced a bill to allow states to opt out.[20] Democrats had retaken control of Congress in 2006, and partisan conflict over both domestic and foreign policy issues, such as the war in Iraq, precluded any possibility for compromise. In the context of a more polarized Washington, traditional education liberals and conservatives were more strident in their calls for unfettered federal resources and a diminished federal role, respectively.[21] "Despite dozens of hearings, months of public debate and hundreds of hours of Congressional negotiation, neither the House nor the Senate has produced a bill that would formally start the reauthorization process," the *New York Times* reported in November 2007.[22] The bipartisan consensus on standards and accountability, for the time being, had lost some of its luster.

THE OBAMA YEARS: BIPARTISAN AGENDA MEETS BIPARTISAN BACKLASH

During his campaign and the start of his presidency, President Obama's political philosophy appealed largely to "unity, compromise, and postpartisanship" and a desire to "transcend politics." The initial appearance of bipartisanship and continuity from the Bush administration's focus on standards, testing, and accountability suggested that this might actually be the case. But again, the appearance of consensus masked the evolution of coalitions, the shifting of power, and the development of new political strategies.[23]

Political scientist John Kingdon famously wrote about the way in which external events sometimes open a "window of opportunity" for policy agendas to shift.[24] Obama's chance to enact education legislation came about in the turmoil of dealing with the economic crisis he confronted upon assuming office, when a window of opportunity opened within the American Recovery and Reinvestment Act (ARRA) in February 2009. Although most of the $100 billion in education funds in ARRA went to preserve teacher jobs, over $4 billion was set aside for "state incentive grants." These grants were also commonly referred to inside the Beltway as "Arne's Slush Fund."[25]

As it became clear that the Republicans in Congress were not going to allow Obama to fully pursue his agenda, Obama and Duncan used those incentive grants to fund Race to the Top (RTTT), which the Department of Education defined as "a competitive grant program designed to encourage and reward states that were creating the conditions for education innovation and reform; achieving significant improvement in student outcomes, including making substantial gains in student achievement, closing achievement gaps, improving high school graduation rates, and ensuring student preparation for success in college and careers; and implementing ambitious plans in four core education reform areas."[26] The basic goals associated with NCLB were still in the forefront, but an important shift had taken place regarding the institutional mechanism the administration would use to pursue those goals, with the federal government moving from the traditional use of formula grants to utilization of a competitive categorical grant with increased congressionally sanctioned Department of Education discretion.[27]

In July 2009, when the Department of Education released the draft regulations for how states could pursue the incentive grants through RTTT, it published the criteria that would be used to judge who would receive the awards while states were applying. Thus, the Department of Education was able to influence state policy making and help reformers challenge the status quo by privileging a set of specific reforms they believed would best advance their goals of accountability plus choice. In essence, they used RTTT to incentivize states to raise standards, limit caps on charter schools, and link teacher evaluations with students' standardized test scores.

RTTT Implementation and "Obama Overreach"

After the publication of these RTTT regulations, much of what is now considered the Obama education legacy developed quickly. Phase 1 applications were due in January 2010 and the two winners, Tennessee and Delaware, were announced in March of the same year. Soon after, in May, the Common Core State Standards were released and immediately woven into RTTT, since states that adopted them by August 2 were reported to have a higher chance of winning grants in the next round.[28] However, after the June 2010 deadline for RTTT Phase 2 applications, various political actors on the left and right began to express louder concerns about RTTT. Anger over high-stakes testing led the NEA to (narrowly) vote "no confidence" in RTTT as "a symbolic slam on the Obama administration."[29] Chester Finn, a conservative voice for the accountability and choice provisions of NCLB but also for a restrained federal government role in education, suggested that states that did not receive grants might not follow through with commitments and instead "just sit on their hands, chill out and say, 'Well, we don't really have the money right now to retrain our teachers.'"[30]

About this time, the broad critique of increased executive action—sometimes referred to as "executive overreach"—began to merge with the commentary on Obama's education agenda.[31] Right-leaning advocates had expressed this concern in previous years (see McGuinn's discussion in chapter 1 on Republican pushback on Clinton and IASA), but it did not gain much momentum during the Bush administration. It wasn't until after the announcement of the first round of RTTT winners that union leaders joined conservatives in expressing their concern about the direction of education policy making more loudly and forcefully.[32] This commentary was then woven into a larger criticism of federal overreach, which had become increasingly salient with the American public.[33] As displayed in figure 2.2, a quick examination of Google Trends data on the term "Obama overreach" demonstrates a clear spike in the use of the phrase in February 2011, followed by a general increase in interest over time. Thus, despite some pockets of concern about federal involvement in education decision making in the early 2000s, the most forceful critique of federal overreach in education appears to have gained momentum in the summer of 2010 and latched on to a broader criticism early in 2011, roughly the same time that Republicans took over control of the House of Representatives.

In the end, all but four states applied in at least one of the three phases of RTTT, but RTTT's actual impact on state policy is difficult to determine.[34] State legislators have claimed that RTTT affected policy decision making, and University of Chicago professor William G. Howell found that, between 2009 and 2014, states enacted 68 percent of reform policies on average, compared to just 10 percent between 2001 and 2008.[35] On the other hand,

FIGURE 2.2   Interest in the phrase "Obama overreach" over time

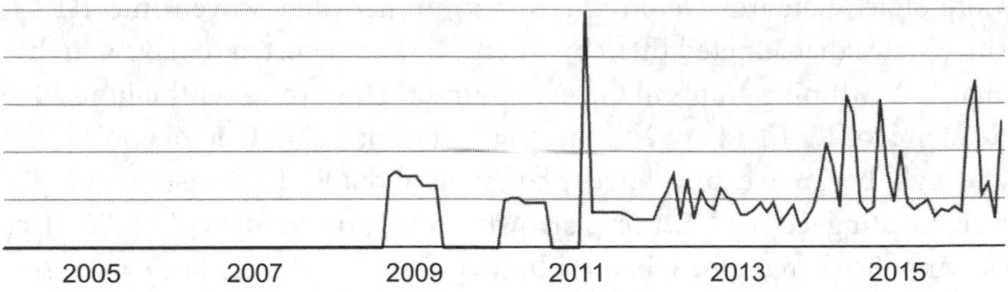

Source: Google Trends, www.google.com/trends.

states might have enacted some of those reforms even absent RTTT and might not sustain some reluctantly promised changes once RTTT funding is no longer in play.[36]

ESEA Waivers as Executive Workaround

With little prospect that Congress would reauthorize ESEA and with RTTT funding running out, the Obama administration found a new way to pursue its goals. It had become clear that something would have to be done because the evidence increasingly suggested that states would not meet NCLB's 100 percent proficient goal by 2014, and states were eager for ways to avoid the tough NCLB sanctions, which were more pervasive than initially anticipated. Thus, in September 2011, the administration unveiled a plan to leverage ESEA waivers as a kind of dollar-free competitive grant: instead of the traditional competitive categorical grant model in which the federal government provides funding to jurisdictions that agree to undertake specific actions, the administration provided relief from NCLB targets and constraints. In a well-publicized 2011 speech, Obama proclaimed, "Given that Congress cannot act, I am acting."[37] By announcing ESEA waivers in 2011, Obama and Duncan were able to use executive action as a lever for change in reaction to the inability to pass legislation promoting their policy goals through the Republican-led Congress.

Trends in the applications of the first eleven states to receive waivers indicated that many of the reforms associated with the Obama administration's preferences were being enacted and implemented, such as state coordination of accountability with federal guidelines, Common Core adoption, and the incorporation of academic growth and other new ways to measure school and district performance.[38] The ESEA waivers were perhaps even more expansive than RTTT. Although the numbers vary somewhat because certain states modified and even withdrew their applications, roughly two years after announcing ESEA flexibility the White House issued a press release revealing that forty states and Washington, DC, had received waivers.[39]

Although it appears that ESEA waivers and RTTT buffered education from the political process in some ways, they consequently sparked a major political reaction. The greatest impact of RTTT and ESEA waivers may turn out to be on the politics of decision making in education, on both the left and the right. For one, although education policy making had previously been somewhat spared from partisan wrangling, during the Obama years education politics intertwined with the increasing polarization of the larger political arena. As the Obama/Duncan administration grew frustrated with Republican efforts to block them on every legislative front, they increasingly relied on workarounds like executive orders. These methods extended to a range of issues, including immigration reform, and combined with growing Republican resistance to Obama and Duncan on education issues to form a broader critique of the Obama administration.

The Intermingling of Noneducation Politics, Unions, and Testing Backlash

Despite the bipartisan language often used in relation to education decisions, there is evidence of partisanship in state RTTT applications and awards. Three of the four states that never applied for RTTT funds had voted for McCain in 2008. Similarly, states that voted for Obama in 2008 on average had RTTT application scores that were roughly 40 points higher than states that did not. As a result, fourteen of the nineteen states that received a RTTT award voted for Obama in 2008, receiving over $3 billion in total. On average, states that voted for Obama in 2008 received roughly $109.7 million in RTTT funds, compared to about $43.6 million for states that did not.

On the right, this partisanship, along with the well-publicized critique of "Obama overreach" that extended to education policies such as Common Core, suggests that education, once an arena considered separate from partisan politics, had become subject to some of the same political battles as other areas like health care. Consider the term "Obamacore," coined by Republicans to link their negative message about the administration's education policy to their broader criticism of the Affordable Care Act. As admitted by New Jersey Governor Chris Christie in 2013, part of the conservative response to Common Core has been based on the "knee-jerk reaction that is happening in Washington . . . if the president likes something, the Republicans in Congress don't . . . It is this mind-set in D.C. right now that says we have to be at war constantly."[40] Terms like Obamacore may have also helped provide cover to the many conservatives who decided to backtrack on their initial support for Common Core. For example, despite New Jersey adopting the Common Core standards in 2010 and even reaffirming them in 2014, Christie later opposed them on the basis of their adoption "200 miles away on the banks of the Potomac River."[41]

RTTT and ESEA waivers also sowed division on the left. Reflecting on both, McGuinn writes that their "greatest impact may be on education politics, and in particular, the relationship between the Democratic Party and the two major teachers unions."[42] The administration's focus on school choice and accountability has led to an increase in the number of charter schools and supporting organizations while disenfranchising teacher unions and potentially even the labor movement more broadly.[43] The Common Core became wrapped up in this fight as well when the national standards intersected with the testing and accountability based on those standards. On April 30, 2013, American Federation of Teachers president Randi Weingarten referenced New York as one of many states where "the assessment has been fast-tracked before the other pieces were put in place" and called for a "moratorium on the stakes associated with Common Core assessments." She continued, "Once . . . an implementation plan and field testing are completed, that's when it makes sense to attach stakes to the assessments. But even then, let's stop this out-of-control fixation on testing."[44] Thus, as the Common Core became increasingly associated with the accelerated implementation of tests linked to the new standards, it fell out of favor with the teacher unions. In the face of teacher frustration based not only on testing but also issues such as equitable funding and local control, teacher unions, once loyal defenders of the Democratic Party, have found unlikely allies such as Republican senator Lamar Alexander.[45]

The Obama administration's policies also alienated affluent and suburban communities that grew concerned about curriculum narrowing and high-stakes testing. Duncan initially reacted by belittling these "white suburban moms who—all of a sudden—their child isn't as brilliant as they thought they were, and their school isn't quite as good as they thought they were."[46] Those parents didn't take that suggestion kindly, and a movement to "opt out" of standardized tests grew. This movement politically revitalized the teacher unions. The education reform movement had promoted the perception that teacher unions were putting their members' interests above those of the children, but the opt-out movement and the sentiments behind it gave the unions an opportunity to reach out to parents and grassroots groups. The unions' resources and organizational expertise joined with the passion and sympathetic appeal of the opt-out movement to give both a stronger voice.

Given this political climate, there was general uncertainty about the likelihood of ESEA reauthorization during Obama's presidency. In 2013 and 2014, years after ESEA was due for reauthorization, there was little hope of a bill passing. Indeed, even as late as July 2015, less than half of "insiders" surveyed in *Education Insider* predicted it would be reauthorized by December of that year. That projection proved wrong, for reasons Alyson Klein details in the following chapter. In December 2015, to the surprise of many, ESEA reauthorization not only rose from the dead; it did so with nearly as much apparent consensus as had marked the passage of NCLB fourteen years before. On December 2, the House voted in favor 359–64 (with 10 not voting); on December 9, the Senate voted in favor 85–12 (with 3 not voting). Of those who voted, every single Democrat supported the law, joining almost three out of every four Republicans.

CONCLUSION

The idea that policy making should be buffered from partisan, ideological, and interest-group politics has deep roots in American political thought. It goes back at least to the Progressive Era slogan that there "is no Democratic or Republican way to pave a street."[47] Instead of party strategizing, ideology, and interest-group maneuvering, the hope of some is to see policy as a province marked by collective learning based on experience and rigorous evidence. This view has had particular resonance in education, where it has been considered particularly important to protect children from the political games of adults.[48]

To someone sharing this perspective, it is tempting to see in this era a nonpartisan, logical progression at work. Other chapters in this volume detail some of the ways in which ESSA differs from NCLB—and times may prove these differences to be important—but both Republicans and Democrats have taken pains to characterize ESSA less as a repudiation of NCLB than as a correction based on learning about the limitations of test-based accountability and the importance of state buy-in and capacity.

As we have suggested, though, the path from NCLB to ESSA was not a straight line, and the various course adjustments were dictated as much by politics as by shared learning. A changing political environment and strategic responses to that environment played key roles in catalyzing contingent alliances that proved fragile. The strong support for both NCLB and ESSA at the time of passage is a story in part of how "strange bedfellows" come together for policy change. Such coalitions obscure differences in values, perceptions, loyalties, and strategic interests that are rooted in party and ideological disagreements and destined to reemerge.

Others have noted ambiguity in major legislative proposals as part of the explanation for why strange bedfellows can unite: legislative negotiators often deliberately allow a bill to have ill-defined concepts and vague commitments in order to make it sufficiently palatable and allow both sides to claim victories. We add to this the phenomenon of "guessing forward." In deciding whether or not to sign on, key actors place bets on a range of complicated matters: the specifics buried in the laws; the ways those specifics will be interpreted in the rule-making process; the vagaries of state and district implementation; the uncertain responsiveness of various private actors, including for-profit and nonprofit providers, foundations, and parents; and the as-yet-unknown external shocks to the system that might come from sudden economic, social, or political changes. The fact that they end up voting together does not mean that strange bedfellows are agreeing on what's needed so much as that they are making different predictions about what will happen next.

How ESSA Passed

The Inside Scoop

Alyson Klein

O n December 10, 2015, schoolchildren, teachers, education advocates, and lawmakers from across the political spectrum gathered to witness and celebrate the signing of the Every Student Succeeds Act.

They had good reason to be jubilant. The bipartisan legislation to replace the withered, nearly universally despised No Child Left Behind Act coasted through both houses of Congress by overwhelming margins—an eye-popping feat in an era of partisan paralysis. It brought together some of the most conservative Republicans in Congress with teacher unions, state education chiefs, and even the coalition of civil rights and business leaders that had been behind NCLB.

The conservative *Wall Street Journal* called ESSA the biggest retreat of the federal role in K–12 education in twenty-five years. The law's Democratic sponsors called it a continuation of the Elementary and Secondary Education Act's civil rights legacy. Remarkably, both were arguably correct.

Amid the celebratory selfies, it was easy to forget that this reauthorization was more than seven years overdue, and that its path was riddled with partisan potholes. There were multiple moments through the course of 2015 when nearly everyone in Washington assumed the effort would falter just as previous attempts had.

As a reporter for *Education Week* for more than a decade, I covered failed attempt after failed attempt. At the beginning of the year, I counted myself among the skeptics. This chapter will give you a front-row seat to how one of the most partisan, deadlocked Congresses in recent history pulled off a long-elusive reauthorization that touched nearly all of their constituents.

THE CAST OF CHARACTERS

Getting the legislation through Congress took a mix of good timing, old-school wheeling and dealing, and just the right collection of characters. Each of the four lawmakers who forged ESSA had been on Capitol Hill for over a decade and commanded respect. Each wanted to get to "yes" on a reauthorization. And each believed that 2015 could offer the best shot at a law that embraced their priorities.

ESSA's architects included Sen. Lamar Alexander (R-TN), the new chairman of the Senate committee on Health, Education, Labor, and Pensions. Alexander, a former US secretary of education and former governor of the Volunteer State, was bent on reining in an Education Department that had begun acting like a "national school board."

He was particularly incensed that Secretary of Education Arne Duncan and his team had attached prescriptive requirements to its No Child Left Behind waivers (see chapter 2 for more on this). More than once, Alexander likened the bureaucratic back and forth to a game of "Mother May I?" between the administration and the states.

And, as it turned out, Alexander had a willing dance partner in Sen. Patty Murray (D-WA), the top Democrat on the Senate Education Committee. Even before ESSA's passage, Murray had a reputation as an ace negotiator. In late 2013, for instance, she worked with Rep. Paul Ryan (R-WI) to craft a fiscal deal that had eluded the rest of their Capitol Hill colleagues.

What's more, Murray had an extra incentive to push forward on reauthorization. Washington State lost its NCLB waiver, thanks to a difference of opinion with the administration on whether teacher evaluation should be based on local or state tests. Murray tried to intervene, to no avail. She never said publicly that Secretary Duncan had been unfair, but she did cite the loss of the waiver as a major reason NCLB needed to be replaced sooner rather than later.

The leaders in the House were equally important. Rep. John Kline (R-MN), chairman of the House Committee on Education and the Workforce, shared Alexander's frustration with the Obama administration's "overreach" on K–12. Kline had already drafted partisan reauthorization legislation that hadn't made it over the finish line. But he'd also worked across the aisle on bills on charter school and workforce development.

Rep. Robert C. "Bobby" Scott (D-VA), the top Democrat on the House Education Committee, stayed on the sidelines at first. But he ultimately played a key role in crafting the toughest compromise: accountability. Scott voted for NCLB in 2001 and wanted any rewrite to maintain a focus on making achievement gaps transparent. But he didn't think the federal government should tell schools exactly how to help historically disadvantaged groups; to his mind, that hadn't worked well under NCLB.

In fact, when I asked Kline why reauthorization finally happened this time, he told me, "The really secret sauce was the fact that everybody was fed up with No Child Left Behind."[1]

THE OBAMA ADMINISTRATION: EXECUTIVE ACTION

The Obama administration, which had stood aloof during the 2013 rewrite effort, had an incentive to play ball this time around. The president had just two years left in office. If Obama moved on without a new ESEA in place, the administration's waivers—which had no grounding in legislation—could be quickly put aside by his successor. The president's entire K–12 legacy might be swept away by a Republican. And even under a Democrat, key elements could be rolled back.

To be sure, Duncan and his team had tried to advance their ESEA renewal vision, releasing a proposal back in 2010. But the administration got much of its K–12 wish list through the American Recovery and Reinvestment Act, which included $100 billion for education.

Part of that money—about $4 billion—went to the creation of Race to the Top, which rewarded a dozen states for embracing the Common Core, test-based teacher evaluation, and more. The stimulus also doled out $3 billion to turn around the nation's worst performing schools by taking dramatic actions, such as replacing the principal and removing at least half the teaching force. Both initiatives were unveiled with great fanfare.

But those good feelings didn't last. Teacher unions, who especially disliked the practice of tying their members' evaluations to test scores while standards and assessments were changing, became some of the loudest critics. Race to the Top and the turnaround program grew increasingly unpopular on the Hill, as did Duncan himself.

Even so, it wasn't until the Obama administration rolled out its waiver plan in 2011, which it called a stopgap solution to a stalled reauthorization, that Congress started considering an ESEA rewrite in earnest for the first time in years.

THE FIRST FAILED ATTEMPTS

An initial draft of a nominally bipartisan bill, written by then education chairman Sen. Tom Harkin (D-IA) and ranking member Sen. Mike Enzi (R-WY), incorporated ideas from the administration's reauthorization proposal, including one of the president's top K–12 priorities: test-based teacher evaluation.

But Republicans on the Senate Education Committee worked in tandem with the National Education Association (NEA) to jettison that provision before the legislation was ever formally introduced. Senator Alexander saw federal interference in teacher performance reviews as overreach. The lack of the requirement helped sour the Obama administration on that attempt.

What's more, civil rights groups were concerned that the bill weakened NCLB's accountability requirements, particularly for underperforming subgroups of students. That was a deal breaker. A Democratic-only bill in 2013 was even less politically viable.

Meanwhile, Kline managed to pass an ESEA reauthorization bill through the House in 2013. The legislation, which became a basis for ESSA, put states and districts in the driver's seat on accountability and slashed dozens of federal programs. It also contained a provision for "Title I portability," which would allow states to use federal Title I funds to create public school choice programs. Portability was popular with Republicans, but others saw it as a backdoor attempt at a voucher program.

Kline also put a personal premium on an issue close to the administration's heart: test-based teacher evaluations. But more conservative members of the House, working at a similar purpose as the unions, forced the education chairman to ditch that provision.

Those past attempts foreshadowed the political dynamic that would ultimately be crucial to the passage of ESSA: the unlikely meeting of the minds between education associations, who typically worked with Democrats, and Republicans bent on reining in the federal role.

ALEXANDER'S PARTISAN OPENING GAMBIT

ESSA ended up as a major bipartisan achievement, but it started off on a decidedly partisan note. Soon after the 2014 midterm election, which gave Republicans control of the Senate and put Alexander at the helm of the Education Committee, he declared that his first priority was fixing NCLB.

Rumors began to fly that Alexander, who had already found common cause with teacher unions over test-based teacher evaluation, was considering getting rid of federally mandated annual testing altogether. It was the move that the civil rights community and the White House probably feared the most. And there was reason to believe that some key players, especially teacher unions, would welcome it with open arms. A crescendo of opposition against NCLB's standardized testing had reached a fever pitch by 2015. As teacher evaluation tests were layered over other federal, state, and local tests, both parents and teachers increasingly decried testing itself.

Parents—some of whom were also wary of new, federally funded Common Core–aligned tests—chose to opt their children out of testing altogether. And in 2014, ahead of the midterm elections, the National Education Association and the American Federation of Teachers backed different House bills to let states test students in certain grade spans instead of every year.

Those bills, coupled with the social media–fueled "opt-out" movement, put civil rights organizations and their Democratic allies in a tight spot. They didn't want to back off NCLB's mandate for annual reading and math tests in grades 3–8. They saw yearly assessments as an essential element in ensuring all students had access to an equitable education. But they couldn't ignore the public outcry.

Democrats attempted to chart a middle course. In December 2014, Rep. Suzanne Bonamici (D-OR) introduced legislation allowing federal funds to be used to rethink state and local tests. The Obama administration quickly backed the legislation. But the strategy didn't work, at least not entirely. The NEA endorsed Bonamici's bill, but continued to beat the drum on grade-span testing.

Meanwhile, Alexander let the question hang in the air. The very first hearing on ESEA reauthorization centered on testing and whether there was too much of it. And in January, Alexander released a "discussion draft" that was similar to the bill that had passed the House in 2013, but with a twist: two options for testing. One kept intact NCLB's schedule of reading and math tests in grades 3–8 and once in high school. The other allowed states to use whatever measures they wanted—summative tests, portfolios, performance tasks—as frequently or infrequently as they wanted. Progressive antitesting groups swooned at the sight of that second option.

Democrats allied with the civil rights community to save the tests. In the process, the debate over whether to preserve a strong federal role in accountability was elbowed out of the spotlight.

A day before Alexander's draft came out, Duncan gave a speech acknowl-edging the problems with overtesting, while making it clear that the admin-istration would not support a reauthorization that cut back on yearly assessments. "I am absolutely convinced that we need to know how much progress students are making," Duncan said. "But we also must do more to ensure that the tests—and time spent in preparation for them—don't take excessive time away from actual classroom instruction."

Meanwhile, some Democratic organizations seemingly panicked. The Center for American Progress, a think tank closely associated with the Obama administration, teamed up with the AFT to endorse an approach that called for annual testing, but accountability only in certain grade spans. If the Obama administration or congressional Democrats had adopted this proposal, it would have been a big concession on accountability, right out of the gate.

Alexander's original plan was to write a GOP-only bill and move it through the legislative process, with most Democrats and the Obama administra-tion joining relatively late in the day. But Murray wanted to be part of the process from the beginning, and the White House made it known it would consider an ESEA overhaul, so long as it was bipartisan in spirit.

In early February, Alexander and Murray made a surprise announce-ment: they'd team up to fix NCLB. Their collaboration may have had a rocky start, but once they decided to work together, it became the engine that propelled reauthorization throughout the year and, finally, over the fin-ish line. "I knew that if we pushed through a partisan bill we would not fix this," Murray told me later.[2]

In the short term, their partnership helped quell fears that the final leg-islation would ditch NCLB's annual testing regime. Murray had already made it clear she wasn't willing to get rid of any of the federally required tests. Nor were Alexander's colleagues in the House; Kline and Rep. John A. Boehner, the Speaker of the House and an author of NCLB, both favored maintaining the tests.

By that point, Alexander was on board, too. He said that he had been persuaded by groups like charter advocates—who told him they needed annual testing data to demonstrate to the public that their schools were of high quality—as well as by Republicans who spoke out in favor of the need for transparency, including Marty West, a Harvard professor who had done a stint in Alexander's office. (See chapter 5 for West's take on ESSA.) In fact, advocates wondered later whether Alexander had ever seriously considered paring back the tests, or whether the proposal had just been a negotiating tactic to get education organizations on his side early on and persuade Democrats to accept a slimmed-down federal role in accountability and greater funding flexibility.

Alexander told me later that, in fact, both were true. "I *was* seriously considering it because we heard more about overtesting than any other issue," he said. "I thought that was an option we should consider—in fact, I thought it would be irresponsible if we didn't consider it. But it also had the effect of shocking people and creating a place for [Democrats] to have a win when we kept it."[3]

To be sure, there were still plenty of testing questions left on the negotiating table: How much would tests matter in gauging school performance, as opposed to other factors, like school climate and teacher engagement? Could districts use their own tests instead of state exams for accountability? Murray, Alexander, and their staff hunkered down to consider the issues.

Meanwhile, Duncan held a series of public events and gave speeches that showcased the administration's other top priorities for the law, including a continued focus on closing the achievement gap, implementing college-ready standards, and providing resources for early childhood education.

REVOLT ON THE RIGHT

For their part, House Republicans moved forward on what was supposed to be an easy step: approving essentially the same party-line bill that had passed two years earlier. That legislation scrapped dozens of education programs by rolling them into a block grant, made it clear that the Education Department couldn't require states to embrace Common Core or any other standards, and allowed for Title I portability. Everyone expected smooth sailing. After all, the main controversy last time was over test-based teacher evaluations, and House leaders had already made that concession.

So, for a few days late in February, Kline and others extolled the bill's local control virtues. Democrats, led by Scott, vehemently but predictably opposed the bill as an attack on the civil rights of the children NCLB had been designed to protect. The White House threatened to veto the bill. Lawmakers adopted, among other changes, an amendment that would have allowed districts to substitute local tests for state exams.

But backstage, the bill's support was shakier than it appeared. The conservative Heritage Action Fund, which had criticized the 2013 version, circulated statements that this measure didn't go nearly far enough. In fact, the group decided to "score" the vote, Washington lingo for factoring it into lawmakers' overall rating on their legislative "report card."

The Heritage Action Fund was especially miffed that its favored amendments were kept from the floor in order to smooth the legislative path. These included an option for federal funds to be used for private—not just public—school choice, and a proposal that would have enabled states to say "thanks, but no thanks" to federal accountability, while still getting federal money. The Club for Growth, an influential antitax organization, joined the effort to defeat the bill. And an anti–Common Core blogger in Utah claimed (erroneously) that the bill mandated the standards. Her post went viral, prompting constituent calls to House conservatives. That didn't help matters.

Eventually, Kline and his allies admitted they simply didn't have the votes, and pulled the bill. "If I made a mistake, and I have to admit that I did . . . I didn't realize how many people didn't know, were not familiar with the debate," Kline told me later. "It took me longer to get people informed, to get them educated, on the education bill, than I had anticipated."[4] Supporters took cold comfort in the fact that the legislation hadn't actually failed to pass; it had simply been postponed. Advocates were despondent. It looked like the effort was dead yet again.

THE SHOW GOES ON IN THE SENATE

But over on the other side of the Capitol, Alexander and Murray pushed on, undaunted. In March, the pair went to the White House, where President Obama outlined his priorities, including annual testing, an early childhood education program, and a requirement that states identify and intervene in the lowest performing 5 percent of their schools.

Murray agreed, and Alexander felt the list was doable, even if all of the president's priorities couldn't be in the initial proposal. "I said, 'Mr. President, in order to get a result, we have to present you with a bill that you are comfortable signing. We'll keep the testing,'" Alexander recalled later. He told the president that he and Murray were sorting through the early childhood issue, and that Congress would do "something on the 5 percent" but they probably wouldn't be able to add it to the bill before conference.[5]

Murray and her staff, meanwhile, were aware that whatever deal they forged would have to take a step backward from NCLB's strong federal role on accountability. But they successfully advocated for a number of additional reporting requirements that they hoped would give districts a clearer picture of how historically disadvantaged students were performing.

As difficult as it was to reach consensus on areas like accountability, it was actually another issue that threatened to blow up the Senate negotiations: early childhood education. Murray, a former preschool teacher, put her foot down, saying she wasn't going to support the bill without an early childhood education program.

Alexander didn't see the rationale for adding a preschool twist to a K–12 law. And he knew a new program, particularly one that bolstered Obama's education legacy, would only make the bill a tougher sell with conservatives. Ultimately, he turned the issue over to Sen. Johnny Isakson (R-GA), who'd worked with Murray before on workforce development legislation. They crafted a preschool amendment, and Alexander agreed to support it in committee.

In April, Alexander and Murray introduced a bill that addressed nearly every one of the most serious concerns that state chiefs, school board members, teachers, and principals had about NCLB. The testing regime at the center of the law remained the same, but states could figure out how much those tests would factor in for accountability purposes. And a small group of states could get permission from the Education Department to pilot new assessments, like performance tasks, in a handful of districts before going statewide. Title I portability was out. There were resources for interventions in low performing schools, but no requirement to turn around a specific percentage of schools, as the White House had wanted. And there was a lengthy list of prohibitions on the education secretary's authority when it came to teacher evaluations, school turnaround methods, and more.

Days later, the ideologically diverse Senate Education Committee passed the compromise unanimously, sending a strong signal that reauthorization was back on track. The panel made a few tweaks in committee—adding, for instance, the early childhood education program. But they left the trickiest issues, accountability and secretarial authority, for further down the legislative road. Lawmakers agreed to save amendments that might have doomed the bill's chances for further consideration—including a bullying amendment and an Alexander-authored voucher provision—for the floor.

Advocates for practitioners and state and district education leaders rushed to embrace the bill and called for quick floor action. The civil rights community, meanwhile, hung back, making it clear that they wanted to see accountability provisions beefed up, particularly for the lowest performing schools and student subgroups. But, unlike in 2011, they didn't attempt to smother the bill. That was partly because some in the community believed 2015 was their best chance to preserve annual assessments and a serious focus on historically underperforming groups of students. It was impossible to guess where the next president's heart might be on these issues, so they wanted Obama to sign and regulate the law.

THE HOUSE BILL GETS DRAGGED ACROSS THE FINISH LINE

Meanwhile, for months, supporters of the rewrite were trying to persuade recalcitrant House Republicans to support the legislation. Kline's staff held roundtables with lawmakers on the fence. It helped that the process was moving along in the Senate; Kline's aides could assure nervous lawmakers they weren't taking a tough vote for nothing. Boehner and other GOP leaders also helped grease the wheels.

Ultimately, the legislation was scheduled again for floor action in July, but not before conservatives had a chance to vote on a package of changes they hadn't been able to consider the first time around. One, which was scored by the Heritage Action Fund, would have allowed states to essentially opt out of federal accountability altogether. It failed to pass but still garnered 195 Republican votes.

Two other changes ultimately made it into the House version of the bill, including one that shortened the "authorization" period of ESEA from five to four years, giving the new president a chance to put their stamp on the next iteration of the law during their first term. The other, which sailed through the chamber with substantial help from Democrats, permitted parents to allow their children to opt out of standardized tests without penalties for their schools.

Even with those concessions, the legislation barely squeaked through the House, passing by a hair-raising margin of 218 to 213, with no Democrats on board. Lawmakers reportedly changed their votes from no to yes in the final minutes. For its part, the Obama administration vowed to veto the bill, and Secretary Duncan said, "House Republicans have chosen to take a bad bill and make it even worse."

THE SENATE MARCHES ON

Shortly afterward, the Senate passed its own NCLB rewrite, after about a week of debate. From the outside, the process on the north side of the

Capitol was almost boring, especially compared to the cliff-hanger in the House. But that was because Alexander, Murray, and their aides had spent weeks smoothing over potential trouble spots. Alexander's education staff, for instance, visited the office of every Republican senator, armed with editorials supporting the bill from conservative-leaning papers like the *Washington Times*. The last thing they wanted was a repeat of what happened on the House side.

Both sides were prepared for a fight over accountability. Sen. Christopher Murphy (D-CT), who had voted for the bill in committee, put together an amendment that included much of the civil rights community's wish list, and had White House backing. It would have called for states to take action in the bottom 5 percent of schools and high schools where less than two-thirds of students graduate, and to identify schools that didn't meet their achievement targets for any subgroup of students for two years in a row or more. And, under the amendment, the secretary of education could tell states how much tests had to count toward a school's performance rating. The amendment was designed to bolster accountability while holding together the bill's coalition of supporters.

Still, the NEA worked to defeat Murphy's amendment. The union said that the requirements would just continue the failed policies of NCLB. In one letter, the NEA warned that it would score the vote, as the Heritage Action Fund had with amendments on the House side. But the Democrats—with Murray's help—muscled up forty-three votes in favor of the changes, including one from a Republican, Rob Portman (R-OH). That wasn't enough to get the amendment over the finish line, but civil rights and disability advocates congratulated themselves anyway. At least it was clear that Senate Democrats favored a more robust approach to accountability.

With that, the legislation coasted to passage on a vote of 81 to 17. A smattering of Democrats, including Murphy, voted against it. So did fourteen Republicans bent on slimming down the federal role in education, including all three Republicans running for president: Sens. Ted Cruz of Texas, Rand Paul of Kentucky, and Marco Rubio of Florida.

By this point, ESEA reauthorization had gotten further than almost anyone had initially expected—further, in fact, than at any point in the past eight years. The clock, however, was ticking. So far, education had flown under the radar in the 2016 presidential contest, but the bills' sponsors assumed that couldn't last. Lawmakers figured they would be best off finishing the bill by the end of the year before it could get mired in election-year politics.

CRISIS AND OPPORTUNITY

And then something happened that seemed to throw a monkey wrench into the proceedings: Boehner announced his resignation as Speaker of the House. For a short time, no one knew who would fill the Speaker's chair. Negotiators put in even longer days, hoping to finish their task either before Boehner stepped down, or more realistically, early into the new Speaker's tenure, when the bill could still credibly be viewed as part of Boehner's legacy. Advocates fretted that months of work would amount to nothing. They feared the new Speaker would be too beholden to hardliners to move a bill to the left of one House conservatives had nearly rejected.

Those fears turned out to be unfounded when Rep. Paul Ryan (R-WI) stepped into the job. Ryan made it known that he wanted a return to old-school legislating, of which the ESEA bill was a prime example. He agreed to bring any compromise to the floor, but hoped to see it finished by the end of the year, congressional aides said.

Meanwhile, negotiators were still searching for the sweet spot on some of the stickiest issues. Civil rights groups and some in the business community found the accountability provisions in both versions deeply unsatisfactory. The legislation would have to move to the left of both bills, at least somewhat, in order to win support from House Democrats, and just as crucially, the White House.

This is where Representative Scott proved critical. "To get Democratic support, we wanted improvements over both bills," he said. "That is unusual in a conference committee because a conference committee is usually just an opportunity to reconcile the differences."[6]

The requirement to turn around the bottom 5 percent of schools was almost a given, since it was the White House's top ask. But Scott knew he had to do something for subgroups of students and schools with high dropout rates. He also knew that some civil rights groups felt the waivers hadn't been strong enough when it came to requiring interventions in schools where at least one group of student—say, English language learners—was struggling to succeed.

At the same time, Republicans were wary of anything that smacked of NCLB. They didn't want prescriptive timelines that told states and districts what they had to do when. And they wanted states to largely be able to decide what constituted poor performance.

Threading the needle wasn't easy. But Scott ended up with an unlikely partner in Kline. The two may have sparred when the House passed its version of the rewrite, but now they worked through the trickiest issue together.

Under their agreement, states would intervene in their worst schools, but they'd get to decide what those interventions looked like. The only schools that would automatically be on the hook would be high schools where less than two-thirds of students graduated. And they wouldn't be subjected to a hard-and-fast timeline, with one exception: states would be required to step in after no more than four years if the lowest performing schools (those with high dropout rates or particularly bad subgroup performance) weren't getting any better.

"We did not compromise at all on the objective that you have to measure and fix achievement gaps," Scott said later. "We just told the states 'you have to get the job done' and they [got] the authority to figure out how to do it."

Kline and Scott presented the plan to the Senate, and it formed the basis of the eventual deal on accountability. "Once we had that, then we really started to roll," Kline said later.[7]

Meanwhile, negotiators were able to sift through equally thorny issues. Title I portability, for example, was out. There would be considerable consolidation of programs—the bill did away with a school counseling program and grants for Advanced Placement courses, for instance—but it didn't go as far as the House bill in slimming down the Education Department. Some of the compromises were dizzyingly complicated, especially on test participation. Under the agreement, states would be allowed to pass laws allowing parents to opt out of standardized tests. But the bill maintained the requirement that 95 percent of students take assessments.

The other major stumbling block was secretarial authority. The Obama administration, naturally, would have preferred to see those prohibitions—some of which read like a barely disguised personal rebuke of Duncan—stripped out. But Republicans refused to budge, even after Duncan announced his resignation in October. There was no way, Republicans argued, that they would have agreed to an accountability system nearly as robust as the one in the bill if the education secretary still had just as much power to interfere in state K–12 systems as he had before. "I didn't trust the Department to follow the law," Alexander told me later.[8]

In the end, the prohibitions remained, but were tweaked in a way that the administration and the bill's Democratic sponsors felt they could live with.

Under the final bill, for example, the secretary would still have the option to give a thumbs up or down to state accountability plans.

But for all the angst over accountability and the secretary's power during the course of the year, one of the last issues settled was early childhood education. Murray dearly wanted to see the president's preschool development grants enshrined in ESSA. Kline didn't think he could sell a new program, especially one with Obama's fingerprints all over it, to his conservative House colleagues.

Instead, negotiators gave Murray a choice: put the program in the US Department of Health and Human Services, which already had responsibility for early education chiefly through the Head Start program, or accept a much smaller investment at the Education Department. She picked the more robust option at HHS, and retained a role for the Education Department in administering the grants.

It had taken marathon negotiating sessions, including at least one that went all night, but the lawmakers arrived at a deal on the timeline they'd hoped for. They hadn't even had a chance to draft actual legislation. A conference committee ended up almost unanimously agreeing to a "framework" essentially consisting of staff notes. The framework was never officially released publicly because no one was sure if the legislation could pass the House, even with Scott fully on board. No one wanted bloggers picking apart the language. Even the Obama administration stayed quiet about provisions it liked—including what it viewed as similarities between the waivers and ESSA's accountability compromise—because it feared that the White House or Duncan could trip up the bill if they hugged it too hard.

The deal was almost immediately embraced by state chiefs, school superintendents, school boards, and teacher unions. The National Governors Association gave ESSA its full endorsement, marking the first time in nearly twenty years that all the nation's governors got behind a piece of pending legislation.

The civil rights community, meanwhile, kept quiet, saying they were waiting for actual legislative language before expressing their views. When the bill was finally released, some three dozen organizations joined the Leadership Conference on Civil and Human Rights in issuing a milquetoast statement of support. ESSA was an improvement over waivers, they said, but not the bill they would have written.

The legislation sailed through the House, 359–64, with the support of every Democrat and the majority of Republicans, and through the Senate,

85–12, with a handful of Republicans dissenting. On the floor, Alexander marveled that the bill was even a reality. He said he'd had dinner the previous night with a Democratic senator who told him he assumed at the beginning of the year that the effort was probably doomed.

CONCLUSION

ESSA, Alexander said, would release "a flood of innovation" in states and school districts. It would also, he predicted, have staying power. "My guess is that this bill and the policies within it will set the standard for policy in elementary and secondary education from the federal level for the next two decades," Alexander said. "It is a compromise, but it is a very well-crafted piece of work. It is good. It is good policy."

To be sure, even then, many of the staffers and advocates who worked so hard to pass the law knew there would be turmoil ahead. Policy wonks puzzled over how the accountability provisions would square with the crackdown on the education secretary. Both sides tried to define the nascent ESSA in the eyes of the public. Republicans hit the local control aspect hard. The civil rights community and Democrats argued that ESSA didn't translate into a free-for-all for states and districts.

Just a few months into the new year, the good feelings at the end of 2015 would begin to evaporate. Alexander would call Duncan's replacement, John King, on the carpet for overstepping his bounds on proposed regulations for a wonky spending provision of the law, "supplement not supplant." It quickly became clear that the new law didn't put a stop to the age-old debates over the federal role in K–12 education. Instead, the same old controversies continued to dog implementation and regulation.

But, for few brief moments in December 2015, all of that was on pause. ESSA was an achievement of which everyone could be proud.

"This is a big step in the right direction," President Obama said moments before signing the legislation. "A true bipartisan effort, a reminder of what can be done when people enter into these issues in a spirit of listening and compromise."

What ESSA Says

Continuities and Departures

Charles Barone

The Every Student Succeeds Act is a 392-page bill with ten major sections, or "Titles." The most important and hotly debated provisions of the law are contained in Title I, a formula grant focused on the "Education of the Disadvantaged." Title I is funded at about $16 billion in Fiscal Year 2016, roughly 70 percent of ESSA's total funding. The next largest program under ESSA is Title II, Part A, on "Improving Teacher Quality," funded at $2.35 billion. The only other Elementary and Secondary Education Act programs for which FY 2016 funding exceeds $1 billion are Title VIII, "Impact Aid," for militarily connected schools at $1.3 billion, and Title II, Part D, "State Grants for Technology," at $1.2 billion.[1]

This chapter will focus on key features in Title I, including provisions regarding standards, assessments, public reporting, school ratings and accountability, and school interventions. We'll also take a brief look at provisions regarding teacher quality and the equitable distribution of effective and experienced teachers.

ESSA is widely known for scaling back many of the prescriptive elements of No Child Left Behind and devolving authority to states and districts. This is true when it comes to NCLB's highly prescriptive accountability goals, school evaluation metrics, timelines, and school interventions. ESSA also completely removed from federal law in place under NCLB any criteria for defining a "qualified" or "effective" teacher. However, ESSA continues some of the landmark policy mandates of NCLB, such as annual testing in grades 3–8, the disaggregation of student data for different demographic groups, accountability and required interventions in low performing schools, and a focus on narrowing achievement gaps. Moreover, while ESSA allows more latitude in the use of outcomes, it also requires states to deploy additional academic and nonacademic indicators both for public reporting and for identifying and intervening in low performing schools.

Before we launch into a review of ESSA's statutory provisions, there are two key points to keep in mind. First, it's often said that there are two things one should never see being made: laws and sausages. There are a lot of ingredients bound together in any piece of legislation, some of higher quality than others, and without the literal force of the law behind them they'd likely crumble and fall apart. That's a necessary product of the compromises that elected officials must make in drafting and passing a bill. Most bills do not make perfect sense, nor are they entirely internally consistent. ESSA is no exception.

Second, federal policy is a blunt instrument. It's a bit of an oversimplification, but we'll distinguish here between two types of statutory provisions: requirements and requests. Requirements—things states and school districts must do if they choose to apply for federal funding—are clear and easy to monitor (e.g., administering a test each year in a particular subject or grade span, or defining a "dropout factory" high school as one with less than a two-thirds graduation rate). Requests are qualitative or leave specifics open to interpretation (e.g., stipulating that professional development activities be "intensive, collaborative, job-embedded, data-driven, and classroom-focused"). While sometimes provisions that meet this definition of a request may have been intended as requirements, they nonetheless tend to have less impact because they are subject to multiple interpretations and are therefore hard to monitor and enforce. For the most part, we'll focus on the bright-line requirements. The other chapters in this volume offer qualitative takes on the elements in ESSA. This chapter will stick to the plain facts, although occasionally it will provide some context or interpretation for explanatory purposes.

TITLE I

Title I has been the centerpiece of the Elementary and Secondary Education Act since its inception in 1965. Title I contains most of the "requirements," and hence the most hotly debated policies, on academic standards, assessments, public reporting, accountability, and school interventions.

As Patrick McGuinn detailed in chapter 1, the Improving America's Schools Act made fundamental changes to Title I, and those changes have been carried over across NCLB, waivers, and now to ESSA. IASA required all states to have academic standards, aligned statewide assessments, performance goals, and interventions in schools that miss performance targets for several consecutive years. NCLB added to and tightened requirements in each of these areas, and the Obama administration's waivers loosened them somewhat, though not quite back to the level of flexibility in IASA. In each of the areas covered next, it may be helpful to think of ESSA as somewhere on the spectrum *between* IASA and NCLB.

Academic Standards

Under ESSA, states must adopt academic standards in at least mathematics, English language arts (ELA), and science. The standards must have at least three levels of achievement and apply to all public schools and public school students in the state. ESSA requires that the standards be "challenging" and that each state demonstrate that the standards are "aligned with entrance requirements for credit-bearing coursework in the system of public higher education in the state and relevant state career and technical education standards."

ELA and math standards have been required since IASA, and NCLB added the science requirement. The requirements that the standards be "challenging," apply to "all public schools" and "all students," and specify three levels of achievement also date back to IASA. The Obama administration's waivers did not substantively change any of these policies. ESSA's requirement that standards be aligned with the requirements of credit-bearing coursework in college is new.

Also new are ESSA's English proficiency standards for English language learners. Each state must establish English proficiency standards that include the domains of speaking, listening, reading, and writing; address the different proficiency levels of English learners; and are aligned with the state's academic standards. "English learners" are defined as those who were not born in the United States, whose native language is a language other than English, or who come from an environment where a language other than English is dominant. ESSA's new English proficiency standards are the foundation for a whole new set of aligned provisions—especially under the "assessments" and "accountability" parts of the law—that seek to help English learners achieve English proficiency.

ESSA allows states to set alternate standards for students with the "most significant cognitive disabilities." Such standards must nonetheless be aligned with the state's academic content standards and promote access to the general education curriculum, as required by the Individuals with Disabilities Education Act. These alternate standards must also be aligned such that students who meet them are on track to pursue postsecondary education or employment, as required by other federal laws related to persons with disabilities.

Limits on Federal Authority

As chapter 2 detailed, the Common Core was one of the most controversial topics in education under the Obama administration. President Obama and Secretary of Education Arne Duncan used the bully pulpit to tout Common Core, and points were given to states under Race to the Top if they adopted multistate (implicitly, though not specifically, Common Core) standards.[2] Conservative congressional Republicans were determined to ensure that the Department of Education could not influence states to adopt any particular set of standards, especially Common Core. Thus, ESSA specifically declares: "the Secretary shall not attempt to influence, incentivize, or coerce State adoption of the Common Core State Standards developed under the Common Core State Standards Initiative or any other academic standards common to a significant number of States, or assessments tied to such standards."

These new provisions did not actually mark a significant change. ESSA provisions with regard to restrictions on federal authority over state standards are fairly similar to those under IASA and NCLB. This reflects the fact that conservative concerns about states' rights on education policy in general and standards in particular, while inflamed by Common Core, are nothing new. Moreover, despite singling out Common Core as a no-go federal policy, ESSA actually goes further than either of the prior two reauthorizations in requiring that standards be aligned with college-bearing coursework in postsecondary education and training, essentially codifying Common Core's underlying aim to promote college and career readiness.

In sum, ESSA provisions on standards enable the secretary of education, if he or she chooses, to enforce the subjects in which each state has standards; that there be three levels of performance; that the same standards apply to all schools and students; and that the standards are aligned with college-bearing coursework. All of these can be demonstrated without the state submitting the standards themselves to the secretary of education. Rigorously enforcing the provision that standards are "challenging," however, is probably not feasible and is therefore largely left to state discretion.

Academic Assessments

Subjects and grades tested

Under ESSA, each state's assessments have to be aligned with the state's academic standards in math, ELA, and science; administered statewide; and be the same tests for public elementary school, middle school, and secondary school students in the state. Tests in ELA and math must be administered annually in grades 3–8 and at least once in the grade span 9–12. Science assessments must be administered annually at least once in each of the following grade spans: 3–5, 6–8, and 9–11.

ESSA's testing requirements are identical to NCLB (though there are some new exceptions, described next). Statewide tests in math and ELA have been required since IASA, though under IASA they were grade-span tests for grades 3–5, 6–8, and 9–12, rather than annually in grades 3–8. The science grade-span testing requirement was first instituted under NCLB and remains unchanged under ESSA.

Exceptions

There are exceptions to some of the provisions just outlined. The state may administer "alternate" assessments to students with disabilities, aligned with the alternate standards previously described. The bill, however, caps the proportion of students who can take alternate assessments at 1 percent, which is equal to about 10 percent of all students with disabilities. This is intended to correlate to the percentage of students with severe cognitive disabilities.[3] Participation in the alternate assessment cannot disqualify a student from attaining a regular high school diploma.

One underlying purpose of these exceptions is to reduce time spent on state and federally mandated testing. First, a state may exempt students from the eighth-grade math assessment if they take an end-of-course math assessment that "the State typically administers" to meet the high school math assessment requirement, and if they take in high school a math assessment that is more advanced than the end-of-course assessment they took to satisfy the eighth-grade math test requirement. The number of contingencies here, and the fact that the exemption applies to a student rather than a school or district, presents a number of challenges in terms of federal and state oversight and enforcement.

Second, to satisfy the high school assessment requirements, local education agencies may, with state approval, choose to substitute a "nationally recognized" assessment in lieu of the statewide assessments in reading, math, and science. This provision recognizes that many high school students already take nationally recognized standardized assessments, such as the SAT or ACT, that are designed to measure college and career readiness. The nationally recognized high school assessment must meet technical criteria established by the state; provide comparable, valid, and reliable data on academic achievement, as compared to the state-designed assessments, for all students and for each subgroup of students; and report results in terms consistent with the state's academic achievement standards.

Assessment quality and technical provisions

ESSA specifies that state assessments must provide coherent and timely information about student attainment of academic standards and whether a student is performing at grade level. Assessments can be used only for purposes for which they are valid and reliable, consistent with relevant, nationally recognized professional and technical testing standards. The statute specifies that assessments are intended to objectively measure academic achievement, knowledge, and skills, not to assess personal or family beliefs and attitudes, or publicly disclose personally identifiable information. ESSA stipulates that state assessments include measures that assess "higher-order" thinking skills and understanding.

IASA and NCLB contained very similar quality and technical guidelines. Outside of widely used terms like *reliability* and *validity*, for which there is clear professional consensus regarding definitions and measurement, these guidelines are very hard to monitor and enforce.[4] From 1994, when assessments were first required of all fifty states under IASA, through the present, there has been widespread criticism that assessment results are not presented in a "timely" fashion and that state assessments do not assess higher-order thinking skills.[5] On the latter point, however, there does seem to be some consensus that new state assessments, such as Partnership for Assessment of Readiness for College and Careers (PARCC) and Smarter, Balanced, are an improvement.[6]

One new wrinkle, not part of IASA, NCLB, or waivers, is the allowance in ESSA that assessments may be "partially delivered in the form of portfolios, projects, or extended performance tasks." A portfolio assessment is a collection of student work that could include virtually anything, such as essays, homework assignments, term papers, quizzes, or drawings. A project or extended performance task could be anything from a writing assignment to a lab experiment to the creation of a video, and may include work that students do either individually or in groups.[7]

Such assessments may promote innovation and better engage students than standardized pencil-and-paper tests. They also present significant challenges with regard to state and local capacity, assessment quality, and comparability. For example, previous attempts to implement statewide systems of portfolio assessments have proven to be both extremely expensive and generally too unreliable for use as summative assessments (i.e., assessments used for the purpose of state accountability systems).[8] Portfolios are almost by definition based and scored in the classroom, so it is also unclear how such assessments would meet the requirement that state assessments be the same ones administered to all students.

A second new feature of ESSA lets states pilot new assessments in a select group of districts before taking them statewide. This pilot program, which up to seven states can test, could portend big changes in state assessment systems. These assessments must meet professional psychometric guidelines; be challenging and aligned with state academic standards and, in turn, with what's required for enrollment in credit-bearing college coursework; and be comparable across all students in the state.

One state—New Hampshire—was given the go-ahead for such an initiative through a waiver issued by the US Department of Education, prior to the passage of ESSA. A couple of years into the program, experts involved in its creation conceded that there were "a lot of technical hurdles to overcome."[9] According to Jennifer Davis Poon, program director of the Innovation Lab Network at the Council of Chief State School Officers: "A particular challenge in New Hampshire is figuring out how to get comparable results across locally developed tasks that vary from one district to another."[10]

English language acquisition

As explained earlier, ESSA contains new requirements—not present in IASA, NCLB, or waivers—to strengthen instruction for English language learners. Each state plan must demonstrate that local educational agencies provide them with annual assessments of English proficiency. These local assessments must be aligned with state standards for English language acquisition. The aligned assessments are a mandatory part of state account-ability systems.

With regard to all of the assessments previously outlined, states must produce individual student reports that allow parents, teachers, principals, and other school leaders to gauge student achievement. These reports must explain and address the specific academic needs of students and be provided to parents, teachers, and school leaders, as soon as is practicable after the assessment is given, in an understandable and uniform format. There are also public reporting requirements, reviewed shortly.

Additional indicator

Another new requirement under ESSA is that each state must have at least one indicator in addition to those already specified. The assessment could pertain to an individual student or, unlike the aforementioned assessments, be a survey of educators, a gauge of parent participation, or a measure of school climate or school quality. This additional indicator may be aca-demic (e.g., postsecondary readiness or student access to and completion of advanced coursework) or nonacademic (e.g., school safety or discipline). States have wide latitude here. The statute merely lists possibilities. ESSA does, however, specify that this indicator must allow for meaningful differ-entiation in school performance; be valid, reliable, comparable, and state-wide; and be the same indicator or indicators used for all students in each grade span.

Public reporting

Each state and local education agency is required to issue, disseminate, and make publicly available a report card that includes a fairly comprehensive set of data on student academic performance and school quality. The report must be concise; presented in an understandable and uniform format; pro-vided, to the extent practicable, in a language that parents can understand; and widely accessible to the public, including being available on a single web page of the state educational agency's website. These provisions are not dissimilar to those under IASA and NCLB and have been proven hard to monitor and enforce. Many, if not most, states have fairly labyrinthine websites that are not easy to navigate. Rarely, if ever, is all the information presented on a single web page.

DATA REQUIREMENTS

Meeting the requirement for concision will prove tricky because ESSA requires reporting of a considerable amount of new data. All data must be reported for the state as a whole, for each school district, and for each school if sample sizes are sufficiently large—as determined by the state—to ensure statistical reliability and to protect the privacy of individual students. Data must be disaggregated for subgroups of students, including students from historically disadvantaged groups, a continuation of one of the landmark policies first instituted by NCLB. All student data must be disaggregated for:

- economically disadvantaged students;
- students from major racial and ethnic groups;
- children with disabilities; and
- English learners.

Other subgroup reporting, depending on the variable, is required for:

- males and females;
- students whose parents are migrant workers;
- homeless children;
- children in foster care; and
- children of military families.

Here is a partial list of data that must be included in state reports:

- information on student achievement for all of the academic assessments described previously
- the percentage of students assessed and not assessed on each of those statewide assessments
- high school graduation rates (four-year cohort rate)
- measures of:
  - school quality, climate, and safety
  - rates of in-school suspensions, out-of-school suspensions, and expulsions
  - school-related arrests and referrals to law enforcement
  - chronic absenteeism (including both excused and unexcused absences)
  - incidences of violence, including bullying and harassment

- the number and percentage of students enrolled in:
  - preschool programs
  - accelerated coursework such as Advanced Placement and International Baccalaureate courses and examinations, and dual or concurrent enrollment programs
- the professional qualifications of teachers and school leaders, including information, disaggregated by high-poverty versus low-poverty schools, on the number and percentage of:
  - inexperienced teachers, principals, and other school leaders
  - teachers teaching with emergency or provisional credentials
  - teachers who are not teaching in the subject or field for which they are certified or licensed
- per-pupil expenditures—federal, state, and local—including actual personnel expenditures and nonpersonnel expenditures for each local educational agency and each school in the state (the "school level" reporting here is a big deal and major policy change under ESSA because pre-ESSA practice was to report only districtwide teacher salaries, a practice that hides seniority-driven salary differences that tend to favor schools with lower percentages of low-income and minority students)

ACCOUNTABILITY

To understand ESSA's accountability system, it's worth reviewing the evolution of federal accountability requirements since IASA.

IASA

Under IASA, states were required to set markers of Adequate Yearly Progress (AYP) based on student progress on statewide reading and math assessments. But those assessments were required to be administered only once in each of three grade spans: 3–5, 6–8, and 9–12. Few states really set annual measurable objectives consistent with the AYP requirement, and for the whole of the reauthorization period, the Clinton administration did not enforce it. Clinton did create accountability incentives by securing more than $100 million in 2000, the last year of his term, for states that identified their lowest performing schools to help with school turnarounds or to provide greater public school choice, including through the creation of new public charter schools.

NCLB

NCLB supercharged the AYP structure that never was truly implemented in states under IASA. In defining AYP, NCLB required states to define annual measurable objectives on reading and math assessments administered in grades 3–8. For high schools, graduation rates had to be part of the equation, as did, for all schools, one additional statewide indicator (most states choose average daily attendance).

Moreover, the annual objectives had to be tied to a goal of 100 percent proficiency by the year 2014 and to the narrowing of achievement gaps between students by race and socioeconomic status, as well as for English language learners and students with disabilities. No school or district could satisfy the AYP requirement if fewer than 95 percent of all students, and 95 percent of students in each of the four aforementioned subgroups, completed the statewide assessments.

NCLB contained a set of graduated sanctions for schools and districts tied to the number of consecutive years they fell short of AYP benchmarks. Students in schools that missed AYP for two consecutive years had the right to transfer to a higher performing public school in the same district. However, research showed that a number of factors—including the availability of higher performing schools in most districts and weak efforts by districts to make parents aware of their options—meant that only a tiny fraction of students actually got to exercise this right.[11] Students in schools that missed AYP for three consecutive years had the right to "supplemental services" (i.e., tutoring options from public and/or private providers), but again, for various reasons, most eligible students in practice did not get access to these services.[12] Schools that missed AYP for four or more consecutive years were expected to take increasingly intensive interventions that, after six consecutive years, could include "restructuring" or school closure. However, according to the US Government Accountability Office and others, there was so much flexibility under the actual language of the statute that for all practical purposes states and districts were free to choose much more peripheral interventions.[13]

Waivers

Pressure built up under the weight of these fairly stringent accountability provisions, and intensified each year beyond the 2001 law's intended six-year authorization window. Even though a "safe harbor" provision rendered the "100 percent proficiency by 2014" goal more or less symbolic, as schools could get credit for AYP well short of being on that trajectory, the goal was held up repeatedly as evidence that the law was unrealistic.[14] By May 2012, according to one report, the percentage of schools nationwide not making two or more consecutive years of AYP reached 49 percent, ranging widely by state, from a low of about 11 percent in Wisconsin to 89 percent in Florida. Even though the law described these as "schools in need of improvement" such schools were widely labeled in the media as "failures," and, to many observers, a 49 percent failure rate for American schools seemed unfair and invalid. By then, the DOE's waiver program was well under way.

Under the waivers, states could dispense with AYP, instead identifying and intervening in "priority schools" that were either in the bottom 5 percent in the state or high schools with graduation rates below 60 percent.

States also had to identify "focus schools," which generally were between the bottom 5 and 15 percent and/or where students from at-risk subgroups were lagging significantly behind their more advantaged peers. This, in effect, made NCLB's gap-closing accountability benchmarks voluntary. The public school choice and supplemental services were stricken completely. States were to choose from among four intervention models, but these were written loosely to allow more or less the same level of flexibility, in practice, as the prescribed interventions in the NCLB statute.

ESSA

ESSA closely resembles the waiver accountability system, though with a few twists. States must identify the bottom 5 percent of all schools in the state for interventions that will be conducted by school districts with state approval. High schools with graduation rates less than 67 percent must also be identified and sanctioned.

Instead of the "focus schools," ESSA requires states to identify a third category of schools, designated as "targeted support schools," in which any subgroup of students is consistently underperforming, as determined by the state. This provision has a slightly stronger tie to subgroup accountability than its analogue under waivers. ESSA requires states to notify the local educational agencies overseeing targeted schools and ensure that those schools are informed of their status. It's then up to staff in that school to come up with an intervention plan to improve outcomes for lagging subgroups. Additional targeted support is required in schools in which the underperforming subgroup tests in the bottom 5 percent. The statute contains flexibility, in terms of subgroup progress requirements that the proportion of such schools identified in any particular state could be significantly higher or lower than the 10 percent of schools identified as focus schools under waivers. Unlike NCLB and waivers, ESSA includes no language—advisory or mandatory—specifying the types of interventions that must be conducted in any of the low performing school categories listed.

Accountability measures

ESSA also significantly changes and expands the number of indicators on which school performance designations are based. For all schools—elementary, middle, and high schools—accountability must be based on long-term goals, including measurements of interim progress toward meeting such goals for the following:

- Rates of student proficiency in math and ELA state assessments, and students' "interim progress" on "long-term goals," both for all students and each subgroup. This is similar to both NCLB and waivers.
- A measure of "student growth" or "another valid and reliable statewide academic indicator that allows for meaningful differentiation in school performance" for all students and for each subgroup. This is similar to both NCLB and waivers.
- English language proficiency for English learners; this, as described previously, is a feature new to ESEA under ESSA.
- An additional indicator of school quality (academic or nonacademic), as described earlier in this chapter. This is also new to ESSA.

In addition, high school accountability systems must be based on the four-year adjusted cohort graduation rate. The four-year graduation rate is defined in a more uniform and rigorous way for all states than it was under the NCLB statute, albeit in a similar way to the definition prescribed in regulations beginning in 2008. State goals must take into account the improvement necessary on such measures to make "significant" progress in narrowing statewide proficiency and graduation rate gaps, meaning that states must set faster improvement timelines for the progress of at-risk subgroups than for all students as a whole. Finally, rates of student participation in assessments must be factored into the state accountability system, but, unlike the system under NCLB, failing to assess 95 percent of students doesn't automatically trigger an identification as "low performing."

Weighting

ESSA also specifies how these indicators are weighted overall and with regard to each other. ESSA specifies that the first three indicators just listed (rates of student proficiency in math/ELA assessments, a measure of student growth, and English language proficiency for English learners), as well as graduation rates, be given, in aggregate, more weight than the fourth (the additional indicator). The secretary of education, however, is prohibited from issuing regulations that attach specific numerical guidelines (e.g., defining "substantial" weighting as 20 percent or defining "greater" weighting to be at least one percentage point higher) to these weighting requirements.

The new accountability system under ESSA departs significantly from NCLB's and its waivers, especially with regard to the number and types of indicators and measures allowed. While there are some bright-line requirements, there are many moving parts, and much is left open to interpretation. States can and likely will move in many different directions, providing many opportunities—and challenges—to study what works and what doesn't.

TEACHER QUALITY

NCLB was the first ESEA reauthorization to put teacher quality requirements into law. It barred Title I schools from being staffed with teachers holding "emergency" or "provisional" certification and required that middle and high school teachers demonstrate subject matter competence either through coursework completion or by passing a subject matter test. Research found these provisions to have some positive effects.[15] But states also found ways to game them.

Between 2002 and 2008, the policy focus on teacher quality shifted from "inputs" to "outputs"—that is, the effect of teachers on student test scores. Race to the Top included heavily weighted incentives to develop new teacher evaluation systems, and these became a requirement under NCLB waivers.

This was probably the single most controversial waiver requirement. In response, ESSA completely eliminates requirements for teacher quality or effectiveness. ESSA does require, however, that states identify disparities in low-income and minority students being disproportionately taught by ineffective, inexperienced, unqualified, or out-of-field teachers; have a mechanism to address these disparities; and notify parents regarding teacher qualifications. Because so little is specified in ESSA as to how to comply with this requirement, it's one to watch as states roll out their new ESSA plans in 2017 and beyond.

CONCLUSION

In many ways, ESSA lives up to its billing as a federal law that transfers considerable authority over education policy back to states and local educational agencies. This is especially true with regard to how states measure student achievement and school quality and to which interventions need to be made in low performing schools. At the same time, the overall structure of ESSA in terms of its system of state standards and assessments, and the identification of low performance based on those standards and assessments, is in many ways remarkably similar to the 1994 ESEA reauthorization (IASA).

Moreover, ESSA maintains NCLB's requirements for annual assessments in grades 3–8 in math and ELA, and NCLB's emphasis on improving the academic achievement of students from historically disadvantaged groups and closing achievement gaps. There is no doubt that over the six-year period of ESSA's reauthorization states will become more different than similar as they avail themselves of the new law's flexibilities. Thus, we are arguably entering one of the most interesting (for some, anxiety fraught; for others, exciting) periods of state and local education policy making in well over two decades.

The Case for ESSA

A Proper Balance

Martin R. West

This much is clear: the enactment of the Every Student Succeeds Act was a political success. The law drew support from more than 85 percent of those casting votes in both houses of Congress, a remarkable development in light of legislators' repeated failures to agree on a replacement for the much-maligned No Child Left Behind Act. The National Governors Association (NGA) offered ESSA a "full endorsement," marking the first time the organization had taken a unified position on a federal law since the 1996 welfare reform act.[1] The NGA's action was perhaps unsurprising, as ESSA's central theme is the devolution of authority over education policy from the federal government to the states. Yet interest groups ranging from teacher unions to the US Chamber of Commerce lined up to urge President Barack Obama to sign ESSA into law (which he promptly did).

But good politics don't always make for sound public policy. Efforts to craft legislation capable of winning broad support can result in a lack of clarity or even incoherence, attributes that may accelerate a bill's progress through Congress only to undermine its effectiveness when implemented. This is especially true when Democrats and Republicans are sharply divided on the underlying issue, as was surely the case when it came to how to revise NCLB during the first six years of Obama's presidency. The administration and many Democrats sought to double down on federally driven school accountability and introduce new requirements on teacher evaluation. Most Republicans wanted the feds out of the picture altogether.

ESSA broke the stalemate with a compromise. The law maintains and even strengthens NCLB's breakthrough transparency requirements while providing states greater control over school accountability and avoiding mandates on teacher evaluation altogether. It continues to require that states test students annually in core academic subjects and report the results of those tests disaggregated by subgroup, along with new information about the resources available to students at each school. Crucially, however, it gives states far more say than NCLB over how schools are identified as low performing and the steps taken to improve them.

This chapter argues that this compromise strikes a new and better balance when it comes to the federal role in American K–12 education. ESSA was assuredly the only politically feasible way to address problems that, if left to fester, could have undermined efforts to hold schools and educators accountable for their performance nationwide. More than that, however, it incorporates and applies the most important lesson from the NCLB era: that the federal government has a constructive role to play in ensuring transparency about student achievement and shining a bright light on lingering inequities, but that it is poorly positioned to dictate the details of states' efforts to improve their schools. Far from a retreat from the federal government's long-standing commitment to support America's most vulnerable children, ESSA represents a new vision for fulfilling that commitment in light of the capacity and resources at its disposal.

To be sure, ESSA is far from perfect. The formulas used to allocate funds for disadvantaged students do a poor job of directing dollars to states that need them most, a problem that dates back to the original Elementary and Secondary Education Act of 1965.[2] ESSA takes only limited steps toward consolidating the myriad categorical programs that have accumulated within that law over the past fifty years. Congress opted not to permit states to let federal aid follow students from low-income families to the school of their choice. In each of these areas, proponents of more far-reaching reforms agreed to step aside so as not to disrupt progress toward a deal on the issues of testing and accountability that appropriately dominated the legislative debate.

On those core issues, however, Congress got it mostly right. This chapter shows how ESSA balances the federal government's obligation to protect the nation's most vulnerable students against the need to provide states more flexibility to innovate not only with respect to school accountability, but also in the areas of school choice, teacher policy, evidence-based policy making, and the use of federal funds. First, though, the chapter lays out in more detail the practical and political problems that ESSA needed to solve.

THE PROBLEMS ESSA NEEDED TO SOLVE

ESSA is, above all, an attempt to fix problems created by NCLB, a law that marked the most dramatic expansion in federal control over K–12 education since the 1965 enactment of the Elementary and Secondary Education Act. Those problems started with a one-size-fits-all accountability system that, thirteen years after NCLB's passage, had long outlived its usefulness.

While the NCLB accountability system was widely perceived as punitive and prescriptive, only the latter adjective truly fits. NCLB did not directly threaten educators' jobs. All that it ultimately required of schools persistently missing performance targets was their public identification and the generation of reams of paperwork in the form of school improvement plans. The law did, however, prescribe a uniform approach to identifying low performing schools based on whether math and reading proficiency rates matched statewide targets on the way to an aspirational goal of 100 percent proficiency by 2014. As that deadline grew closer, this approach became increasingly unworkable.

By 2015, however, that system had largely been replaced as a result of the Obama administration's 2011 decision to offer waivers to states willing to comply with a set of conditions aligned with its own reauthorization priorities: college- and career-ready standards, a narrowed set of federally defined options for turning around schools in the bottom 5 percent, and test-based teacher evaluations. The waiver program addressed the NCLB accountability system's most salient flaws but only fueled concerns that had emerged over the past decade about federal overreach and the role of standardized testing in American education. With teacher unions increasingly embracing a growing movement among parents to opt their children out of state tests, members of Congress were inundated with constituent demands that they do something about the perceived scourge of overtesting.

As the 114th Congress took up ESEA, then, it faced multiple challenges. Perhaps most fundamental was a need to reclaim authority over education policy from the executive branch, where it had in effect resided since the Obama administration began issuing waivers in 2011. Setting aside any doubts about the waiver program's legality and the desirability of the policies it had pushed states to adopt, the approach had clearly created an atmosphere of uncertainty that hindered states' ability to engage in long-term planning. In order to reclaim authority, however, Congress had to reach agreement on a replacement for NCLB—a task that had proven elusive in multiple previous attempts since its scheduled end date of 2007.

The question was not whether any new legislation would reduce the federal government's footprint in K–12 education; it clearly would. The question was whether, in their understandable efforts to rein in Washington's influence, legislators would find a way to preserve those aspects of the federal role that fulfill functions that would otherwise go unaddressed within our multilayered system of education governance. In several key respects, ESSA accomplished that goal.

STATE AND LOCAL LEADERSHIP ON ACCOUNTABILITY

The internal and external pressures to reauthorize ESEA in 2015 forced legislators to revisit first principles about the federal role in K–12 education. While NCLB's testing and accountability mandates had typically been viewed as a single package, the ESSA compromise rightly recognizes that they are distinct—and that this distinction matters when considering the appropriate federal role. This enables the new law to address its predecessor's most serious flaw—a prescriptive, one-size-fits-all accountability system—while building on its most important contribution: the provision of greater transparency about the academic achievement of American students.

Enhanced Transparency

ESSA's efforts to promote transparency start with maintaining the federal requirement that states test students annually in reading and math and report the results of those tests at the level of the state, district, and school, both overall and disaggregated across ten student subgroups. The law also broadens the information available to judge school performance, requiring that states report for each school and subgroup (1) a second indicator of academic achievement (which for high schools must be graduation rates); (2) a measure of English language learners' progress toward English proficiency; and (3) at least one other indicator of "school quality or student success" to be selected by the state. In addition, states are required to publish report cards that include detailed information about the resources available in each school, including such indicators as advanced course enrollment rates, teacher experience and qualifications, and per-pupil spending.

These requirements recognize that the federal government has a natural role to play in ensuring the provision of timely, accurate data on the performance of local schools and the resources available to them. Not only is such a role consistent with the federal government's capacity, those best positioned to produce good information on school quality—namely, local and state governments—may not find that it is in their own interests to be transparent about the performance of the institutions under their control. If the federal government does not demand that they do so, citizens will be hindered in their ability to make informed school choices and hold local education officials accountable for results.

Moreover, ESSA ensures that the performance of students on comparable tests of their skills in core subjects will remain central to federal efforts to promote transparency in public education. The skills measured by these tests are closely aligned to the schools' central mission of helping students master academic content, and ample evidence confirms that the scores that students receive on them are predictive of important later-life outcomes, such as postsecondary success, employment, and earnings.[3] Of course, schools also contribute to students' success in ways that are not captured by test scores and are therefore harder to measure—a fact ESSA acknowledges with its requirement of an additional indicator of school quality or student success.[4] However, any effort to promote transparency about school performance that did not include data on student learning as measured by tests that are comparable statewide would have been badly compromised.

The decision to maintain NCLB's annual testing mandate remains controversial among antitesting activists, teacher unions concerned about the use of test results in teacher evaluation, and conservatives who believe the mandate exceeds the federal government's authority. As an alternative, these groups proposed requiring states to test students once in each grade span (i.e., elementary, middle, and high school), as had been mandated (but not consistently enforced) under the 1994 Improving America's Schools Act. But eliminating annual testing was not necessary to address concerns about overtesting in American schools and would only have made it harder for states to address the most important flaw of the NCLB accountability system: its exclusive reliance on student performance levels as a measure of school performance.

Eliminating annual testing was unnecessary to address concerns about overtesting because the tests required under NCLB typically accounted for less than half of the total amount of time students spend taking standardized tests. For example, a 2015 Ohio Department of Education audit found that the seventeen NCLB-mandated tests were responsible for just 32 percent of testing time in that state.[5] The rest was devoted to state- and district-mandated tests and to assessments developed as part of the teacher evaluation system the state was implementing under the Obama administration's waiver program. Some of those additional tests may have been indirectly attributable to NCLB, due to the pressures it placed on educators to prepare students for the state test. However, ESSA's architects rightly concluded that this response was driven more by the unrealistic expectations of the NCLB accountability system than the testing requirement itself.

Under that accountability system, whether a school made Adequate Yearly Progress was determined primarily based on the share of students who were proficient in math and reading in a given year—a level-based measure of student achievement. Achievement levels are a poor indicator of school quality, however, as they are heavily influenced by factors outside of a school's control. Measures based on the amount students learn from one year to the next can provide a more accurate gauge of schools' contributions to student learning.[6] These kinds of measures are only possible, however, when students are tested annually.

ESSA both ensures that states gather the raw material needed to construct measures of achievement growth and enables them to use growth measures as the second indicator of academic achievement with which they evaluate schools' performance. While it may have seemed preferable to *require* states to use achievement growth for this purpose, the enthusiasm with which states sought the opportunity to do so under a Bush administration pilot program suggests that most are already likely to do so. Any requirement would also have necessitated that regulators at the Department of Education define what constitutes an acceptable growth measure, an unsettled question best left to states.

ESSA's transparency requirements remain firmly tethered to the federal role in ensuring equitable access to educational opportunity for vulnerable students. A return to grade-span testing would have all but eliminated school-level information about the achievement of student subgroups, as testing a single grade within each school often results in sample sizes for groups such as racial or ethnic minorities, English language learners, and students with disabilities that are too small to generate reliable information.[7] By incorporating the rate at which English language learners achieve proficiency into the evaluation of schools' overall performance, the law signals that serving such students is an integral component of school quality. Finally, ESSA recognizes that transparency about the achievement of students with disabilities is meaningless without a cap on the number of students who can be excluded from regular testing. It eliminates states' ability to allow up to 2 percent of students to take tests aligned to less rigorous proficiency standards and maintains the current 1 percent cap on the share of students in each state who can be given alternative assessments due to severe cognitive disabilities.

Flexibility on Accountability

Despite ramping up transparency, ESSA offers states considerable discretion when it comes to identifying schools as low performing and near-complete latitude over how they address those schools' problems. States are required to use the aforementioned indicators to differentiate schools according to their performance. They must identify at least the bottom 5 percent of schools based on overall performance, high schools with graduation rates below 67 percent and schools with persistent achievement gaps for "comprehensive support and intervention," and an unspecified number of additional schools for "targeted support and intervention" based on the underperformance of student subgroups. Yet the law does not dictate the precise weight that states must assign to indicators when judging school performance, stating only that academic indicators must be the predominant criteria.[8] Once schools are identified for comprehensive support, states must simply ensure that their school districts, in partnership with local stakeholders, develop a plan to improve student outcomes that includes evidence-based interventions. States are required to set aside 7 percent of the funds they receive under Title I to support these school improvement efforts, but they may deploy those funds as they see fit.

The flexibilities ESSA affords to states make good sense in light of our limited understanding of how best to design school accountability systems to improve student outcomes. One rarely acknowledged consequence of NCLB was to slow the pace of innovation in the design of educational accountability systems and other reform efforts. In prescribing a uniform approach to the identification of low performing schools, NCLB needed to select an approach that all states had the capacity to implement. The introduction of this lowest-common-denominator approach appears to have produced modest gains in student achievement in states that the law required to introduce consequential school accountability for the first time.[9] Lost in this calculus, however, are any effects the law had on states with the capacity to pursue more sophisticated approaches to evaluating school performance—and therefore the rate of learning from their varied experiences. At this point, we know a great deal about the strengths of the NCLB approach and even more about its weaknesses, but far less about those of potential alternatives.

Consider the issue of basing the identification of low performing schools on achievement growth rather than achievement levels. As explained earlier, emphasizing academic growth provides a more accurate indicator of how much schools are contributing to student learning and is therefore fairer to educators in schools serving disadvantaged students. At the same time, some in the civil rights community have criticized proposals to judge schools based primarily on growth measures, as doing so could allow high-need schools to avoid sanctions even if the pace of their students' progress is insufficient to close achievement gaps. This is a legitimate concern, and state policy makers may want to strike a balance between achievement levels and growth when deciding where to focus improvement efforts.

The elimination of federally prescribed interventions in low performing schools is a concession not just to our limited knowledge of what works, but also to the challenges confronting federal efforts to drive school improvement at the local level. We don't yet know how best to turn around persistently low performing schools, as evidenced not just by the disappointing results of school restructuring efforts under NCLB but also of the decidedly mixed track record of the Obama administration's more prescriptive School Improvement Grant (SIG) program. The most promising results under SIG appear to have occurred in school districts that used the program as an opportunity to replace a school's principal and more than 50 percent of its staff.[10] Such an approach is unlikely to be successful in districts with a limited supply of human capital, however, and a federal mandate to pursue that approach far exceeds the bounds of political feasibility in an education system in which the federal government accounts for only 10 percent of spending.

In short, rather than follow NCLB's lead in prescribing a uniform approach to school accountability nationwide, ESSA provides states both space and incentive for experimentation. The new law clearly represents a setback for those who would prefer to see the federal government continue to offer what amounted to a guarantee of academic success for all students. But what good is a guarantee that exceeds the government's capacity to deliver? The simple truth is that we do not yet know which approach to evaluating school performance is most likely to drive improvements, nor how best to address the challenge of turning around persistently low performing schools. By ensuring transparency and directing states to take action to improve their worst schools without dictating the actions they must take, ESSA provides an opportunity to find new answers to these questions.

STATE AND LOCAL LEADERSHIP ON SCHOOL CHOICE

At first glance, ESSA would appear to be a setback for the cause of school choice. As Chad Aldeman laments in the next chapter, the law eliminates the requirement that school districts offer students in persistently low performing schools the option to attend another school, a requirement that at its peak made NCLB the nation's largest school choice program. Congress also rejected proposals to administer Title I as a portable grant program under which funds follow students from low-income families to the school they attend, potentially including private schools.

These setbacks are less consequential than they seem. More than anything else, NCLB's public school choice program illustrates the federal government's limited capacity to drive reform when it must rely on school districts to implement its ideas. Most school districts did a poor job of notifying families of their eligibility for choice, burying relevant information deep within long letters championing the various initiatives under way to improve their local school's performance.[11] Because the program required only that families be given the option to choose another nonfailing school within the same district, it was meaningless in many places and did nothing to increase the supply of high-quality schools. Whether due to a lack of information or a shortage of attractive alternatives, participation rates in public school choice were consistently low, hovering around 1–2 percent of eligible students each year.[12]

Proposals to make Title I funds portable have been advanced by conservative lawmakers and presidential candidates for decades but face at least two challenges. First, at less than $1,000 for each eligible student, grants funded solely through Title I would likely be too small to help most low-income families access out-of-district or private schools. Second, the administration of the grant program would inevitably fall to school district officials with strong incentives to keep Title I funds within their own schools, casting doubt on the chances of successful implementation. Presenting portability as an option to states rather than a mandate could increase the likelihood of buy-in, but it is doubtful that more than a small handful would opt in.

The simple truth is that, as a 10 percent investor without the capacity to directly oversee school assignment policies, the federal government's ability to promote school choice on a national basis is severely constrained. ESSA's architects were therefore wise to pursue a series of more focused efforts to advance choice within willing states and school districts.

ESSA preserves the ability of districts to use federal funds to offer public school choice to students in low performing schools and gives states new tools to encourage them to do so. For example, a new provision enables states to reserve up to 3 percent of Title I funds (amounting to roughly $450 million annually nationwide) to make competitive grants to school districts for so-called direct student services, which may include academic tutoring and transportation for public school choice. States can allocate the 7 percent of Title I funds they are required to set aside for school improvement activities as competitive grants, presenting an opportunity to incentivize districts to provide new options for students assigned to low performing schools. Finally, a pilot program in the law will allow up to fifty school districts to include federal funds in weighted student funding systems under which dollars follow students to whatever public school they attend, a model that could facilitate the implementation of districtwide school choice. Even if only a small fraction of districts take advantage of these opportunities, either on their own or due to encouragement from their states, the net result is likely to help many more students than NCLB's attempt at a fifty-state strategy.

ESSA also continues the federal Charter Schools Program (CSP), which offers competitive grants to states to open new charter schools, and updates it in key ways. For example, it codifies a stimulus-era program through which the Department of Education has provided grants directly to charter management organizations to support the replication and expansion of high performing schools. It also outlines new competitive priorities for states applying for CSP funds, emphasizing policies designed to create a level playing field between charter and traditional public schools, such as equitable funding, facilities access, and the availability of nondistrict authorizers. At least in the short run, the CSP will support the development of new school options only for families in states and cities willing to expand their charter sectors. But that is precisely where federal dollars are apt to do the most good.

STATE AND LOCAL LEADERSHIP ON TEACHER POLICY

ESSA's approach to teacher policy provides another example of addition by subtraction—and of avoiding the temptation of federal overreach. The law eliminates the pleasant-sounding but ineffectual NCLB requirement that states ensure that all courses in core academic subjects are taught by a "highly qualified teacher." And it does not incorporate the waiver program requirement that states establish teacher evaluation systems that incorporate measures of student achievement growth. The law permits states to use federal funds to improve teacher and school leader evaluation systems, but it does not require them to do so.

The strategies the federal government pursued under NCLB and the waiver program reflect alternative attempts to regulate the way to a better teacher workforce. NCLB's highly qualified teacher requirement focused on inputs, demanding that all American teachers have the right paper credentials, defined as a bachelor's degree, full state certification, and demonstrated mastery of their subject. Such indicators, however, are weak predictors of teachers' effectiveness. The requirement that all teachers be highly qualified thus served only to reinforce state certification regimes that do a poor job of ensuring teacher quality and create barriers to entry for talented individuals who lack proper credentials. It also complicated state efforts to develop alternative certification programs that permit teachers to complete certification requirements after they begin teaching, the status of which was unclear in the statute and the subject of repeated litigation.

Through Race to the Top and the waiver program, the Obama administration pushed states to shift to an outcome-based approach to regulating teacher quality. Mounting evidence had confirmed that teachers vary widely in their effectiveness, and that this variation matters a great deal for students' success in school and later in life. And the teacher evaluation systems in use throughout most of the United States were clearly broken, assigning only a fractional share of teachers unsatisfactory ratings and offering them little in the way of feedback to improve their practice. The case for local experimentation with new approaches was clear.

Less clear, however, was whether the federal government was well advised to attempt to drive this activity. We have very little evidence on how best to design evaluation systems that differentiate among teachers' effectiveness while avoiding unintended consequences. Moreover, reforming teacher evaluation systems is a classic example of a policy where what matters most is likely to be how well any particular approach is implemented. Addressing the technical and political challenges inherent in altering long-standing practices that directly affect educators' work lives requires strong commitment from local leaders. By demanding that states desperate for flexibility from NCLB take on this task, the administration's policies fostered shallow buy-in from key stakeholders and, as a result, all but guaranteed ham-fisted implementation and political backlash.

While avoiding further federal efforts to regulate teacher effectiveness, ESSA does provide a small window of opportunity for states interested in a deregulatory approach. Specifically, it permits states to use a small portion of their federal funds to launch new "teacher preparation academies" operated not by traditional schools of education but by nonprofits and other public entities. The law also reauthorizes an existing competitive grant program, the Teacher and School Leader Incentive Program, that provides resources to districts willing to experiment with paying educators based in part on their effectiveness or willingness to teach in hard-to-staff schools. With these programs, and by authorizing the use of federal funds to develop new teacher evaluation systems, Congress found a way to encourage innovation while avoiding the drawbacks of a federal mandate.

LOCAL CONTROL OVER FUNDING

ESSA offers a promising new tack on what is arguably the most enduring challenge in federal education policy: ensuring that federal dollars to support the education of disadvantaged students reach their intended targets. The law dramatically simplifies the rule known as "supplement not supplant," which prior to ESSA required schools to demonstrate that each and every purchase made with Title I funds would not have been purchased had federal aid not been available. In addition to requiring copious staff time and paperwork, this approach often led schools to avoid spending funds in ways most likely to benefit students out of fear that a federal audit would conclude that they had engaged in supplanting. As economist Nora Gordon explained, "They buy 'interventionists' instead of teachers, or 'supplemental' curricular materials rather than 'core' ones, and are discouraged from investing Title I funds in technology."[13]

ESSA replaces the cost-by-cost method for enforcing supplement not supplant with a simple requirement that districts demonstrate that they allocate state and local funds to schools without regard to the federal funds that each school receives. It then states plainly that districts need not prove that every single purchase they make with those funds is supplemental, in a narrow and restrictive sense. This approach, which will dramatically reduce the compliance burden on districts, is attentive to the need to ensure that districts do not reduce their own spending on schools receiving federal funds while giving educators in those schools the autonomy to use those funds in the ways they believe will best help students succeed.

Consistent with its overall emphasis on transparency, ESSA also requires that states engage in new reporting on school resources, including for the first time publishing per-pupil spending levels in each school based on actual dollars spent rather than budgeted staff positions. This requirement reflects a concern that there are often large disparities in what is spent across schools within the same district that lead disadvantaged students to receive fewer resources than their more advantaged peers. One well-documented source of these disparities is the migration of more experienced and therefore better-paid teachers to schools with more advantaged students.[14] Requiring states to publish accurate school-level spending information should, at a minimum, ensure that citizens are informed of these patterns and may create pressure on districts to address the policies and contract provisions that drive them.

At the same time, Congress rejected proposals to close the so-called comparability loophole that permits districts to use budgets based on staff positions when demonstrating that the services available in Title I schools are comparable to those in schools serving more advantaged students. While this loophole may well mask disparities, legislators were concerned that the proposed cure could end up being worse than the disease. They were appropriately reluctant to reach so deeply into the finances and staffing policies of the nation's fourteen thousand school districts without first developing a better understanding of the scope of the problem and its causes—something that the new transparency requirements should accomplish.

STATE AND LOCAL LEADERSHIP ON EVIDENCE-BASED POLICY MAKING

ESSA doesn't just empower states and school districts to take ownership of more decisions; it equips them with new resources to learn from them. ESSA is the first federal education law to define the term *evidence-based* and to distinguish between activities with "strong," "moderate," and "promising" support based on the strength of existing research. Crucially, for many purposes the law also defines as evidence-based a fourth category comprising activities that have a research-based rationale but lack direct empirical support—provided, that is, that they are accompanied by "ongoing efforts to examine [their] effects" on important student outcomes.

NCLB also sought to make the American education system more data-driven, famously using the term *scientifically based research* some 110 times in an attempt to limit the use of federal funds to activities with proven results.[15] It also defined scientifically based research narrowly, emphasizing the need for experimental or quasi-experimental studies (and expressing a clear preference for the former). The problem was that, on many topics, there simply weren't any studies that met the law's criteria. Its evidence requirements became mere words on a page.

This is what makes ESSA's more inclusive definition of evidence-based activities potentially so powerful. When using federal funds to improve low performing schools, the law requires school districts to include interventions that meet at least the "promising" standard. Elsewhere the law encourages states and school districts to adopt evidence-based programs but permits them to do so by subjecting novel programs to ongoing evaluation.

To be clear, these provisions do not require that funds be spent on evidence-based activities. Doing so is simply listed as an allowable use of funds allocated for a particular purpose, such as improving teacher quality, engaging families, or meeting the needs of English language learners. But the clear implication is that states and school districts may use a portion of their federal funds to pay for the ongoing evaluation of untested programs; otherwise, the evaluation activities would constitute an unfunded mandate.

Like so much in the law, the opportunity to use federal funds for evaluation purposes will matter only if state and local officials use it. Some states—perhaps most—will lack either the appetite or the capacity to engage in this new model of evidence-based policy making. But ESSA may well prove to be a shot in the arm to states and school districts committed to learning about what works in their schools over time.

CONCLUSION

Ultimately, of course, ESSA should be judged based on its results—on whether its implementation improves the performance of American schools so that more students emerge prepared for college, careers, and life. Yet even this standard may prove to be murky. Fifteen years after the passage of No Child Left Behind, scholars continue to debate whether the gains the law produced in core subjects were enough to offset unintended consequences stemming from its exclusive reliance on math and reading test scores to evaluate school performance.

What is already clear is that ESSA will succeed only if state officials make good use of their newfound authority. The law's most vocal critics contend that states will fall down on their responsibilities, especially when it comes to ensuring equity for students of color and from low-income families. They worry that, absent stronger federal oversight, a combination of inertia, complacence, and political pressure will prevent states from taking aggressive action to improve the schools these students attend or to give them the opportunity to choose an alternative. They note that, for all its shortcomings, NCLB did provide political cover for reformers eager to drive much-needed change across a broad swath of American schools, not just those at the very bottom.

These concerns are not unfounded. States' failures to ensure equity for vulnerable children have been the key driver of federal involvement in education. ESSA does not offer a compelling answer to the question: What about Mississippi? Or California? Or other states where inertia, complacence, and interest-group politics have consistently stifled equity- and performance-oriented reform?

Yet a closer look at the history of the federal role provides cause for optimism. As Patrick McGuinn documents in chapter 1, the only previous reauthorization of ESEA to have reduced federal involvement, enacted under President Ronald Reagan in 1981, produced not a stagnation of reform activity, but rather the emergence of the standards-based reform movement. This movement was facilitated by the Department of Education's 1983 publication of *A Nation at Risk*, demonstrating that mandates and regulation are not the only tools at the federal government's disposal to drive education policy change. This activity eventually became the basis for NCLB, which sought to take what had emerged as best practices in leading states and impose them on the nation as a whole.

NCLB overshot the mark in terms of prescriptiveness, however, and led to the federal government taking on tasks that it was ill equipped to accomplish. The law's implementation revealed that federal mandates can be constructive when simply requiring states to execute a basic task is enough to effect positive change. This was arguably the case when it came to the law's testing requirements, where asking states to administer assessments and report results was sufficient to provide a framework for public transparency about student achievement. Federal mandates are less effective, however, in situations where what matters most is the on-the-ground quality of implementation, as illustrated by the limited success of the law's directives that states restructure low performing schools and develop robust systems of public school choice.

In refocusing federal policy in a way that reflects those lessons, ESSA also sets forth a flexible framework that allows for the evolution of state education policies over time. This is critical, as another obvious lesson from NCLB is that federal education laws can remain on the books in their current form far longer than expected, even when there is agreement on the need for change. ESSA itself lays out a schedule for reauthorization after just four years, presumably to allow the next president an opportunity to weigh in. Soon after ESSA's passage, however, the law's principal Republican architect, Senator Lamar Alexander, projected that it would "govern the federal role in K–12 education for ten or twenty years." Unlike with the education system under NCLB, there's little reason to fear that he may well be right.

6

The Case Against ESSA

A Very Limited Law

Chad Aldeman

When the 114th Congress took up education, it did so with near consensus that the federal government had overextended itself. The No
Child Left Behind Act's well-intentioned provisions had aged poorly, and
the perception that it was a punitive, one-size-fits-all law fueled a backlash
from left-leaning Democrats. From the right, Republicans chafed at the
Obama administration's use of executive power to issue large-scale waivers
from NCLB that enacted the administration's preferred reforms on standards, accountability, and teacher evaluations.

Still, in the politically tumultuous environment of 2015, it was not at all
clear that congressional leaders could fashion a compromise that President
Obama would sign. But they did, and Congress passed the Every Student
Succeeds Act with large bipartisan majorities. Obama happily signed it just
one day after it cleared the Senate.

While it may be tempting to see this level of bipartisanship as good in
itself, political consensus isn't always a signal of policy merit. NCLB's flaws
were becoming more apparent with time, and the Obama administration's
waiver initiative was fraying under the weight of too many one-off, tempo-
rary decisions. But rather than trying to fix those things, ESSA throws up
its hands and chooses no rules over smarter rules. Moreover, ESSA veers
in directions that reflect common perceptions about NCLB that weren't
grounded in the actual text of the law or how it was actually being implemented. For all its warts, NCLB wasn't nearly as prescriptive as was commonly asserted.

Moreover, ESSA is far more muddled than any of the law's champions would admit publicly. During the legislative phase, Congress relied on ambiguity as a way to build compromise, and that ambiguity is part of why the law gathered such a large majority. But the end result is a Rorschach test of a law, and political battles over how to interpret its provisions are already well under way. Those fights may eventually spill over into the courts, but regardless of the outcome of those battles, ESSA's vagueness will make it even more challenging to implement than its predecessor.

Worse, ESSA places all the burden of school reform on state and local leaders. It gives no political cover to those leaders who would like to take strong action, and it provides little protection against backsliding or obfuscation. In a number of key policy areas, including accountability systems, school choice, teacher policy, and evidence-based policy making, ESSA gives broad discretion to state and local leaders. Absent strong federal protections, the students most at risk from this arrangement are historically disadvantaged groups of students: black and Hispanic students, English language learners, and students with disabilities. While some states and local communities will choose to fill the void left by the removal of federal requirements, history suggests that, due to lack of capacity, local politics, or simple inertia, many will not. Whether state and local leaders act in the best interest of students will ultimately determine whether the Every Student Succeeds Act lives up to its lofty name. This chapter outlines the risks as that process begins.

HOW ESSA WON ITS BIPARTISAN COALITION

Critics from both sides of the political spectrum weighed in against the compromises needed to secure ESSA's passage. Conservatives like the Heartland Institute's Joy Pullmann called the final version of ESSA a "mess of a bill, a veritable Christmas present to every education special interest except the most important (parents and teachers)."[1] From the left, the New America Foundation's Conor Williams seized on the law's ambiguities, arguing that it "combines a thin veneer of civil rights equity with excruciating complexity and uncertain accountability. It takes a relatively simple federal accountability system, removes the teeth, and layers on a bunch of vague responsibilities for states."[2] In a statement, the Education Trust's Kati Haycock praised the law's inclusion of accountability for low performing subgroups but cautioned that, given the long history of state and local decisions shortchanging vulnerable students, the flexibility in the law was "cause for serious trepidation."[3]

In signing the bill, Obama made clear that he interpreted the law as giving the federal government the "oversight to make sure [state] plans are sound."[4] Outgoing Secretary of Education Arne Duncan offered more candid remarks. In an interview with Politico, he declared the administration's intent to implement and regulate on the law and expressed his belief that the Department of Education's lawyers were "much smarter than many of the folks who were working on this bill."[5]

But as soon as the Obama administration signaled its intent to regulate the law's requirements on spending and accountability, Republican senators challenged its interpretation of the law. Senate Health, Education, Labor, and Pensions Committee Chairman Lamar Alexander asserted he would use "every power available to him" to stop the regulations.

There's reason to think this is not just typical political posturing but actually reflects fundamentally different interpretations of what the law means. But regardless of how the political battles end in Washington, the law depends on fifty different states looking at this fuzzy picture and deciding what to make of it. The law's ambiguity is likely to hamper those state and local implementation efforts.

STATE AND LOCAL DISCRETION ON ACCOUNTABILITY

ESSA's proponents say that it's a long-overdue replacement for NCLB's one-size-fits-all system. But that's an argument based on a myth. While NCLB's rules were indeed the same for every state, states had wide discretion in how they implemented those rules. An academic paper titled "Fifty Ways to Leave a Child Behind: Idiosyncrasies and Discrepancies in States' Implementation of NCLB" documented all the choices that state accountability systems reflected. States had discretion over everything from choosing their own standards and setting their own performance benchmarks to more technical decisions like how many students must be part of a group in order to hold the school accountable for that group (called the *n-size*). The results were wildly divergent, and school failure rates ranged from as low as 1 percent to as high as 80 percent. The study concluded that "purposefully or not, some states used loopholes that made it much easier for schools to meet targets."[6]

Actual state outcomes also varied widely under NCLB. In a 2015 paper for the Urban Institute, Matt Chingos showed that, even after controlling for changing student demographics, some states made significant progress in reading and math in the NCLB era, while others lagged behind.[7] Chingos dug into various factors affecting student outcomes and determined there was as much variation *across* states as across school districts *within* states. In terms of contributions to student achievement, states were only slightly less important than individual schools and teachers. In another paper looking at state-level National Assessment of Educational Progress (NAEP) data, John Chubb and Constance Clark found wide variation in student achievement gains after NCLB.[8]

In other words, even with the strong federal role under NCLB, state-level decisions mattered immensely. That is likely to be even more applicable when states operate in a looser accountability environment under ESSA. And if results under NCLB were far from uniform, we should ask the more honest question: does ESSA set states up for success, or leave too much to variation?

Designing an Accountability System

ESSA requires each state receiving federal funds to create a "statewide accountability system" with a "state-determined methodology" to "meaningfully differentiate" among schools. In addition to the state's own priorities for its accountability system, ESSA also imposes rules on the type, quantity, and quality of the measures selected. On type and quantity, ESSA says that each school must be rated on at least four factors. Those factors must include achievement rates, as measured by proficiency on the state's annual assessments; some other "valid and reliable" academic indicator, such as student growth (for high schools this must be graduation rates); progress in achieving English language proficiency; and at least one other indicator of school quality or success.

States can add measures beyond these four, but ESSA also imposes quality rules on any measure included in state accountability systems. All measures must be reported separately for all students and for each of ten subgroups of students (males, females, white students, black students, Hispanic students, Asian students, American Indian students or Alaska Natives, students with disabilities, students with limited English proficiency, and low-income students). Additionally, each indicator of school quality or success must also "allow for meaningful differentiation" across schools and be valid, reliable, and comparable statewide.

ESSA does not explicitly guide states on how many measures they should use, but they must give "substantial weight" to each of the academic indicators, and the academic indicators must, in the aggregate, be given "much greater weight" than the measure(s) of school quality or success.

These rules may be individually less prescriptive than any of NCLB's—ESSA has no "bright lines" that 100 percent of students meet a predetermined proficiency benchmark, or that all schools with a single subgroup failing to meet that target must be identified for improvement—but ESSA may lead to even more complicated accountability systems. The danger is that states create such convoluted systems that they fail to provide clear information to parents and the general public, or that they offer no clear directions for how schools should improve.

NCLB was attacked for its overemphasis on reading and math and the subsequent unintended consequences that flowed from that. But if states aren't careful, they now have many more opportunities to encourage their own, new set of unintended consequences. For example, there's a large body of research suggesting that students who are suspended or expelled are less likely to persist in school. There are also wide disparities along race and class lines in terms of these disciplinary events. But holding schools accountable for reducing suspensions and expulsions may be counterproductive, because it could lead schools to simply recategorize the disciplinary events rather than dealing with the root causes. This is just one example, but there are now hundreds of decisions that each state must make over which indicators to include, how to measure them, how to incorporate subgroup results, and how to cobble together the chosen measures into some sort of rating system or dashboard that's coherent for parents, teachers, and school leaders.

Finally, as states contemplate new accountability systems, they may run into similar problems as they did under NCLB. For example, one problem with NCLB was that it identified low performing schools based on tests that measured each student's status on a given day, while ignoring how much they had grown over time. But due to fears of federal overreach, ESSA does not require states to change this focus, and it allows, but does not require, student growth to be included in state accountability systems. If states don't change their focus from status to growth, they'll continue judging schools based more on their student demographics than the quality of education they're actually delivering.

Identifying Low Performing Schools

States must use their accountability systems to identify "comprehensive support" schools made up of the bottom 5 percent of schools, any high school with a graduation rate below 67 percent, and schools with persistently large achievement gaps. School districts with comprehensive support schools must draft a plan for the school to improve student outcomes. Additionally, states must also identify another category of schools based on large achievement gaps, called "targeted support" schools. Upon identification, targeted support schools must craft their own improvement plan.

ESSA also changes the federal government's answer to the question of whether all schools need to improve or just the worst ones. NCLB put all schools on notice that they needed to ensure all students were learning. It held every school and every subgroup in that school accountable for meeting objective standards for performance, and no matter how many schools or subgroups failed to meet that standard, all of those that failed were told they needed to improve. Over time, as expectations rose, so too did the number of schools failing to meet them. At its peak, more than nineteen thousand schools—about two-fifths of Title I schools and one-fifth of all public schools nationally—were placed on lists of schools "in need of improvement" and were subject to NCLB's cascading sanctions.[9]

The Obama administration's waiver initiative shifted from a criterion-referenced system where any school could fail to a norm-referenced one with schools identified based on how they compared to their peers. The number of schools told they needed to improve began dropping immediately, from a high of 19,270 after the 2011–2012 school year, the last full year of NCLB, to 16,548 in 2012–2013, the first year under waivers. As a few more states collected waivers and moved to their own relative ranking systems, the numbers dropped again in 2013–2014, down to 15,536.[10]

Under ESSA, states have the option to identify only the absolute bottom 5 percent of schools receiving federal funds, leaving the remaining 95 percent of schools without any pressure to improve. By the time the law is fully implemented in 2017–2018, states may identify just the worst of the worst 2,750 schools. At that point, states could let almost seventeen thousand schools off the hook for needed improvements.

This is a big deal. Perhaps NCLB's greatest contribution was its reach into all types of schools, telling every school when it wasn't serving each of its students. Multiple studies have borne out the idea that schools will respond to the threat of identification. For example, Thomas Ahn of the University of Kentucky and Jacob Vigdor of Duke University analyzed the impact of NCLB's accountability sanctions on school performance in North

Carolina. They found that the "strongest association between failure to make AYP and subsequent test score performance occurs among those schools not yet exposed to any actual sanctions."[11] In this case, the threat of imminent sanctions was a catalyst for schools to improve. For those schools that failed to make progress for multiple years, the threat of the "ultimate penalty"—implementation of a restructuring plan—also had a strong positive impact on test scores.

Similarly, a study out of Texas found that low performing students benefited when their school was at risk of being identified as "low performing." Those benefits included short-term gains on test scores as well as higher college-going rates and higher early-career earnings.[12] In other words, there are positive effects behind the mere act of notifying schools in need of improvement that they face the potential of sanctions.

State policy makers have very few tools at their disposal that can boast similar outcomes, but it requires the right mix of incentives. The Texas study, for example, found that a reward for high performing schools led some schools to push out low performing students. Those students had *worse* long-term outcomes. Accountability systems can lead schools to change their practices in ways that improve long-term student outcomes, but only if those systems are well designed.

Intervening in Low Performing Schools

Unlike NCLB or subsequent efforts like the School Improvement Grant program, ESSA does not include federal rules on what the interventions in low performing schools should be. States themselves have approval authority over local improvement plans, and must monitor and review local implementation of those plans, but ESSA relies heavily on local will to change behavior. States may adopt their own requirements on local interventions, but they would be acting on their own authority.

Since ESSA shifts toward a more relative accountability system, where schools are compared against one another, a strategy focused on fixing the toughest problems hinges not just on the identification process but also on the desire and ability to actually do something about persistent poor performance. ESSA requires little in this regard. It asks each district with a low performing school—these are low functioning districts that let the school flounder in the first place—decide what's best for them. Federal law no longer requires consequences for inaction, does not provide an escape for affected students, and does not give political cover to local leaders who do want to make aggressive interventions. These decisions will be left entirely to state and local politicians.

LOCAL DISCRETION ON SCHOOL CHOICE

Like other areas, ESSA relies on local discretion to decide whether families should be given a choice of public schools. For example, ESSA updated the federal Charter Schools Program (CSP), a competitive grant program supporting the expansion of charter schools that traces back to the 1994 ESEA reauthorization. ESSA authorizes $270 million for CSP in fiscal year 2017, and up to $300 million in fiscal year 2020. Unfortunately, this represents a slight decline from 2016, when Congress allocated $330 million to the program, and by the time ESSA expires, it will be quite a bit less in inflation-adjusted terms.[13] What's more, CSP's competitive nature relies on states and cities that actively want to open and expand charter schools. But some states don't have charter schools at all, and some local communities are hostile to school choice. A competitive grant program offers dollars to places that are already interested in expanding charter school offerings, but it's not a fifty-state strategy to reach all fifty million K–12 students.

This stands in contrast to NCLB, which included a mechanism to correct for market failures anywhere they arose. As part of its intervention strategy, NCLB's Public School Choice program required all schools that failed to meet performance benchmarks in reading or math for two consecutive years to offer families the option to transfer to another school in their district.

There were some obvious flaws from the beginning with this strategy. Beyond simple logistics—some districts were so small that they had no other schools to choose from—the program was a federal mandate forced on state and local bureaucrats who had little incentive to make it work well. As a result, the required letters informing parents of their choices tended to bury the most important information—school choice with free busing—in obscure form letters.[14] Consequently, the take-up rate for the program was never all that high. As a percentage of eligible families, not even 3 percent of students accepted a transfer offer.[15]

Still, with millions of kids eligible for a transfer spread across all sorts of communities, the total number of students served was quite large. About 48,000 students took advantage of the option to transfer schools the first year it became available, in 2004–2005. Those numbers eventually rose to

167,000 students. At the time, it was the largest school choice program in the country.

Under pressure from local school districts, state education bureaucrats couldn't wait to end the program. The Obama administration gave them that chance starting in 2012, when it began granting waivers for states to avoid the most onerous aspects of NCLB. Without any federal mandate, states elected to drop the school choice provision and the number of students offered school choice fell dramatically.

Under ESSA, the school choice provision remains an allowable use of federal funds, but the waiver experience suggests the clunky, bureaucratic federal mandate mattered a great deal. In the end, there was simply no natural constituency supporting the Public School Choice program, and it didn't expand the pool of good schools available to parents, like the Charter Schools Program does. Still, this example illustrates what is likely to happen under ESSA: local school districts will gain more control over their student assignment patterns, but thousands of children will lose the option to transfer out of their assigned low performing schools.

STATE AND LOCAL DISCRETION ON TEACHER POLICY

ESSA severely diminishes the federal push for better teacher policies. It allows, but does not require, states and districts to spend federal funds on improving teacher and principal evaluation systems. It requires states and districts to enact plans to ensure students have equitable access to "highly qualified" or effective teachers, but it has no accountability mechanisms to make sure those things happen. It permanently authorizes an existing program (previously called the Teacher Incentive Fund, or TIF), but it freezes funding at the prior level ($230 million), which will wear away over time in inflation-adjusted dollars.

Now, it's hard to argue the federal government's interventions on teacher policies over the last two decades have been implemented well. First, after NCLB began holding schools accountable for the distribution of teachers deemed "highly qualified," districts exercised loopholes under which nearly all existing teachers met the standard. The Bush administration allowed states to use this definition in lieu of looking more closely at inexperienced, unqualified, or out-of-field teachers, which allowed districts to paper over any inequities, and NCLB's toothless "equity plans" imposed no meaningful consequences even on districts with large disparities.

Meanwhile, evidence mounted about the importance of, and variance across, teacher quality. When the Obama administration took office, it used its Race to the Top competition, and then its waiver initiative, to push states to create more nuanced evaluation systems for teachers and principals. As part of its comprehensive NCLB waivers, states were no longer required to hold districts accountable for NCLB's highly qualified teacher provision, but were instead required to design evaluation systems that included student growth, in significant part, in every teacher and principal's evaluation rating, and districts had to use those ratings in making personnel decisions.

Those evaluation systems eventually fueled a backlash on two fronts. At the state level, they created animosity against the simultaneous implementation of the new Common Core standards, and the additional tests needed to measure student growth helped fuel a movement for parents to opt their children out of state assessments. At the federal level, conservatives argued that it wasn't the federal government's place to dictate state policy on teacher and principal evaluation systems. These two camps, represented by traditionally more liberal teacher unions and more conservative federal legislators, eventually combined forces to pass ESSA, which ended the federal government's role in teacher evaluation systems.

Regardless of what one thinks of the federal government's role in teacher evaluations, they were the Obama administration's effort to ensure that all schools were accountable for all students. This level of accountability existed under NCLB—theoretically any school could fail to meet its performance targets—but under the Obama administration's normative-based accountability system, only a select group of schools were at risk of accountability. Teacher evaluations and the focus on student growth were another way to ensure all students were learning every year. ESSA doesn't embrace that goal. Unlike NCLB or the waiver initiative, ESSA has no mechanism for ensuring all students are learning.

Besides, the federal push for better teaching had a number of positive side effects. In response to federal incentives, states made a number of important policy changes, including building new data systems that can link teachers with their students, adopting tougher licensure standards, and creating and expanding alternative routes into the teaching profession. On evaluation systems alone, the National Council on Teacher Quality found that two-thirds of states strengthened teacher evaluation policies between 2009 and 2012.[16] By 2015, more than forty states planned to include some objective measure of student achievement in teacher evaluations.

In the absence of federal oversight, states may choose to revamp their evaluation systems with less emphasis on student growth, use lower-quality measures of growth, or delay the rollout of their systems. Although taking such steps may be popular with teachers, it would represent a decline in the quality of those evaluation systems. That would be a shame, because teacher evaluations today are better than they have ever been. Critics have seized on the fact that 98 percent of teachers are still rated "satisfactory" or better, but schools and districts have shifted from binary educator evaluation systems where everything was black or white—whether an educator was "satisfactory" or not—to multitiered evaluation systems that differentiate excellent teaching from mere mediocrity and mediocrity from ineffectiveness. Moreover, teachers and principals are receiving more frequent, more differentiated feedback than ever before.[17] Most state and district evaluation systems are still works in progress, but they're better now than before the federal government got involved.

LOCAL DISCRETION ON EVIDENCE-BASED POLICY MAKING

Champions of ESSA point out that it embeds "evidence-based policy making" into its very fabric. Indeed, ESSA's authors sprinkle the term *evidence-based* seventy times throughout the bill. School districts will have to make "evidence-based" decisions when they select interventions for low performing schools, as they design professional development for teachers and principals, and when they engage parents, among other things. The law defines *evidence-based* as "an activity, strategy, or intervention that demonstrates a statistically significant effect on improving student outcomes or other relevant outcomes or demonstrates a rationale based on high-quality research findings" provided that it "includes ongoing efforts to examine the effects of such activity, strategy, or intervention." Harvard professor Martin West argues that these provisions "hold the potential to create and provide resources to sustain a new model for decision-making within state education agencies and school districts," if they are "taken seriously and implemented with care."[18]

There's reason to doubt ESSA's evidence-based provisions *will* be taken seriously and implemented with care, because similar provisions in NCLB were ignored. The authors of No Child Left Behind preferred a different term, *scientifically based research*, but they used it in nearly the same way ESSA's authors used *evidence-based*. NCLB referenced scientifically based research over one hundred times, and applied it to the same types of activities as ESSA now does.

To give one concrete example, No Child Left Behind allowed school districts to use their teacher professional development funds on class size reductions. But it also required those districts to conduct a needs assessment and describe how their planned activities would "be based on a review of scientifically based research and an explanation of why the activities are expected to improve student academic achievement." There's a broad academic literature on class size reductions, and it is quite clear that class size reduction efforts matter most in the early grades and when class sizes are brought down significantly. In contrast, class size reductions in later grades and in places that only marginally reduced class size have not had any observable effects.[19] And yet states did not require districts to rely on this body of evidence in making decisions about how to use their federal dollars.

ESSA will likely result in more of the same. It says school districts may use their federal funds for reducing class sizes if it's to a "level that is evidence-based." The authors of ESSA are relying on local actors to interpret the "evidence-based" language differently than they did "scientifically based," but there's no reason to think it will lead to different results. If history serves, districts will likely continue to ignore the suggestion, just as they did under NCLB.

LOCAL CONTROL OVER FUNDING

Although money can be an important lever for reform, ESSA represents a missed opportunity to use federal dollars to target the places most in need of support. Tracing back to the original ESEA in 1965, the federal role in education has always been primarily in service of providing additional resources to low-income schools. The amount of money and how it's distributed have evolved over time, but federal Title I dollars are some of the nation's most targeted investments in low-income students. Still, there are flaws in the Title I formula that tend to drive budget allocations disproportionately toward larger districts. And within districts, a provision called the "comparability loophole" allows them to award Title I dollars without considering any resource inequities across schools. Although these issues have been well documented, ESSA's authors punted and left the existing formulas and the comparability loophole intact.

ESSA also won't mean any new money for schools. In fact, ESSA will lead to a decline in federal education spending in real, per-pupil dollars. ESSA authorizes a nominal Title I increase of 7.8 percent over the four years of the bill, but that's less than even a modest inflation assumption (compounded over the same four years, a 2 percent annual increase in inflation would equal a total increase of 8.2 percent). That amount assumes congressional appropriators award Title I its full authorization amount, and it doesn't factor in any rise in student enrollment. The National Center for Education Statistics projects that total public school enrollment will rise 2.2 percent over the same time period, mostly due to a rapid increase in Hispanic students.[20]

ESSA did, however, add a new reporting requirement mandating that all states report actual per-pupil expenditures of federal, state, and local funds for each public school and district, data that will help shine a light on any disparities. Its inclusion in the final bill foreshadowed a fight in rule making on another funding rule called "supplement not supplant." Supplement not supplant is designed to ensure that federal funds are applied on top of any state or local funds. This concept has always been a difficult one to demonstrate, but the tracking of actual school-level expenditures may help identify places where federal funds are merely being used to replace state or local dollars, rather than adding to them. Still, because Congress declined to mandate this approach, it will be left to the executive branch to regulate, or for local advocates to make use of the new fiscal transparency to push their own reforms.

CONCLUSION AND POSSIBLE PATHS FORWARD

The theory of action behind ESSA relies on transparency, vague nudges, and the best intentions of state and local policy makers. As this chapter has laid out, there are reasons to believe that ESSA has not set up state and local actors for success when it comes to holding schools accountable for the progress of all students, creating educator evaluation systems that treat teachers and principals as professionals, or offering students in low performing schools a way out.

Still, what's the right direction for the federal role? NCLB offered one answer—that standardized federal rules would set a floor for all states and ensure that "no child was left behind." That law failed to live up to its potential, and its strict theory of action wasn't right either. It was too tight on means and not tight enough on ends. But there are gradations between NCLB and ESSA that offer other potential directions for future federal education policy.

One is that federal policy could be even more focused on transparency. Under NCLB and now under ESSA, the federal government has required states to create their own academic standards in reading, math, and science; measure school and district performance in those subjects in a comparable way; and then report the results to the public. The federal government even has rules on what those report cards must look like, where they should be posted, and what they must include.

This sort of forced, fifty-state transparency is unique to the United States and could be done better by the federal government. Most countries have set clear national standards in key subjects and have standardized methods to measure all students and schools against one common yardstick. The National Assessment of Educational Progress (NAEP) already serves this purpose for states and large school districts, and it could be expanded. There's also precedent for this sort of expansion: participation in NAEP was voluntary for states until NCLB required it.

To be clear, expanding NAEP would not entail the federal government meddling in local decisions about how best to teach or operate schools, but it would accept that the only way to get truly comparable results is to have one national benchmark. The recent battles over the Common Core suggest this is not a politically viable option at the moment, but NAEP manages to avoid most of those conflicts by being strictly apolitical and low stakes. Its goal is to provide high-quality, nationally comparable data in a low-cost and transparent way. The federal government plays this role in many different areas of life, ranging from producing official employment statistics to predicting weather patterns and collecting nationally comparable data on America's citizens through decennial censuses.

Federal policy could also play a much larger role in research and innovation. Although the Department of Education's research and evaluation arm, the Institute of Education Sciences (IES), is authorized in a separate piece of federal legislation, that bill, the Education Sciences Reform Act, is also due for reauthorization and hasn't been updated since 2002. The federal government is uniquely situated to conduct large-scale research projects, but the IES budget of $574 million represents less than 0.1 percent of the $600 billion K–12 industry. IES received a one-time infusion of money from the 2009 Recovery Act, but overall its budget has not kept up with inflation.[21]

Second, although the federal government is not in a situation to *mandate* improvement efforts, it is uniquely positioned to provide incentives for local actors to change their practices. Going back to an earlier example, in 2015 the advocacy group Democrats for Education Reform estimated that the Charter Schools Program, under the Obama administration alone, had given out grants that led to the creation of seventy-two thousand new seats.[22] Those seats would not have been created without the federal investment. ESSA keeps the Charter Schools Program, as well as competitive grant programs for transforming educator evaluation and compensation systems, investing in innovative practices, and coordinating neighborhood social services. But all of these had been in operation since at least 2009, and ESSA more or less preserved their existing structures and funding levels; it did little to advance innovation efforts.

Third, the feds should seek a middle ground on accountability between a strict rules-based system like NCLB and the more flexible ESSA. Such an approach would focus the federal government on verifiable evidence of positive educational outcomes, while leaving the details over accountability systems, interventions, and finances up to each state. This "compact" approach would represent an important departure from current practice. Instead of a rules-based system like NCLB, a performance compact system would focus on states' outcomes—are low-income students, for example, making gains in reading—as opposed to what reading program schools will be required to implement. That would present states with a deal: dollars in exchange for results. States would not be entitled to federal dollars, nor would they be required to follow strict federal rules, but they would have to demonstrate positive results. Such a proposal would rely on some form of federal oversight, be that the Secretary of Education or a nonpartisan governing board analyzing a set of predefined outcome metrics.[23]

ESSA follows none of these three paths. It fails to ensure national transparency and actually includes new provisions that will erode within-state comparability. It does preserve a few existing programs that attempt to accelerate local innovation efforts, but those are generally small investments. Worse, ESSA's loose, ambiguous rules create the appearance of accountability without any real underlying substance. The law leaves the federal government little recourse in the event that states take federal dollars and fail to show any real progress. In the end, ESSA's faux accountability may prove worse than no accountability at all.

7

ESSA and State Capacity

Can the States Take Accountability Seriously?

Arnold F. Shober

U S Senator Lamar Alexander (R-TN) presented US Secretary of Education John King with a litany of ills in a testy Senate hearing in early 2016: "Local school boards, classroom teachers in states, had gotten tired of the US Department of Education telling them so much about what to do . . . the Department of Education had become a national school board, telling Kansas what their standards must be, telling Tennessee how to fix failing schools, telling Washington State how to evaluate teachers."[1]

Alexander left no doubt that the US Department of Education had become an albatross. In his view, the Every Student Succeeds Act is a good south wind, pushing federal policy away from its suspicions of the past. For fifty years, federal education policy assumed that states had little will and less capacity to improve American education. Federal policy was prescriptive, categorical, and rigid.[2] The epitome of this distrust toward states came with No Child Left Behind in 2001 as states were handed strict requirements about standards, assessment, and the consequences of both.

For all their suspicion, however, federal policy makers have had little progress to show for their efforts. A racial and ethnic gap in academic performance has remained stubborn and wide. Disparities in quality between teachers, schools, and districts have remained large. Skeptics on the right and left have wondered whether federal policy is now a stumbling block. Perhaps the states could show leadership. Some already have: Tennessee, Massachusetts, California, and other states have innovative assessments and school choice programs. Maybe the states could perform. In this, ESSA *is* a watershed. It surrenders federal leadership to the states.

Ironically, most states can exhibit such initiative only *because* of earlier federal leadership. Fifty years of federal direction has imbued many state and local officials with a desire for quality equal education. The success of the Common Core State Standards by 2014 spoke to the near-universal desire of governors and state boards of education to give all students some semblance of quality education. Governors have been on board this train for close to twenty years.[3] Fifty years of federal tutelage has also endowed the states with the technical capacity to design, measure, and advance achievement. Despite its critics, NCLB dramatically improved states' data-collection and processing abilities.[4] But a secondary accomplishment of the federal standards regime was to uncover wide disparities among the states. The median students in Massachusetts, New Jersey, and Minnesota have outperformed the best students in Alabama and Mississippi. Latino and African American students have continued to lag behind those in other groups. Further, the dramatic decline in "proficient" test scores from Common Core–linked tests has created an unenviable crucible for state officials. Paradoxically, fifty years of federal compliance has helped give states the capacity to drive student learning. But without federal oversight, it's uncertain whether they can transform compliance into creativity.

ESSA'S POTENTIAL

ESSA's architects have great expectations for the states, but the states will succeed only if they do not squander their inheritance. First, states have a tremendous opportunity to replace NCLB's simplistic performance metrics with multiple measures that are honest about individual students' learning and the role that schools and teachers play in that process. Indeed, rules implementing the law inserted the requirement that the measures be "fair" to participants in the process.[5] Alternatives including surveys, scale scores, and student growth matrices all hold promise to this end, but any changes will require careful thinking in the statehouse and state bureaucracy. States will be tempted to tinker with existing systems and continue the fairy tale of unbelievably high proficiency rates.[6]

Second, ESSA opens new frontiers for the use and understanding of student data. Student data may sound esoteric, but states have the opportunity to leverage data to benefit teachers' practice. Yet states will be tempted to yield too much of the assessment process to teachers and districts, potentially undercutting the data's promise. These groups have little incentive to report on failures, and if they're given too much leeway, ESSA could obscure academic inequities more than they often already are.

Third, ESSA allows states to move beyond NCLB's "short list" of school remedies (school choice, tutoring, or reconstitution). NCLB created a significant research base for states on school turnarounds. Combined with new, more flexible turnaround spending in ESSA, the states could significantly improve their services to low performing schools. Still, any aggressive interventions will prompt local backlash, and ESSA will not allow the states to shift blame to the federal government. Real turnarounds will require bold—and risky—leadership from state politicians.

Performance Metrics

The first, and easiest, opportunity for states is the design of better performance metrics. NCLB's Adequate Yearly Progress (AYP) was widely panned as unrealistic, statistically unsound, and subject to political manipulation. And it was. ESSA abolished that system, but retained the commitment to school-level transparency and specified two well-worn measures of academic proficiency: performance on state tests and graduation rates.[7] States will have little trouble extending these elements. Tony Evers, the president of the Council of Chief State School Officers and Wisconsin state superintendent, suggested that states' existing work created "an emergent research base to show what might work well and how a state could begin to implement these type of innovations."[8]

But *can* the states be innovative? They have shown remarkable reticence. They were given an opportunity, not a mandate, to act when the Obama administration's NCLB waivers offered them the chance to experiment with multiple, alternative measures. Eighteen states took the opportunity, but they were decidedly uncreative. Of these, twelve used ACT or SAT scores or participation rates, ten used attendance rates, and, in a throwback to the 1980s, seven used a count of advanced course taking in high school.[9]

Each of these measures had a real and measurable correlation with school-level or student performance, but none suggested that states were willing to experiment with *better* ways to identify schools (or students) who need the most help. Fortunately, two promising "inside-the-box" reforms—a "transition matrix" of student performance, and an index of social and emotional learning—have been tried in real public schools and so are part of Evers's "emergent research base."

Transition matrices eliminate the unintended consequence of categorizing students' performance into levels. NCLB categorized students' performance as below basic, basic, proficient, or advanced. But NCLB led many school officials astray. Because it required schools to show improvement over time, some school officials directed their best efforts toward students who scored just below the proficient cut score. There was no payoff for schools if higher or lower performing students scored better; those students would not "improve" into a new performance category. Transition matrices thwart this temptation by creating per-student growth plans. Instead of rewarding or sanctioning schools for a snapshot of overall student performance, students receive "points" for raising their test score enough to move to the next proficiency level compared to the previous year's test. To find a school's score, the state finds the mean student growth score for all students in a school and compares that number to state growth targets. This is not a statistically savvy approach, but it is tailored to effective implementation. The matrices are easy to explain to teachers, principals, and parents.

Second, policy analysts and a few school districts have experimented with a variety of tests to measure "social and emotional learning" (SEL). These tests ask students or their teachers a battery of questions about students' social awareness, self-management, and decision-making skills. Not only are they currently available from a variety of universities and vendors, but most of them have already been carefully studied for their relationship to academic performance, school completions, or at-risk behaviors that would impair school performance. The best-known examples are the Devereaux Student Strength Assessment (DESSA), the Comprehensive School Climate Inventory (CSCI), and the Social Skills Improvement System (SSIS).[10] These tests provide individual-level data and could be easily paired with student assessment data, allowing districts to control adequately for different school populations.[11] Neither of these measures is revolutionary, but that's central to their appeal. Even when states were offered the opportunity to think differently about assessment by the US Department of Education, none launched truly experimental measures. The benefit of transition matrices and SEL tests is that they've been used at scale in the last decade, so states can look forward to lower startup costs should they adopt them.

Data Education

NCLB and prodding from the Obama administration's Race to the Top program unquestionably improved the states' technical capacity to collect, report, and analyze student assessment data. While that data generated value for some researchers and forced measurable improvements, it also provoked anger and misunderstanding. No one truly knew how schools or teachers should respond to a 35 percent proficient rating, because no one really knew what that meant; most believed that failing to meet AYP was at least as much a statistical artifact as a genuine failure. Louisiana State Superintendent John White was emphatic that data was central to all successful school leadership: "You have to start with essential facts, a set of essential facts, and tell a story with them to support a vision for change in education. The worst things will happen with ESSA if it becomes an exercise in box checking. You have to have data-driven leadership."[12] Compared with NCLB, ESSA offers states a way to provide meaningful data training, longitudinal reporting, timely reports, and curriculum links to the Common Core. All of these could improve both the acceptance of assessments as useful pedagogical tools and offer practical improvements in data use.

The challenges of state data are substantial given the transient nature of many students, especially in low-income neighborhoods. Even administrative data like attendance, gender, and poverty status is notoriously error-prone, undermining its use for either identification or instructional support. In the waning years of the Obama administration, a handful of states banded together under the banner of "data quality" to improve the situation and to build "a school culture in which data help school staff make informed decisions about instruction and school programs."[13] The Data Quality Campaign (DQC), an organization encouraging states to boost the availability and integrity of educational data, suggested that forty states had taken substantial steps toward a robust use of data, including generating meaningful educational research, maintaining a statewide data repository, and creating progress reports for students.[14] ESSA comes at a fortuitous time for testing technology. States could employ shorter but more frequent assessments as part of their school quality measures to support teachers in the classroom, and multiple firms have launched scalable tools to emphasize teacher understanding of data.

Finally, ESSA will allow states to complete what has long been a quixotic errand in education circles: tying state assessment to classroom curriculum. States have been chasing curriculum alignment without much success since the 1970s. Local districts used widely divergent curriculum and held students to a variety of graduation standards. Assessment in the 1980s and 1990s turned away from curriculum, testing students against their peers or against state standards in the hopes that districts would align to those standards. Today, the near-universal adoption of the Common Core by school districts (even in states that never adopted it or rescinded their participation) all but guarantees that teachers will know what their students are supposed to learn. If the states incorporate those standards into their assessments, teachers could receive meaningful feedback for their daily practice. Further, transient students can all expect assessments to test consistent material in any district. Combined with better longitudinal tracking, student growth can follow these students throughout the state.

Fifty years of federal compliance, with its substantial record-keeping requirements, has provided states with a base of technical competence. ESEA built local constituencies for standards and accountability across all states in the last twenty years. The Obama administration's Race to the Top program pushed states into quick adoption of a common curriculum *and* better-quality assessments. Now ESSA has given states the opportunity to make them their own, but that will require leadership, not compliance.

Turnarounds

ESSA offers states a third opportunity: to remedy the overly broad approaches that NCLB took to improve lagging schools. As with alternate measures of performance and data education, some states and districts have a long history of "turnaround" efforts tied to school finance cases from which to draw lessons. NCLB also provided states with a real research base for studying school improvement. ESSA significantly increases the flexibility of turnaround funding, giving states additional resources to implement creative and research-based school improvement.

The richest source of state capacity comes from four decades of school finance litigation. After the Supreme Court washed its hands of school finances in *San Antonio Independent School District v. Rodriguez* (1973), advocates of higher funding turned to state courts to remedy unequal or inadequate funding.[15] Plaintiffs rarely need to look far to find schools that fail some test of "adequate" educational performance, and they have compelled state legislatures and state bureaucracies to address low scoring or poorly funded schools. Indeed, NCLB bolstered adequacy arguments by giving advocates the federally required "proficient" benchmark. If schools could not meet these standards, they were obviously not adequate. One adequacy proponent noted that "from a litigating point of view, this stuff is dynamite and the more extreme NCLB gets, the better it is for us plaintiffs."[16] In the aftermath of these cases, a handful of states have taken measures suggesting they *could* implement turnarounds even without a judgment against them.[17]

Beyond school finance, states can look to ten years of turnaround research from NCLB. In that time, approximately 4 percent of all Title I money was available for federally specified turnaround efforts through School Improvement Grants (SIGs). SIG funds were meant to boost persistently low performing schools, but the money was tightly restricted. Funds could be used for closing a school (and reopening it), converting it to a charter school, firing and hiring half of a school's personnel, or one of a handful of less intense "transformative" strategies, including performance pay or longer school days. Despite these options, most states, many districts, and major interest groups thought the program straitjacketed local leaders, many of whom wanted more freedom to build school- or district-level collaboration.[18] ESSA addresses this critique in a big way: not only does it boost improvement funding to 7 percent, but it removes many restrictions on what the funds can be used for. They have to be for "innovation," but the states can decide what that innovation looks like. This change will "open up possibilities for real creativity on the spending side," according to Louisiana's John White. "The funds come with enough discretion to pursue turnaround models that we know work."[19]

The SIG research generated decidedly mixed results. Data indicated that 54 percent of schools first funded by the SIG in 2011–2012 had gains in mathematics scores in the next academic year, but 40 percent had losses (non-SIG schools' numbers were 45 percent and 47 percent, respectively).[20] Nevertheless, proponents noted that for the three years of the program, SIG schools were more likely to post gains than losses and more likely to post gains than non-SIG schools. The modest gains appeared to coincide with consistent elements, including persistent monitoring of student and teacher data and local buy-in. With data and local support on hand, schools could adjust curriculum, pace, and goals.[21] States' new assessments, especially if they are not once-a-year summative tests, could easily assist this goal.[22] Looser controls on turnaround financing can give districts—through the state—incentives to enhance these activities, especially as state-centric reforms typically yield the weakest results.

Although much of ESSA only codifies flexibility already available through waivers, states now have some legislative certainty that their experimentation is not tied to a particular presidential administration. States have a formal opportunity to embark on new measures of success, improve local communication about results, and tune turnaround efforts to local conditions.

And states and districts *have* embraced innovation.

Ironically, ESEA put state departments of education in a much better position to serve districts and schools than they would have been without federal pressure. Although federal legislation guaranteed that state departments of education would be implementing an odd mix of compliance-driven policy, creative state-level assessment, and district service, some states were able to leverage federal mandates to provide genuine innovation.

Some education departments were able to design accountability measures in a way that was attentive to teachers and parents. Some states built ties to local interest groups—in education and in the business community—to ensure that education work would have local political support. In some cases, local groups helped design state measures that then helped provide field training for schools and districts.

POLITICAL REALITIES OF STATE CAPACITY

All this suggests that state departments of education *can* provide meaningful guidance and oversight of academic quality in schools and states *if* they have politically capable leadership and the technical capacity to do so.[23] ESSA will be a boon to these states, but there are serious technical and political barriers that may impede the law's success in other states.

The first is a subtle shift from accountability to collaboration. Second, federal education policy has spent fifty years fostering compliance-driven state bureaucracies; ESSA is unlikely to shift that mentality. Third, contrary in spirit to much of the bill, ESSA imposes additional requirements to protect student subgroups and special education students. Whatever their benefits, the requirements place limits on what states can do.

Turning Around or Tuning Out?

The most striking shift is in language after a decade of exhaustion with data-driven public accountability. Instead of "accountability," many state officials have begun to talk about "responsibility" and "collaboration." Kansas Commissioner of Education Randy Watson was explicit: "Academic skills are important, but not to the exclusion of other things . . . You don't do test prep for four months for one test that doesn't matter."[24] Wisconsin's Tony Evers told the Senate HELP Committee that his Department of Public Instruction would begin with "stakeholder engagement" as an "opportunity to hear multiple perspectives of what is working in the state, what needs to be changed, and how people envision flexibility in practice."[25] California's school leaders took this kind of rhetoric to heart and created a dashboard of school measures instead of calculating a single measure of school quality. California State Board President Michael Kirst argued that the state should not prioritize some educational outcomes over others—that should be left to parents and other stakeholders. "If you're smart enough to look at five things on the dashboard of a car and still drive, you should be able to understand a school," he said.[26] It may be simplistic or presumptuous to assign a single A to F grade to a school when stakeholders have many goals for education. An A collapses all of those goals into a single metric, but that can focus attention on the best and worst like nothing else. Multiple measures may allow teachers, staff, administrators, parents, and the public to focus on what they value most, but will also detract from the pursuit of academic performance.

While there were problems with NCLB's accountability metrics, ESSA's softer focus may replace meaningful school improvement with politically palatable local "collaborations" or simply excuse poor performance as a local problem. The danger is especially acute because 95 percent of federal turnaround funding is to be sent to school districts, precluding some bolder reforms, including charter schools and alternate school district arrangements. District-led strategies can provide excellent political buy-in from the stakeholders who are more directly affected—the teachers, support staff, and administrators. But the premise of "turnarounds" is that *these* personnel are somehow part of a school's academic problem. Thus, according to Andy Smarick, a fellow at the Thomas B. Fordham Institute, direct federal spending on districts "muddies authority, undermines good governance, and has the potential to inhibit state experimentation and slow emerging state innovations."[27] If schools are to prepare students for college or career in the future, collaboration now may be a less powerful motivator for change than starkly low student performance. District-based efforts may improve the district, but they are unlikely to address core problems or try substantial innovation.

Data for Decision Making?

A second risk is states' well-honed compliance mind-set. ESSA gives states the chance to change the way they manage and service data. But years of operating in compliance mode makes it more likely that they'll treat data collection as routine paperwork rather than as an opportunity for innovation.

Despite the NCLB-induced improvements in data gathering and processing, states' focus remains thoroughly pragmatic. Kansas's Data Quality Certification is typical. The state's program was highlighted by the Thomas B. Fordham Institute as making "solid advances in [its] education data system," but its program included substantial training on data entry and navigation of state and federal databases—including which school is responsible for entering data for which students—rather than actually thinking about data.[28] Pennsylvania's 2015 Department of Education Data Summit acknowledged this natural rut. The conference, themed "Moving Beyond Compliance: Getting Value Out of Data," highlighted "data dashboards," "early warning systems" for dropout prevention, and database basics for retrieving data.[29] Both of these programs, and similar ones in other states, provide necessary fundamentals, but they indicate that states have only started to help districts analyze student data and have done little to help parents or teachers understand how psychometric exams, growth models, or cut points work. If data training found a champion in the state legislature or executive mansion, it's possible that some states would offer innovative and robust training. A handful of states did this very thing in the 1980s under performance-minded governors. But it was personality-driven and short-lived. Absent the federal lever, state departments appear unlikely to reinvent how they look at data.

Yet even if they wanted to use data—to track individual progress, for example—other hurdles would remain, especially states' current interpretation of the Family Educational Rights and Privacy Act of 1974 (FERPA). This act was meant to prevent abuses by government officials—especially school officials—in the midst of widespread government abuse in Watergate, including the use of tax records to target political opponents. (FERPA was signed by Gerald Ford twelve days after Richard Nixon resigned.) Since that time, threats to student privacy have morphed from unwitting school secretaries letting something slip to domestic and international hackers looking for identities to steal. Here, the Department of Education has undermined real opportunities for good practice. Regulations and litigation have placed the privacy of student data at the forefront of professional development for practitioners.[30] Thus, FERPA has replaced thinking about data with thinking about regulatory compliance. If ESSA's new measures are to yield better benefits that NCLB's simplistic school- and district-based measures, federal policy makers will have to clarify *when* student privacy is actually threatened.

Limits of Universality

A third limitation to state capacity comes from ESSA itself. Despite the act's generally open-handed flexibility, it doesn't offer relief from categorizing students by subgroup or for testing children receiving special education services, both major components of NCLB's testing regimen. These should be the easiest of the reforms from ESSA, but its continuing requirements create practical limits on how innovative states can be.

Civil rights groups and many Democrats in Congress were adamant that states' assessment measures remain in force for "all" students. Their intention was for schools to remain politically (and financially) accountable for on-standard performance even by small demographic groups of students. This was a deliberate choice. Before ESSA, the US Department of Education had allowed states to combine multiple groups of students into larger pools (as "supersubgroups"). ESSA removes that option. As a result, state accountability measures may suffer the high variability characteristic of small populations. That variability was the genesis of a major critique of NCLB—that a school or district could miss AYP purely from statistical artifacts in small subgroups. The performance measures used by the states will have to account for small-group variability carefully.

A potentially greater challenge for states lies in ESSA's treatment of special education students. A core component of federal accountability legislation is that all students in a state will be held to the same standards, regardless of their income, race, or academic ability. Some special education students fit uncomfortably in this framework because their learning trajectories may be substantially different than those of their peers. The law recognizes this and allows states to give alternative tests to students with "severe cognitive disabilities," so long as they comprise no more than 1 percent of students (about one-tenth of all special education students). Learning-disability interest groups lobbied hard to keep this cap low to prevent schools and states from sidelining special-needs children. They succeeded, and in this area, ESSA's regulations are stricter than they were under NCLB; Evers argued that the waiver requirements from these rules were even more "onerous" than NCLB's.[31] Part of the reason is that states are held to a standard that individual districts are not. The law requires that of all students tested in a state, no more than 1 percent may be alternate assessments, yet districts may exceed the cap. Of course, for a state to meet ESSA's requirements, every district that gives more than 1 percent of its students alternate assessments will have to be balanced by districts that give fewer alternate assessments. The states can try to mitigate this difficulty by defining what "severe cognitive disabilities" are, but after pressure from civil rights groups, ESSA regulations prohibit states from linking "disability" to school performance, English language proficiency, or (solely) behavior in school. Because "all" students must be given the same tests—even those with less severe cognitive disabilities—state policy makers will be tempted to lower standards across the board to ensure that test passage rates are politically tolerable.

Despite the seemingly open-handed nature of ESSA, these statistical mandates have made *genuine* state leadership difficult. Neither requirement is flexible, and some stakeholders see them as even less flexible than NCLB's prescriptions. These requirements guarantee that at least part of ESSA's implementation will be compliance-driven. Although well meaning, these requirements risk setting up the rest of ESSA for an unimaginative, cookie-cutter implementation. Without careful thought and concerted effort, these may undermine ESSA's broader possibilities for creativity and innovation in the states.

ESSA: PROMISE OR PERIL?

ESSA's promise is not that every state will suddenly become Massachusetts, Texas, or Delaware. Instead, it is that states will be able to borrow—or pool—measures, data education, and school improvement strategies from similar states and build on other education consortia, whether those are the assessment consortia built into Smarter Balanced, PARCC, ELPA21, ACCESS, or something else. The federal government "borrowed strength" from state capacity to implement NCLB; it relied on state bureaucracy to be able to design or purchase state tests, build up a meaningful assessment framework, and monitor schools for data quality.[32] ESSA gave states the opportunity to "borrow strength" from one another. The public is ready, too. In 2015, some two-thirds of the public continued to support the NCLB-era annual testing in math and reading, and states and localities received the lion's share of support (about 81 percent) for assessing and revitalizing low performing schools.[33] States may have great expectations for new-found freedom from federal oversight, and their success will be reflected in their cooperation.

But will they take their opportunity? Political challenges to ESSA loom large: states will no longer be able to shift blame easily, the work of schools may shift, and testing may reopen political wounds.

When states faced technical trouble or political pushback from NCLB, it was convenient and sometimes true that the fault lay with the federal government. The National Education Association made this argument consistently, and Connecticut (unsuccessfully) sued the federal government on the charge that NCLB was compelling state spending. When states came under pressure in late 2014 over Common Core–aligned tests, state lawmakers made a show over withdrawing from federally funded testing consortia.

There will be no such out with ESSA. ESSA's potential new measures create opportunities to highlight disparities in the provision of education, and that could generate a new wave of school finance litigation. Under duress, state defendants have occasionally admitted that academic performance should be comparable within their states. When *Rose v. Council for Better Education* (1989) and a handful of school finance cases in other states suggested that states should equalize nontested factors, no one knew how to measure them. Now, defendants would be unhappy to discover that they have created a measure—classroom climate, parental involvement, or student perseverance—for courts to require equity. The push for standards, accountability, and transparency was meant to empower parents, teachers, districts, and the public to ensure that all children were served by public education. An unintended consequence of ESSA might just be that education policy is placed even more firmly in the hands of state judges. The result would not be innovation, creativity, or even local democracy; ESSA could instead paralyze state education policy.

Second, new measurements will reshape how schools do their work and create new political puzzles. Just as NCLB successfully pushed math and reading to the core of schooling and made testing student performance a prominent feature of education policy, ESSA's codification of flexible measurement may permit schools to retool their approach to career education and work skills. These may be worthy goals, but such a shift would exacerbate a decades-long debate over tracking and schools as "sorting machines." Critics on the left have already decried business influence in education; prioritizing work skills would only heighten their anger. Common Core was a long-term project of the business community and governors of both parties, but it reshaped state political alliances, especially on the right. ESSA may do the same, this time potentially on the left.

Third, if lawmakers choose to add new, creative measures, they will face the risk of inflaming opponents of school testing. Although most parents do not support their students opting out of tests—*Education Next* found 67 percent support for accountability testing in schools—legislators caved to pressure in 2015 and 2016 and curtailed tests in Arizona, Indiana, Georgia, Ohio, and South Dakota, and others imposed time limits on academic testing.[34] Gov. Terry McAuliffe, fêted for reducing Virginia's exams related to its standards of learning, said, "I think we've heard from the students [that] these tests don't really help us prepare for college, or more importantly, they're really not helping us prepare for life."[35] This attitude was widespread as ESSA rolled out, suggesting that *meaningful* performance testing, only recently accomplished, could be ephemeral. "Better" assessment may be better from a psychometric perspective, but without political support, ESSA-inspired metrics are unlikely to succeed.

CONCLUSION

Still, these risks should be tempered by the larger truth that "policy" can only do so much. State leaders have to supply a vision for quality education. NCLB's theory of action was largely that measurement and reporting of academic performance would prompt teachers and schools to change. There is evidence that NCLB got states partway there. But policy makers in the states, the US Department of Education, or Congress cannot depend on policy alone to improve learning in America's schools. States can design new measures, educate teachers and parents about their students' progress, and think creatively about school turnarounds, but ESSA will not win the long game. "We have to stop fetishizing policy," John White said. "We need an authentic vision for students tailored to a mission of improvement. In my experience, policy is neither a tremendous opportunity nor a tremendous barrier. It is a system to be shaped."[36] Some states turned in far-reaching, innovative reforms under NCLB because key state leaders dreamed an impossible dream *in spite* of the law. ESSA has expanded the frontier of possibilities, but state leaders must grasp their freedom to take others with them.

8

ESSA and State Policy

What's Next for Education Policy?

Ashley Jochim

O ver the last three decades, the influence of federal education policy on states, districts, and classrooms has grown. The No Child Left Behind Act ushered in an era of test-based accountability, expansion of school choice, and a new focus on school and district turnaround. More recently, the Obama administration's Race to the Top (RTTT) program and NCLB waivers pushed and pulled states to establish statewide systems of teacher evaluation, Common Core standards, and evidence-based school turnaround approaches. While these efforts were largely crafted and implemented by states and districts, they were initiated and constrained through federal policy.

If history provides any insight, the Every Student Succeeds Act is likely to drive new changes to state policy, with renewed focus on some issues and fading interest in others. This chapter discusses the likely impacts of ESSA on state education policy. It will focus on the six areas that have been central to recent reform efforts: standards and assessments, test-based accountability, school turnarounds, teacher quality, school choice, and school finance. Based on the changes likely to follow, the chapter concludes with recommendations on how states can best leverage ESSA and mitigate its likely challenges.

HOW FEDERAL POLICY SHAPES STATE POLICY

The framers of the US Constitution sought to balance the interests of those who favored a stronger central government with those who believed more power should be vested in the states. The relationship between states and the federal government evolved over time, shaped by court decisions, practice, and changes in the national political climate.

Federal influence has grown substantially in the twentieth century. Some of this influence stems from federal regulations. But increasingly, the federal government shapes state policy through grants. According to the US Census Bureau, federal grants make up between 20 and 40 percent of state general fund revenues.[1] Unlike regulations, grants offer states funding in return for compliance with programmatic requirements, though a full accounting of costs is rarely pursued and it is not always clear whether the benefits outweigh the compliance costs.

Federal support for public schools has increased since World War II. In 1945, federal funds were just 1.4 percent of total education spending; by 2011, during the height of the Great Recession, they were 12.5 percent.[2] Some states rely on federal funding more than others. As figure 8.1 depicts, federally supported spending on K–12 education ranges from a low of 4 percent in New Jersey and Connecticut to a high of 16 percent in Mississippi.

While federal dollars for K–12 education are dwarfed by state and local spending, states have come to rely on federal funds to support key components of their educational programs. The largest of these investments stem from the Elementary and Secondary Education Act of 1965. Title I, the law's signature program, sought to improve the achievement of low-income children by providing states with funding to support supplementary educational services. Subsequent reauthorizations added new support for other state and locally administered programs—including special education programs for children with disabilities and bilingual education programs for non-native English speakers—and grants to states to support improvements in teacher and principal quality.[3] In 2010, the Government Accountability Office counted 229 federal programs spread across 20 agencies, with the vast majority operating as grants to states or districts.[4]

Federal grants have grown more prescriptive over time. As political scientists Susan Welch and Kay Thompson suggest, "Prior to 1960 most such grants were designed to help states and localities achieve their own goals; since then, federal grants have been mostly designed to help states and localities accomplish national goals."[5] The National Center for Policy Analysis reports that the total number of regulations procured by the Department of Education grew from two thousand in 1980 to nearly eleven thousand in 2010.[6]

FIGURE 8.1 Percent of education spending funded by federal government, 2012–2013

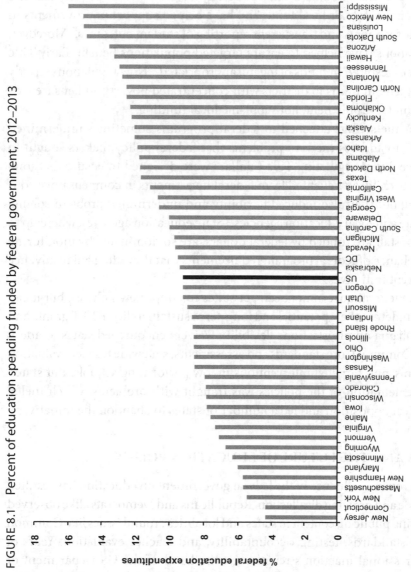

Source: National Center for Educational Statistics, Revenues and Expenditures for Public Elementary and Secondary Education: School Year 2012–13 (Fiscal Year 2013).

The proliferation of programs and regulations was often well intended, as policy makers sought to get states to address long-neglected problems in local K–12 public school systems. Sometimes, these efforts were successful. Federal education funds are more strongly targeted to high-poverty districts than either state or local funds and have helped support improvements in state assessments and transparent reporting of student outcomes.[7] Moreover, regulations have helped to ensure targeted populations benefit. Early Title I abuses resulted in funds being misappropriated.[8] Now regulations strictly target federal funds to districts with concentrated poverty and ensure federal funds "supplement, not supplant" local funding.

But the strings attached to federal programs sometimes undermined efforts to address the very problems that federal policy makers sought to resolve. Rules regulating Title I dollars were designed to ensure that low-income children benefited from federal investments in compensatory education, but they also reduced flexibility and undermined problem solving in state and local education agencies.[9] State education agencies, where up to half of staff are funded by federal dollars, are so dominated by monitoring compliance of federal program requirements that they often fail to advance coherent initiatives.[10]

The federal government can get states to adopt new policies, but it can also undercut their potential and long-term sustainability. RTTT grants and the Obama administration's flexibility waivers encouraged states to adopt new Common Core standards and assessments, statewide teacher evaluation systems, and targeted interventions in low performing schools. But states' implementation of the policies was fraught with problems, which fueled political opposition and led a number of states to abandon the initiatives.

ESSA AND THE FUTURE OF EDUCATION POLICY

The growing influence of the federal government on education has resulted in wide and growing disaffection. Republicans and Democrats alike observed growing public discontent in states and localities around issues like Common Core standards, testing, accountability, and teacher evaluation. Years of congressional inaction strengthened the hand of the US Department of Education, thereby further distancing federal law from state priorities. The passage of ESSA had its roots in these concerns.

Many observers lauded the law for returning control over education back to the states. The *Wall Street Journal* reported the law signified "the largest devolution of federal control to the states in a quarter-century," while the *New York Times* said it "represent[s] the end of an era in which the federal government aggressively policed public school performance, and return[s] control to states and local districts."[11] Utah Governor Gary Herbert, speaking for the National Governors Association, said the law "is a clear example of cooperative federalism" and provides states and localities the "freedom" they need.[12]

The devolution narrative, however, does not capture how the new law is likely to constrain states moving forward. ESSA maintains federal oversight in key areas like accountability and establishes new guardrails that are likely to limit what states do in the future. As Kelly McManus of the Education Trust observed, "Instead of playing in one section of the yard, [states] can play in the whole yard. But [the yard is] still fenced."[13] A larger yard provides states with more freedom of action to try new things. But the fence of federal regulations will continue to circumscribe state policy. In this sense, ESSA does not represent a federal retreat from K–12 schools and federal policy will continue to shape what states do.

Common Core, Standards, and Assessments

Beginning with the 1994 reauthorization of ESEA (the Improving America's Schools Act, or IASA), federal law has required states to adopt academic standards and assess student progress. IASA, however, and its successor, NCLB in 2001, left states in charge of developing their own standards and assessments. Because states were also charged with bringing all students up to "proficiency," state standards often lacked rigor and the quality of assessments varied widely.

In 2009, the Council of Chief State School Officers and the National Governors Association set out to address the shortcomings in states' standards. They launched the Common Core State Standards Initiative to develop common English and mathematics standards. US Secretary of Education Arne Duncan used the carrot of $4.35 billion in federal funding in the RTTT competitive grant program as well as relief from NCLB to encourage states to adopt the standards and aligned assessments. These efforts were successful in getting many states to adopt the standards. But they also transformed the bipartisan effort into a political football: conservatives expressed concern over the federal government's role, and liberals worried about how the standards would fit into state accountability systems.[14]

Common Core was on the minds of lawmakers when they drafted ESSA. Senator John McCain praised the law for "[doing] away basically with

Common Core."[15] ESSA explicitly prohibits the secretary of education from forcing or even encouraging states to adopt a particular set of academic standards. But, of course, the law could not do away with the standards because the federal government only ever indirectly controlled states' participation.

Despite the political controversy, Common Core is going nowhere. The few states that "abandoned" the standards typically engaged in only modest revisions. States looking to adopt new standards would need to make substantial new investments in curriculum, professional development, and testing, an unpalatable proposition in an era of tight budgets. As well, the law's requirements for standards to meet entry requirements for higher education institutions will make it difficult for states to return to their old standards. Data from the National Council of State Legislatures suggests that the conflict over Common Core standards is simmering down with opt-out bills on the decline—thirty-four bills in 2016 compared to forty-nine bills in 2015.[16]

But while Common Core is here to stay, the future of the aligned assessments is uncertain. The Obama administration invested $350 million in two consortia, Smarter Balanced and the Partnership for Assessment of Readiness for College and Careers. The consortia were charged with developing next-generation Common Core–aligned assessments, and forty-five states initially signed on to participate. But as controversy swirled, loyalty to the consortia weakened. By 2016, just twenty states were poised to implement the consortia-designed assessments.

The consortia's challenges have been fueled in large part by a broader public backlash over standardized testing. Frustrated by the impact of testing on students, parents in many states are increasingly opting out of traditional standardized tests. Teachers and their unions helped to fuel the public backlash as states introduced new test-based teacher evaluation systems.

ESSA provides states new flexibility around assessments, allowing states to expand the use of student work portfolios, extended performance tasks, or multiple interim assessments. The law also provides districts flexibility to use nationally recognized assessments like the SAT for high school students with state approval. The enhanced flexibility will likely spur significant changes and introduce more variation into state assessment programs.

ESSA's improved flexibility gives states new options to ensure assessments do more than "test and punish." As New Hampshire Department of Education Deputy Commissioner Paul Leather said, "We hear about over-testing because we really have two accountability systems: the state system is required by federal law but may not help us improve teaching and learning. Schools administer their own tests for that."[17] According to the National Council of State Legislatures, states introduced about five hundred bills related to assessment in the legislative session immediately following the passage of ESSA.

While assessments are likely to change, it is unclear whether states will use their newfound flexibility to create more streamlined, responsive, and useful systems. The challenge for states is particularly acute given that state assessment programs aim to both inform policy makers and parents about the performance of public schools and improve teaching and learning. Whether states are able to achieve these ends will depend on their ability to work with stakeholders to identify problems and the availability of innovative, high quality, and cost-effective assessments in the marketplace.

Test-Based Accountability

Accountability systems provide the glue that connects state standards to school practices. What states choose to measure is likely to incentivize changes in the behavior of districts, schools, teachers, and even parents.

NCLB spurred substantial changes to states' accountability systems. States varied considerably in their embrace of accountability prior to NCLB—fewer than half gave annual assessments in reading and math in grades 3–8, and fewer publicly reported on the results.[18]

But the law's accountability requirements had unintended consequences. The exclusive reliance on standardized test scores to judge school quality led many schools to narrow their offerings and focus much of their effort on tested subjects and grades. In some schools, educators focused on test preparation over higher-level learning and targeted "bubble kids" who were on the cusp of proficiency, spending less effort on children well below or above proficiency benchmarks.

ESSA explicitly seeks to address what was maligned with NCLB accountability systems. Like NCLB, ESSA requires states to track student achievement across student subgroups and publicly report on the results. But the law significantly broadens the set of indicators that states must include. All states will now be required to include five measures in their accountability system and disaggregate these indicators by major student subgroups:

- proficiency on annual assessments
- a second measure of academic achievement for elementary and middle schools that allows for "meaningful differentiation" in school performance (e.g., student growth)

- graduation rates for high schools
- progress of English learners toward English language proficiency
- another indicator of school quality (e.g., access to rigorous course-work, school climate, or socioemotional learning)

While state flexibility over the design of these metrics is likely to be further constrained by DOE regulations, these changes will require many states to broaden their set of accountability measures. This presents both opportunities and risks—the former because states can work to tailor their accountability system toward local priorities, and the latter because not all states are equally well equipped to design and select new, often novel measures of student outcomes.

While many observers point to the inclusion of student growth measures in the law, ESSA's embrace of growth reflects the ongoing trend in states. According to the Center for American Progress, forty-six states already include a measure of student growth in their accountability system.[19] These systems are likely to continue to evolve as states fine-tune them. Perhaps the most exciting prospects stem from opportunities to measure growth across the achievement spectrum (i.e., both high and low achievers), incentivizing schools to better serve students who already meet proficiency benchmarks.[20]

The fourth and fifth indicators are likely to spur the most substantial changes to accountability systems. While NCLB required states to measure progress toward English language proficiency, accountability strictly targeted districts, not schools, and was divorced from states' traditional account-ability system. As a result, just six states currently incorporate a measure of English language proficiency into their accountability systems in any way. By moving English language proficiency into their accountability systems, states will shine new light on these students.

Perhaps the most promising element in all of ESSA is that it enables states to experiment with more nuanced methods of assessing school quality. Before ESSA, states varied tremendously in whether they include non-achievement-based measures of school success in their accountabil-ity systems. Some states tracked school climate or access to coursework, but few disaggregated that data by student subgroup. ESSA allows states to use measures of school climate to address some of the undesirable impacts of accountability under NCLB, including a narrowing of the cur-riculum and a focus on test preparation over higher-level learning. States might choose to measure students' access to a well-rounded curriculum, providing schools an incentive to expand their offerings in arts, music, and physical education.

The devil, of course, is in the details. States that lack capacity to develop new measures may turn to existing metrics that largely mirror the existing accountability system. Alternatively, states may use measures that lack an evidence base and find themselves with an accountability system that fails to reliably assess outcomes. The latter issue is a particular risk with the fifth indicator, which has not historically been a component of state account- ability systems and where experts warn that assessment systems are still in their infancy.

Draft regulations released in June 2016 added further constraints to the fifth indicator. DOE has proposed that all measures in this category be backed by research that shows they contribute to student achievement or gradua- tion rates, leaving some observers to worry that the opportunity to include broader, nonacademic measures of school quality would be circumscribed.[21]

School Turnarounds

NCLB was widely criticized for inaccurately deeming a large number of schools "in need of improvement" and for prescribing how districts and states must intervene when schools failed to meet targets.

ESSA explicitly addresses much of what critics found wrong with NCLB's approach to school turnaround: it enables states to create locally defined improvement targets for all schools and subgroups, rather than defining an arbitrary set of goals for all states and localities; it requires states to identify the lowest performing schools but leaves the method of identification (e.g., how to weight the indicators) up to states, subject to some regulatory con- straints; and it abandons prescribed methods of turnaround, instead favor- ing locally developed approaches.[22]

The improved flexibility empowers states to take a much more thought- ful approach to the work of identifying schools in need of improvement. States could choose to differentiate schools based on a weighting scheme that is tied to state priorities, such as the number of English language learn- ers or the desire to encourage schools to improve non-achievement-based measures of school quality.

States will also be positioned to better leverage local expertise in the work of school turnaround. The law continues support for school improvement efforts by reserving 7 percent of states' Title I allocation. But it provides substantial new flexibility in how states support local districts. States are allowed to distribute these funds to districts on either a competitive or formulaic basis. A competitive basis would enable states to capitalize on work already happening in local districts and reward districts that put forward the best proposals.

Of course, flexibility also introduces risk. States may forgo the opportunity to develop local solutions to performance gaps and choose instead to do nothing (see chapter 7 for more on the challenges facing state education agencies). Or states could act aggressively and impose their own, one-size-fits-all solution that's just as removed from the school as the old federally prescribed turnaround strategies.

While the historic debates over ESEA often focused on the plight of urban schools that serve large numbers of low-income students, ESSA could increase attention toward suburban schools. The law requires states to identify schools in need of improvement where "any subgroup of students is consistently underperforming." This may result in the identification of schools whose overall performance is strong but where deep achievement gaps exist. The change in identification may push more suburban districts to acknowledge achievement gaps and do more to address the needs of struggling students. While NCLB also targeted suburban schools, as growing number of schools failed to make Adequate Yearly Progress, the law's more prescriptive requirements for turnaround strategies helped to fuel backlash in these communities. ESSA allows districts to take the lead in identifying improvement strategies, possibly mitigating some of the potential political opposition. It also requires documentation of resource inequities, thereby empowering historically disadvantaged groups with data that may help them drive changes in school- or district-level practices.

Improving Teacher Quality

NCLB made a big investment in improving teacher quality. Title II required 100 percent of teachers in core academic subjects to be "highly qualified teachers" (HQT), which it defined largely in terms of teacher education and certification standards, and appropriated nearly $3 billion to support improvements in teacher quality. Most states were successful in getting the vast majority of teachers certified as highly qualified, but there is little evidence that these efforts improved teacher quality or low-income students' access to quality teachers.

The HQT provisions of NCLB were an outgrowth of a large body of evidence that suggested teachers could have substantial impacts on student learning and that not all credentialed teachers were equally effective at supporting students' academic progress. But policy makers had long wrestled with how to improve the quality of the teacher workforce, given the challenge of identifying effective teachers and developing strategies for improving teacher training and professional development.

The Obama administration sought a new path toward improving teacher quality by shifting attention from teachers' qualifications to their impacts on student learning. This approach eliminated the need to define effective teaching, relying instead on student achievement to identify ineffective teachers. This shift was enabled by the successful expansion of state data systems, driven in large part by NCLB's accountability requirements, and new value-added measures of student growth. The administration incentivized states to adopt new systems of teacher evaluation in which student achievement was a significant factor through RTTT and NCLB waivers. These efforts spurred substantial changes in states' evaluation systems and resulted in a threefold increase—from sixteen to forty-three—in the number of states that required student achievement to be included.[23]

But the use of student achievement data in teachers' evaluations spurred substantial controversy. Teachers and their unions rejected the heavy reliance on student achievement data, while many conservatives believed that the Obama administration overstepped its authority in requiring states to adopt the policies in the first place. As a result, it is no surprise that ESSA does away with federal rules that require the use of student achievement data in teacher evaluation systems.

The new law also abandons NCLB's highly qualified teacher requirements and substantively changes the focus of state reporting away from teacher qualifications and toward teacher effectiveness. States will now be required to demonstrate that low-income and minority children are not served at disproportionate rates by "ineffective, out-of-field, or inexperienced teachers" and publicly report on progress in addressing gaps. But states will define what makes a teacher effective or ineffective.

States are likely to revisit the systems put in place to define and measure teacher effectiveness. There are signs that states are already looking to revise or abandon their current systems for evaluating teachers. New York and Oklahoma announced delays to the use of student achievement data in teacher evaluation, while state leaders in Georgia have expressed interest in deemphasizing the indicator.[24] Despite these challenges, Daniel Weisberg, the CEO of TNTP, a leading advocacy group for including student achievement in teacher evaluation, expressed optimism. He observed that while "[s]ome states may roll back evaluation laws in the short term . . . it'll be a longer discussion in the bulk of the states."[25]

Regardless of what happens, the challenges states have confronted in implementing statewide teacher evaluation systems are also likely to rear their head as states seek to improve low-income and minority students' access to effective teachers. As Montana Superintendent Denise Juneau expressed, "The state does not control the hiring and placement of teachers in our schools. These decisions are made by locally elected boards of trustees, not the states."[26]

But while states can't control the hiring and placement of teachers, they can help shed enough light to empower advocates and communities to act. States could keep pressure on local districts by putting forth rigorous, but fair, definitions of teacher effectiveness and tracking basic data on how effective teachers are distributed across schools and districts. Local groups are better positioned than states to use this data to press for substantive changes in collective bargaining agreements and teacher hiring decisions.

A less noticed provision of the law is likely to increase pressure on higher education institutions (HEIs) that sponsor teacher preparation programs, thereby driving changes to teacher quality on the supply side. Teacher preparation programs are widely criticized for inadequately preparing teachers for the demands of their jobs.[27] ESSA enables states to do an end run around HEIs by allowing the use of Title II funding to develop new "teacher preparation academies" that are sponsored by nonprofits or other public entities. In addition to providing funding, the law also dictates requirements for these programs to ensure that they do not face unnecessary regulatory requirements (e.g., "obligating the academy's faculty to hold advanced degrees or conduct academic research") and that teachers (or principals) trained through these academies are recognized with degrees that are similar to other programs (e.g., a master's degree). These provisions will position state education agencies that remain independent from higher education institutions to reshape K–12 teacher and principal pipelines using Title II, rather than engaging in protracted fights.

School Choice
NCLB substantially expanded the role of the federal government in increasing access to school choice in local school systems through both charters and traditional public schools. The law explicitly authorized states to reconstitute

low performing schools as charter schools, offered additional funding to support charter expansion, and required districts to provide transportation to students attending a school "in need of improvement" to a higher performing school of their choice.

These efforts had mixed effects. The investments in charter schools helped to expand the sector in some locales and create new authorizing capacity in state education agencies, but few states or districts converted failing public schools into charters. In addition, despite ever-growing eligibility for transportation and alternative placements, very few families took advantage of the opportunity to transfer to a higher performing school.[28]

ESSA largely sustains much of NCLB's legacy with regards to school choice, with minor modifications. Support for charter schools will continue through the Charter Schools Program. An expanded set of entities will now be eligible for state grants, a change that could empower other entities to support charter schools where state education agencies are reluctant to get into the fray. The law will no longer require districts to offer students a transfer to a higher performing school, but this option will remain an allowable expense under Title I school improvement funds.

But ESSA is likely to shape state policy around school choice in other ways. The law also enables states to set aside up to 3 percent of their Title I funding to develop direct student services in districts. Districts could use the funding to support access to online courses, career-tech education, credit recovery programs, academic acceleration programs, and personalized learning programs. Some states and districts are already operating programs like these. Louisiana operates a course access program that enables students to take courses through providers that are approved by the state, and many rural districts sponsor programs like these to ensure students have access to rigorous and specialized college preparatory coursework that is not always available in settings where economies of scale are limited. The 3 percent set aside is likely to support these efforts and catalyze new investments in local school choice programs. Because the programs will be operated by districts, local communities will have a chance to weigh in on what kinds of improved access will be most beneficial, whether that be expanded support for homeschooling students, investments in personalized tutoring services, or improved access to Advanced Placement and International Baccalaureate programming.

Of course, for school choice programs to be of any use to families, states and districts must do more to notify families about the opportunity to choose. In many districts, parents' access to choice remains hamstrung by a lack of information. While ESSA continues NCLB's mandate for states to publicly report on school performance, few states have made the investments in report cards that would enable families to readily access information, understand differences across schools, or take advantage of opportunities to choose. The law's requirement for states to develop a school rating system may spur the development of "parent friendly" report cards that equip families to better evaluate schools in the school choosing process. But whether these efforts are successful depends not just on the data that states report on but also how they present that information to families. Few states have engaged in systematic efforts to use their reporting responsibilities to inform parent choice. Illinois and Louisiana are two noteworthy exceptions.

School Finance

Because the federal government provides comparatively little of what states and localities spend on K–12 education, federal law has not typically spurred substantial changes to how money is allocated. Even as states have stepped into funding disputes to refashion how money is allocated between districts, it has struggled to exert influence over local spending. Because the vast majority of education dollars goes to fund staff—teachers, principals, and administrators—many of those decisions are made via collective bargaining and/or negotiation with local teacher unions.

ESSA has the potential to reshape local education spending profoundly. States have historically reported on expenditures according to federal requirements, but an accounting loophole enabled them to use average, rather than actual, salaries for personnel. As a result, districts could meet federal requirements by showing staff-to-student ratios that were comparable. But this obscured the fact that teacher salaries tend to vary systematically across schools, with schools serving large numbers of disadvantaged children typically employing teachers at the bottom of the pay scale. Accounting for these salary differentials reveals substantial differences between the per-pupil spending in high- and low-poverty schools.[29]

ESSA requires states to publicly report on per-pupil expenditures for each school, including actual personnel expenditures. Parents and communities will be able to see a school's funding alongside its academic results. This is likely to generate what Marguerite Roza has deemed the "sunlight effect"—unearthing indefensible inequities and providing advocates with data to fight for further changes to spending locally.[30]

CONCLUSION: HOW STATES CAN MAKE THE MOST OF ESSA

The Every Student Succeeds Act provides states and localities with substantial new flexibility to pursue reform grounded in local priorities. Gone are many of the prescriptive elements of NCLB and the Obama administration's flexibility waivers.

While states have more space to innovate, however, federal regulations continue to limit what they can do. The yard is larger, perhaps less intensely supervised, but it remains fenced. As detailed in this chapter, requirements for multiple measures, targeted interventions in low performing schools, set-asides for school choice, and improved transparency in school finance are likely to spur changes to K–12 education and its politics.

How ESSA shapes education policy in the future will also depend in large part on how states take advantage of the flexibility that the feds have provided. As one observer noted, ESSA may be an instance of the "dog catching the car."[31] States wanted more flexibility; now that they have it, the burden falls on them to define their priorities for K–12 education and act on them.

None of this is a given. The Obama administration provided states the flexibility to develop multiple measures for use in their accountability systems through its waiver program, but just eighteen took advantage of it.[32] As detailed previously in this volume, states often fail to fully leverage the power they already have to improve conditions for school and district leaders. Providing flexibility creates a window of opportunity, but it does not guarantee that states will utilize it.

In order to fully leverage the opportunities that ESSA provides, state policy makers and their supporters must double down on efforts to enhance the capacity of state education agencies, which are likely to lead much of the work of crafting new accountability systems and overseeing the work of improving schools and districts. These agencies are rarely adequately equipped in either technical know-how or political skill and are likely to need help.

ESSA's most significant implications may rest in politics. Devolution will make education policy subject to the shifting political winds of state elections and the priorities of state legislatures and governors. The law is also likely to mobilize new groups in the fight over education policy, as accountability systems and public reporting requirements shine light on problems that have often escaped public view. These changes will no doubt spur renewed pressure for evolution in federal law, much as NCLB did more than a decade ago.

As states leverage their newfound flexibility to craft a new approach to K–12 improvement, they should take stock of the lessons learned from the last decade of school reform. The efforts of the federal government to improve public schools have always been limited by the fact that it does not (and cannot) directly control the individuals whose behavior it seeks to influence.

States are often no better positioned than the federal government to direct improvement efforts. They can provide data, flexibility, and the ownership over results that encourage local educators to improve. But the success of these efforts ultimately depends on the cooperation of teachers, principals, and administrators.

9

ESSA and Urban Public Schools

Ambivalence and Opportunity

Michael Casserly

The Elementary and Secondary Education Act of 1965 is a critical pillar of federal support to the nation's urban public schools, but in 2015 the law's reauthorization, the Every Student Succeeds Act, presented urban districts with a complicated set of choices.

At the outset of reauthorization, urban school districts were warier than others because the new bill presented unique risks for the very schools and students that the original legislation was intended to help. As Richard Carranza, the superintendent of the San Francisco Unified School District, put it: "We have a lot to lose if this reauthorization goes badly."[1] These risks ranged from problematic technical and operational issues to big-picture strategic concerns. Of course, ESSA also offered relief from some of the ineffective and counterproductive burdens that districts faced under 2001's No Child Left Behind Act. But from the vantage point of an urban school system, ESSA represented a fundamental shift toward state autonomy that threatened to override the strategic alignment of urban schools and the federal government around support for the nation's neediest students.

As the authorization process dragged out, urban districts found themselves fighting to preserve what they saw as the central tenets of ESEA. Now that the law has passed, districts are taking account of the victories that were won, as well as the challenges they now face. ESSA's reliance on the will and capacity of individual states to implement its framework effectively has done little to assuage the initial ambivalence felt by many big-city school districts. Urban school leaders remain concerned that new state power may be mishandled or abused. On the other hand, ESSA may pave the way for important new partnerships between districts and states as they work together to implement various aspects of the law. Only one thing is clear: the ultimate success of the new education law will depend on how well it serves our nation's neediest and most disenfranchised students—students who are most likely to call a big city home.

SETTING THE STAGE: URBAN DISTRICTS AND NCLB

Understanding urban school districts' ambivalence toward ESSA requires taking a step back to assess where these districts have been over the years in the quintessential American debate over federal versus state control. While some might assume that local school districts would be natural opponents of a strong federal presence in the oversight of local schools, urban school leaders have come to rely on the federal government over the years as a key partner and ally in pursuing reform and serving poor children and children of color.

During President Johnson's War on Poverty in the 1960s, big-city schools often found themselves on the side of the federal government, working to boost resources for poor and minority urban students even as they struggled with civil rights groups to reshape systems that were built to sort and track students by race, language, income, and disability. At the same time, these schools often found themselves at increasing odds with other broad-based education groups and with states that were not seen as having the interests of urban areas in mind, or the capacity to help them.[2]

This uncertainty about state leadership was rekindled during the Reagan administration, when greater educational decision making was returned to the states during the 1981 ESEA reauthorization. In this case, the administration proposed consolidating the federal Title I program and the Education of All Handicapped Act, the precursor of today's Individuals with Disabilities Education Act (IDEA); eliminating all federal desegregation aid under the Emergency School Aid Act and block-granting other programs; and dramatically cutting federal aid. After all the legislative wrangling was over, the nation's urban schools had lost almost 20 percent of their federal assistance, and would not soon forget how unresponsive the states were to urban needs during this period. It took urban school systems much of the remaining 1980s and 1990s to claw their way back.[3]

By the early 2000s, there was growing public impatience with what sounded like excuse making by educators about poor results, and urban school leaders were eager for opportunities to reverse the public's sense that they were stuck with the status quo. So when NCLB was unveiled, the nation's urban schools broke ranks with other education groups and endorsed the law. They were joined in that support later by major civil rights groups, but from the start the nation's urban schools saw the measure as an opportunity to demonstrate their support for better academic results and stronger accountability.

Of course, urban school leaders saw the same operational problems with NCLB that everyone else saw, but concluded that the opportunities for reform outweighed the law's technical flaws.[4]

Ultimately, NCLB succeeded in spurring a greater focus on student achievement and advancing the reform efforts of many big-city school systems. But the poorly calibrated operational details of the law—and the side effects it created with instruction and testing—eventually caught up with it. By the time the Obama administration came along, big-city school systems were looking for relief like many others were. This was when—and why—the waiver process launched by the Department of Education was popular with many urban school districts. The waivers provided districts with relief from having to provide costly and questionably effective supplemental services, and they allowed some urban districts (like those in California) to pursue reforms that the state would not support.

Of course, not everyone was eager to see the new administration pursue the waivers. Urban school leaders don't respond any better to being told what they can do than anyone else, but they also knew that the federal government was pushing urban school districts in directions they wanted to go anyway. Where states were waffling about new college- and career-ready standards, big-city schools were all-in on the Common Core State Standards—as was the administration. Where teacher organizations were hostile to test-based teacher evaluation, urban school systems had been experimenting with various accountability systems for years—something the administration wanted to expand. And while states were struggling to develop coherent data systems, urban school systems were well down that path already. In other words, many big-city school systems shared the administration's priorities.

Big-city schools also seized on the waivers as an opportunity to rid themselves of the supplemental education services (SES) provisions of

NCLB—provisions they felt were a waste of Title I resources, a sop to private-sector interests, and an ineffective mechanism for raising student achievement. In fact, the nation's urban schools worked aggressively behind the scenes with US Secretary of Education Arne Duncan to ensure that scrapping SES was included in the waiver package.

The new waiver program thus became part of the calculation being made by big-city schools about whether they wanted a reauthorization. The trade-off between ESEA reauthorization—with its unforeseeable results—and NCLB with Duncan's waivers had become, for urban districts, a question of sticking with the devil they knew.

However, big-city concerns over reauthorization amounted to much more than a fear of the unknown. A new bill held the potential to weaken the historic relations between the federal government and the big cities and to dilute the long-standing targeting of federal aid for poor urban areas. These fears were well founded. Various proposals to alter Title I funding formulas had already been introduced in Washington, and were backed by rural and small-town interests. And there was an emerging consensus in Congress and among numerous interest groups that new legislation was needed to roll back what was perceived as federal overreach by the Obama administration.

This budding consensus to return greater decision-making authority to state and local school systems had been building steadily for some time. No one had to lobby the issue. Members of Congress from both parties had been hearing for years that constituents were tired of the NCLB straitjacket. In addition, Congress was skeptical of an administration that it viewed as operating outside the law; governors wanted greater control to set educational priorities; state school superintendents were tired of negotiating waiver provisions with the Department of Education; local school boards and administrators didn't like being told by the federal government what they could do; and teachers wanted relief from waiver requirements on test-based teacher evaluation.

Almost everyone wanted out of NCLB for one reason or another. Almost everyone, that is, except for urban school districts, who were wary of state control and had found a way to make the waivers work. So the big cities were not clamoring for a new bill with the same enthusiasm as other groups. On the other hand, most state and local education interests were eager to replace NCLB with almost anything because they saw almost anything as being better than current law. The nation's urban schools, however, weren't confident that just any bill would be an improvement.

PASSING ESSA: THE FIGHT TO MAINTAIN TITLE I

These clashing priorities were front and center in the minds of big-city school districts as reauthorization neared in 2015.

Paramount among the issues for big-city schools were the Title I aid proposals, which have resulted in significant financial losses to the nation's urban schools in ways that were reminiscent of the losses under Reagan. Both the proposed Title I formula changes and Title I "portability" were seen by the cities as attempts to shift federal aid out of major urban areas.

The fight over the formula, in particular, played out almost entirely behind the scenes until it emerged on the Senate floor. Very few people even knew about the struggle. But the nation's big-city schools were fully engaged and universally opposed to the proposals—even when they periodically benefited from various versions of the formula changes. The specter of having federal Title I aid to the cities cut by over half a billion dollars under the House-proposed formula at the same time that greater authority was being returned to the states was a prospect that no urban school system wanted, no matter how much local flexibility it might gain.

There were numerous twists and turns in the road that ESSA traveled, but from the outset, greater state autonomy was predestined. But the outcome of the Title I formula struggle was not inevitable. Here the big cities won a major victory in keeping the Title I funding formula intact. The House bill went into conference with the Senate containing both a portability provision and placeholder language for a formula change that, on its own, had no effect on how funds were distributed, while the Senate bill included a formula change that would not take full effect for years. It was not easy getting to that point. At the end of the day, the two formula proposals were irreconcilable, and ESSA emerged from conference committee with neither a formula change nor portability in its final version.

Ultimately, ESSA resulted in a split decision that left urban districts in a quandary. The new law shifted greater authority back to the states. On one hand, cities could point to the unequivocal benefit of having retained the targeting of federal aid. The cities were convinced they would soon relearn what they knew before NCLB: states don't have the capacity or sometimes the political will to manage education reform. Ultimately, the big cities believed that if they had to start the reauthorization process over again, they might not be able to cut a better deal—particularly on the formula—the second time around.

One thing was clear: had the targeting of Title I funds not been preserved, big-city schools would have actively opposed the bill—and just might have brought it down.

ESSA AND URBAN SCHOOLS: WHAT IT GOT "RIGHT"

There were a number of other potential pitfalls the final bill *avoided*—proposed changes that would have made the bill difficult for the big-city schools to support. The final bill did not, for example, include significant changes to federal maintenance of effort provisions that would have allowed states to lower their financial support to public education; it maintained the "supplement not supplant" requirements for schoolwide programs; and it kept the current comparability provisions mostly in place. (The US Department of Education would subsequently rule extensively on the provisions.) And ESSA *could have* frozen federal program funding levels—curtailing any appropriations increases for the remainder of the decade.

The bill kept the 40 percent poverty threshold in place for Title I schoolwide programs, the lowering of which would have diluted the targeting of aid. It also maintained transferability provisions that allow school systems the flexibility to move Title II and Title IV funds to and from each other or into Title I. In addition, the bill did not require Title I funds to be used in high schools with poverty levels as low as 50 percent, which might have required local school systems to transfer Title I funds away from much poorer elementary schools. Finally, the bill did not consolidate programs, which might have reduced the federal focus on students with very specialized needs.

Furthermore, the bill eliminated NCLB provisions that the cities and others ultimately saw as counterproductive, duplicative, or destructive. For instance, the bill scrapped federal Adequate Yearly Progress (AYP) targets, the 20 percent Title I set-aside for SES, and redundant accountability provisions for English language learners in Title I and Title III. The bill also dispensed with the federal definition of "highly qualified teachers"—an ineffective, burdensome paperwork exercise that had failed to improve teacher quality.

ESSA also included language that the big-city school systems were pleased to see, including requirements that states adopt challenging academic content and achievement standards; English language proficiency standards aligned to a state's general academic standards; and alternative academic standards for students with the most profound cognitive disabilities.

The bill also retained annual testing in reading and math in grades 3–8 and once in high school, along with grade-span testing in science, NCLB subgroup reporting, and the 95 percent testing mandate. The cities were also glad to see a focus on the 5 percent lowest performing schools; the ability to count former English language learners for up to four years after exiting ELL status; and a new preschool development program.

In other words, there were plenty of provisions in ESSA that the big-city schools were happy about. Still, there were also provisions where additional state discretion raised significant concerns for them. These provisions fall into four broad categories: accountability, reporting requirements, resource allocation, and assessment. The following section will explore each of these areas, as well as the overarching concern at the heart of district ambivalence over the new law: whether states have the capacity to properly execute their new authority in any of these areas.

ESSA: KEY AREAS OF CONCERN FOR SCHOOL DISTRICTS

Accountability

The accountability provisions of ESSA created substantial contention during the reauthorization process. ESSA requires states to develop a differentiated accountability system that is applied to all schools and subgroups in the state. These accountability systems must include five key indicators: academic proficiency, growth or another academic indicator, graduation rates, English language proficiency, and another lesser-weighted, nonacademic indicator of school or student success. It also requires that 95 percent of students participate in the state assessments. In addition, ESSA requires a three-tier state accountability system. States must identify schools in one of several categories:

- Targeted Support and Improvement (TSI) for schools, including all non–Title I schools, where a subgroup meets the state-determined definition of consistently underperforming. TSI requires the school to develop and implement a plan to improve student outcomes that is approved and monitored by the district.
- Additional Targeted Support and Improvement (ATSI) for any TSI school where the underperforming subgroup(s) is large enough to affect the performance of the entire school. ATSI requires that the

district develop an intervention plan for boosting the achievement of the school while the state determines exit criteria and timelines.

- Comprehensive Support and Improvement (CSI) for the 5 percent lowest performing Title I schools in the state, any high school with less than a two-thirds graduation rate, and any ATSI school that is both Title I and has not met state-determined exit criteria after a state-determined number of years. CSI requires that the district, school, and state agree on a comprehensive support and improvement plan.

- More rigorous state action is required if state-determined exit criteria are not met, and action may include changes to school-level operations, governance, and organization.

Where do states have discretion in defining accountability? States are allowed to establish the minimum number of students constituting a subgroup (n-size), an area that was subject to substantial manipulation and gamesmanship by states under NCLB. It was often used to ensure that small school systems or school systems with small subgroups were not held accountable for student results, placing most of the accountability burden onto big cities with larger subgroups. In addition, states have the discretion to define both long-term goals and interim progress measures.

States can define the aforementioned five accountability indicators and how they are measured. And they can determine if academic growth is measured at the high school level and whether graduation rates beyond the traditional four years of high school can be calculated. The federal government approves the state accountability plan, but the law is silent on what happens if a state does not follow that plan or inappropriately makes exceptions to the plan.

States are also left to determine the weights applied to each of the differentiated accountability indicators as long as the weights applied to the school-quality indicator do not outweigh the other four. Moreover, states can develop the methodology for identifying TSI, ATSI, and CSI schools—and determine exit criteria and the timeline by which local school systems must improve the schools without risking state-defined intervention. States also specify the criteria for identifying districts for local education agency (LEA) improvement. Finally, states will define the nature of the assistance they provide to school districts, if any.

Reporting Requirements

ESSA also contains an extensive new array of Title I and Title III reporting requirements. Both district and individual school report cards will now be required to include new data on:

- student achievement for homeless, foster care, and active-duty military family status along with the existing disaggregation of data by race, language status, poverty status, and disability;
- indicators of school quality, school climate, and safety, including data on in-school suspensions, out-of-school suspensions, expulsions, school-related arrests, referrals to law enforcement, chronic absenteeism, and incidents of violence (including bullying and harassment);
- per-pupil expenditures of federal, state, and local funds, including actual personnel expenditures and nonpersonnel expenditures disaggregated by source for each school system and school (Title I and non–Title I);
- numbers and percentages of students with the most significant cognitive disabilities taking an alternative assessment by grade and subject; and
- numbers and percentages of students in ELL programs who are making progress toward achieving English proficiency in the aggregate and disaggregated for ELLs with disabilities, ELLs attaining English proficiency based on state English language proficiency standards by the end of each school year, and ELLs not attaining English proficiency within five years of initial classification.

In other words, Congress advertises ESSA as more streamlined and less intrusive, but on the ground, local school officials may actually find that the act requires them to do much more than under NCLB.

Resource Allocation

Under ESSA, school districts also face new challenges concerning resource allocation. One example involves the private school provisions. This new language changes the allocation of Title I–funded services for private school students by calculating the private school share based on a school district's total Title I allocation rather than on the funds that LEAs provide to schools in eligible attendance areas. In addition, school districts previously could set aside Title I funds for SES, choice initiatives, school improvement, and other activities and then calculate the private school share based on the remainder. They can't do that under ESSA. The upshot: these changes are likely to substantially decrease the public school system's share of Title I dollars and significantly increase the share for private schools.

Another concern involves the increased state set-asides under Title I and Title II. The new law compensates for Congress's decision not to reauthorize the Department of Education's School Improvement Grant (SIG) program by increasing the state Title I funds set aside for school improvement from 4 percent to 7 percent. The result is that urban school districts will see their Title I allocations decrease by somewhere between $100 and $200 million, although some of it will be returned in state discretionary grants. On top of that, ESSA allows states to take an optional 3 percent additional set-aside for *Direct Student Services* grants, which may include SES, choice, and other activities. Finally, states have the option of reserving 3 percent of their Title II funds for various leadership-oriented discretionary grants to local school systems. The combination of all these set-asides, along with the increased allocations for private schools, is likely to put a substantial dent in the formula grants that urban school systems fought to protect.

This latter example of the set-asides, in particular, presents an early test case of sorts for whether the theory behind ESSA will actually work on behalf of big cities. The harm they do is palpable, but the benefit is only speculative. It is entirely possible that these increased state set-asides could drive worthwhile, well-targeted state interventions. But it is only a possibility at this stage. In fact, it seems more likely that these set-asides will not live up to their promise unless urban school systems see productive and collaborative state leadership, which most have not experienced historically.[5]

Assessments

In the area of testing, states have the discretion to use a single summative assessment or multiple statewide interim assessments rolled into an aggregate index of performance or growth. ESSA also gives states the discretion of using alternative assessments for students with the most significant cognitive disabilities, as long as the total number of students doesn't exceed 1 percent of the state's enrollment. Moreover, states have discretion over developing and administering computer adaptive assessments and can limit the aggregate amount of time devoted to assessments. Finally, states can make their own exceptions for testing recently arrived English language learners.

That's a lot of responsibility for states on assessment issues where they sometimes lack experience or expertise. Of particular concern are English language learners. Title III of ESSA requires states to establish and implement standardized, statewide program entrance and exit procedures for ELLs. States are also required to define English proficiency and determine the timeline by which ELLs attain that proficiency. In addition, states are allowed the aforementioned testing exception for recently arrived ELLs who have been enrolled in US schools for less than twelve months, by which these students can be excluded from one administration of the state reading or language arts assessments or by which the test results can be excluded from accountability calculations.

Unfortunately, these new ESSA requirements could easily lead states to set uniform entrance and exit program criteria—rather than procedures— for ELLs in cases where they have vastly different language acquisition needs at the local level. And it is not hard for city schools to envision situations where states would establish one-size-fits-all criteria for programs exiting without considering individual factors (e.g., students' content mastery, time in program, formal education in their countries of origin, specific language, or over-age for grade-level status), instead relying on a single English language proficiency test score.

In addition, it is not clear how states, which typically don't have senior-level staff specializing in ELL issues, will craft their new Title I accountability systems with ELLs in mind now that Title III accountability requirements have been folded into Title I. These and other circumstances that require more nuanced and case-by-case consideration at the local level will be difficult for states to define, but they will disproportionately affect big-city schools, which enroll some 30 percent of all ELLs in the nation.[6]

In theory, states should be better suited to making these decisions because they are closer to the ground—but they are not that close. Ultimately, the theory behind ESSA may fall short in practice, because making good decisions often requires more than familiarity with broad policy requirements; it also requires localized expertise that state leaders frequently don't have. Thus, states may have asked for something in this reauthorization that they are not always able to provide.

Another worrisome example of state discretion involves students with disabilities. ESSA allows states to develop alternate achievement standards and assessments for students with the most significant cognitive disabilities. However, the new law places a 1 percent cap on the total number of these students statewide who can be assessed. At the same time, it forbids the secretary of education or the states from placing a district-level cap on the percentage of students tested in this way—although districts exceeding 1 percent must provide the state with an explanation.

This requirement could put states in an untenable bind. Currently, about twenty-seven states have identification rates above 1.14 percent. How will states bring down their numbers to 1 percent when they are not represented in local IEP meetings, can't cap local school systems, and have limited control of disproportionate identification? To big-city school systems, the situation would seem to invite states to implement the provision clumsily. Urban schools could be disproportionately affected, because cities often attract families with children having the most significant cognitive disabilities due to the wider availability of medical services, and are often the first stop for refugee families whose children may be the victims of violence and war in their native lands.[7]

States could do real damage to ELL children and students with disabilities if they don't take individual circumstances into account. One can easily see students misdiagnosed, placed in inappropriate programs, or stripped of needed services if state assessment systems and program guidelines are too blunt or undifferentiated. Ultimately, issues such as these will test the proposition that states are capable of addressing the needs of disadvantaged students.

The Underlying Issue of State Capacity

Above all, urban districts fear that increased state discretion coupled with limited state capacity will lead to ineffective implementation and potentially ruinous results. The initial ambivalence of big-city schools toward ESSA was based on concerns that they would be ceding important reform ground gained only as a result of strong federal oversight. The reauthorization process had "wins" and "losses" for urban school districts, but this central question still hangs in the balance. If ESSA depends on the will and capacity of fifty individual states to implement it, how can big-city schools ensure that they are maintaining the momentum that has been building to improve educational outcomes for *all* children?

It's fair to ask whether big-city schools would really rather have the federal government control and define accountability, assessment, and other items. The answer is yes, and no. Some of ESSA's discretion seems reasonable on its face, and doesn't necessarily lend itself to the argument that the

Department of Education should define all the rules governing each provision. It is also more than clear that the DOE often does not know when to stop regulating. At a recent hearing of the Senate Health, Education, Labor, and Pensions Committee, Des Moines superintendent Tom Ahart made it clear that the department often thinks it is being helpful with its regulations but instead is often restrictive and unduly expansive.[8]

Yet most big-city school systems trust the federal government more than their own states to treat them fairly. The feds aren't the only ones who can overregulate; many city school districts find that their states will misinterpret the law or add requirements that Congress never intended.[9] Unfortunately, the law actually makes it harder now for local school systems to apply to the federal government for their own waivers without first going to the state.

In addition, the US Department of Education is also less likely in the eyes of urban school systems to involve itself in local political issues than state departments of education, and less likely still to target large cities for interventions they wouldn't apply to other districts—as states often do. States are well known for passing legislation that applies only to big-city schools and no one else in their jurisdictions, something that the federal government does only rarely. Missouri, for instance, requires that the Kansas City school district have nine school board members, but does not mandate the same for anyone else in the state.[10] Other examples include charter laws that apply only to the biggest cities in a state or tax caps that affect only the biggest city school systems.[11]

The federal government has also historically set a higher priority on aiding poor and minority students and is more likely to target aid to those students in greatest need, where many states are often more likely to spread funds around or to cap funds to large districts or schools. The argument that states can spend funds in a smarter and more targeted way than the federal government fell on deaf ears in most cities. In the 1980s some states smeared money around under the old Chapter 2 program that replaced the more targeted school desegregation aid, and many current urban school administrators recall how in the 1990s and early 2000s states dispersed the SIG program funds with little regard to need—situations that added to big-city-school skepticism about the increased state set-asides under ESSA.[12]

Finally, cities view the federal government as more likely than the states to keep even pressure on accountability, given the crosscurrent of statewide interest groups and the ever-present pressure to water down accountability provisions. For example, under NCLB many states exempted schools and school districts with small numbers of racial and language subgroups from their accountability systems, or created "supersubgroups" under the waiver process that consolidated NCLB categories. The result was an uneven application of federal accountability provisions.

This does not mean to suggest that urban schools are always simpatico with the federal government or that the US Department of Education always has greater expertise. The opposite is true in many cases. Ample evidence of this was on full display in negotiated rule-making sessions when DOE staff had little clue about the operational chaos that their proposed comparability regulation would create.[13] In addition, the department's insistence on pursuing its four reform models under the SIG program was another example of a policy that had no basis in either research or good practice. Nonetheless, urban schools have often found a valuable partner in the US Department of Education. Orlando school superintendent Barbara Jenkins put it this way, "Over the years, many big-city school leaders have been able to count on the federal government to keep the concerns of urban communities in mind when others have not."[14]

CONCLUSION: RISKS AND OPPORTUNITIES AS URBAN SCHOOLS MOVE FORWARD

When all was said and done, urban school districts, under the auspices of the Council of the Great City Schools, endorsed ESSA, but with decidedly mixed emotions. In many ways the legislation is a masterful patchwork of compromises, but many of those compromises represent new challenges and potential hurdles that big-city schools will have to clear.

Some observers have argued that the new law takes the pressure off of big-city schools to improve and reform. States are freer than they were under NCLB or the waivers to move away from the most rigorous standards, and will have considerable latitude to ease up on accountability measures. And apart from considerations of will, states may lack the capacity to compel better student outcomes.

Perhaps no one is more concerned with these risks than big-city school districts, which often find themselves the targets of poorly conceived state— and federal—interventions. Still, few entities in public education have taken their own improvement as seriously as have urban public school districts. This doesn't mean that urban schools are teaching their students to college- or career-ready levels or that full equity and access have been achieved. But urban school systems are not waiting for someone else to fix them. Instead, they have created a strong peer culture to improve their academic and operational performance.

This culture of support is evident in the hundreds of technical assistance teams that urban school districts have provided one another over the years. It is also apparent in the unique performance management system that urban school districts have built to benchmark their performance, better inform instructional decision making, and spur efficiencies. And it is obvious in the initiation and recent expansion of the Trial Urban District Assessment of NAEP—an initiative proposed by urban districts to stimulate better results.[15]

So, while other groups might be relieved at the prospect of less federal control and oversight, urban districts are now looking for ways to accelerate the pace of reform on their own. These big-city school and district leaders hold the most intimate, practical knowledge of how implementation of education policy works—and how it doesn't—and are keen to improve their academic performance and noninstructional operations. With ESSA, they now have the chance to use this expertise to help inform and guide states on how to exercise their new discretion.

Many big-city school leaders are eager to transform what they once saw as risks into opportunities. The law presents urban districts with a unique chance to forge new partnerships with their state departments of education—at least in some places. At the national level, relations between the Council of the Great City Schools and the Council of Chief State School Officers has never been better, and both groups have pledged informally to help each other with the many implementation challenges to come—despite state and big-city tensions over the years. This budding relationship is likely to be very uneven, but it does hold the potential of easing implementation problems with ESSA in some jurisdictions.

Of course, the ability of districts to work within the new ESSA framework to effect positive change will require more than episodic bouts of collaboration. It will take the sustained commitment of districts, states, and the Department of Education to open a dialogue and a shared understanding of what is likely to work in and for our inner-city schools and students. Just as the passage of ESSA—and its support from big-city schools—rested on a key set of compromises made during the reauthorization process, its success now rests precariously on the decisions that are made as the law is implemented. Passage of the law could one day be pinpointed as the beginning of a period marked by political turmoil and stalled progress in the educational reform movement. But it could also be a turning point—an opportunity for urban schools to demonstrate their expertise and leadership, and to build lasting partnerships with the states that serve to propel education reform and improvement forward. Given the position urban schools hold on the front lines of education reform, how well these districts are able to adapt and thrive under the new ESSA framework will play a major role in the ultimate impact and legacy of the new legislation. For the sake of America's children, hopefully the leap of faith that urban school districts have taken in supporting ESSA pays off.

10

From ESEA to ESSA

Progress or Regress?

Cynthia G. Brown

T he Elementary and Secondary Education Act of 1965 began with soar-
ing hopes. But four years later it was judged wanting:

> For the first time, the national government recognized the necessity of
> providing Federal aid to elementary and secondary schools. For the first
> time, the special needs of poor children were recognized and effective
> ameliorative action promised through special assistance to school systems
> with high concentrations of low-income children. Our hopes that the Nation
> would finally begin to rectify the injustices and inequities which poor
> children suffer from being deprived of an equal educational opportunity
> have been sorely disappointed. Millions of dollars appropriated by the
> Congress to help educationally deprived children have been wasted, diverted
> or otherwise misused by State and local school authorities.[1]

THEN TO NOW

At the time of ESEA's passage—the height of the civil rights movement—
I went to college and graduate school, and I became inspired to work for
social justice. In 1966, I went to work in the Office of Equal Educational
Opportunity Programs in the Office of Education, now the Office for Civil
Rights in the US Department of Education. There I met Ruby Martin and
Phyllis McClure. They left shortly thereafter and turned their attention from
school desegregation to Title I of ESEA, writing in 1969 the seminal work *Is*

It Helping Poor Children? ESEA Title I. A Report. Eventually I joined them out of government at the Washington Research Project (which became the Children's Defense Fund), working to improve Title I as well as to continue pursuing school desegregation.

ESEA and civil rights school desegregation were connected from the beginning. They still are for advocates like me. The well-known story of Presidents Kennedy and Johnson wanting to get federal dollars to high-poverty schools, especially in the South, in exchange for desegregation led to the passage of both Title VI of the Civil Rights Act of 1964, which prohibits discrimination in federally funded programs on the basis of race, color, and national origin, and then of ESEA in 1965. These laws set up the federal carrot-and-stick approach that continues to this day.

I spent most of my career alternating my focus between the carrots and the sticks. In 1977, I returned to the Office for Civil Rights as deputy director. There were by then additional laws prohibiting discrimination on the basis of gender and disability. There was also a much broader array of issues—desegregation of public postsecondary institutions, education of English language learners, intercollegiate women's athletics, and others. When President Carter created the Department of Education in 1980, he appointed me assistant secretary for civil rights. But I didn't serve for long because of the election of President Reagan.

In the late 1970s and early 1980s, federal court rulings and congressional prohibitions deeply constrained school desegregation, but ESEA continued and grew. I realized that it is very difficult to achieve equity for low-income students and students of color from the federal level. My focus turned to the state level, and in 1986 I joined the Council of Chief State School Officers (CCSSO) as the director of its Resource Center on Educational Equity. I stayed in the position fifteen years, interacting with the Department of Education, states, and Congress.

Today, after fifty years working on educational equity, I find myself discouraged. Very large education achievement gaps persist. Schools with large proportions of low-income students remain underresourced by elected and appointed officials at all levels. True, many African American and Latino students gained access to a good education, excelled, and moved into the middle class. But many others have been left behind. There were times when I was very encouraged, but backlash always seemed to ensue. I still believe there must be federal leadership, but with no civil rights law prohibiting discrimination against students based on family income, or a right to quality education law, real progress seems far in the distance.

But I've jumped ahead. Early developments in ESEA implementation remain important today, and they show important attempts to make progress.

IN THE BEGINNING

In 1969, Phyllis McClure and Ruby Martin wrote their devastating analysis of the early implementation of Title I. The authors collected information and interviewed numerous officials at all levels of Title I's operation. They also interviewed Title I parents. They found "faulty and sometimes fraudulent" ways of Title I operation in many parts of the country. Specifically, they found:

- use of Title I funds as a general aid in many school systems, including for the purchase of services, equipment, and supplies made available to all schools;
- use of Title I funds in both the North and South to supplant rather than supplement state and local expenditures;
- use of Title I funds to purchase "massive amounts of equipment" and "excessive construction of facilities";
- lack of concentration of funds on children most in need of assistance with programs "of sufficient size, scope and quality to provide reasonable promise of substantial progress"; and
- failure to meet the needs of educationally deprived children "in order to raise their educational attainment to levels normal for their age."[2]

This report made a huge splash when it was published. The Office of Education beefed up its monitoring of states, issuing audit exceptions and sometimes requiring state refunds. Congress amended Title I to prohibit supplanting; require states and districts to maintain their funding levels and operate programs of sufficient size, scope, and quality; and "provide services in project areas which, taken as a whole, are at least comparable to services being provided in areas in such district which are not receiving funds under this title."

But the comparability provision never worked out as advocates had hoped. A northern congressman from Chicago, Roman Pucinski (D-IL), then chair of the House Education Subcommittee, pushed the Office of Education to establish a major loophole: excluding teacher "longevity pay," salary increases given to experienced teachers, from calculations of comparability between schools receiving Title I funds and those that were not. Pucinski wanted to protect the ability of urban districts to assign the newest, weakest, and poorest paid teachers to African American and Hispanic schools, but still show comparability with the less needy, non–Title I schools in the district, which tended to attract more experienced teachers. Over the years there's been tinkering with the comparability provision, but the loophole remains. Battles over it are as heated as ever; today Senator Lamar Alexander (R-TN), chair of the Senate Education Committee, is the loophole's key advocate.

THE MIDDLE YEARS

Initially advocates and federal leaders believed that lack of funding was the primary cause of inadequate schooling for disadvantaged students. They were convinced that federal funds could make a significant difference. But they—we—were wrong. It turns out that it matters *how* funds for education are spent. The amount of money matters too. Federal funds alone have never been enough, and in many states, districts, and schools, there are obscene funding shortages compared to more affluent jurisdictions. During the 1970s and 1980s there were several reauthorizations of ESEA and national evaluations of its effectiveness. By the late 1980s, National Assessment of Educational Progress (NAEP) data showed a narrowing of achievement gaps, though experts have never determined if Title I or school desegregation was the main factor. No matter, because gap closing ceased. During those two decades, I engaged in some advocacy for Title I improvements, but much of my attention was focused on civil rights enforcement, both in and out of the federal government. In 1986, as I've mentioned, I joined CCSSO as its director of the Resource Center on Educational Equity.

Shortly after I was hired, Gordon Ambach, the commissioner of education in New York State, became CCSSO's executive director. Throughout his fourteen-year tenure, Ambach engaged CCSSO in very active lobbying around ESEA, especially Title I. He also voiced his unhappiness that Congress had eliminated ESEA Title V, which provided federal funds for state education agencies.

In late 1986, David Hornbeck, Maryland's state superintendent of education, was elected CCSSO's president. Hornbeck wanted CCSSO to become a visible advocate for the improvement of schools for disadvantaged students. Ambach assigned me to work closely with Hornbeck to operationalize his agenda. Together we raised funding to produce a policy document, a model state statute, and a report on the work of states on behalf of at-risk children. In November 1987, CCSSO members unanimously adopted a statement entitled "Assuring School Success for Students at Risk." Thus began an almost fifteen-year run of major CCSSO policy statements directed at national and federal issues and mostly focused on educationally disadvantaged students.

The Department of Labor then awarded CCSSO $400,000 to operate a competitive grant competition among states to promote state-level guarantees of educational and related services for at-risk students.

THE EDUCATION REFORM MOVEMENT GETS SERIOUS

By the late 1980s, shortly after I joined CCSSO, the focus on racial discrimination diminished somewhat and policy makers turned their attention to education quality and achievement gaps. The push really started with the publication in 1983 of *A Nation at Risk*, the report from President Reagan's National Commission on Excellence in Education. It was quite a wake-up call. In 1989 President George H. W. Bush convened forty-nine governors in Charlottesville, Virginia, and they agreed to six education goals. The Bush administration in 1990 created the National Education Goals Panel. Among other things, the panel pushed for national standards and voluntary national tests. The standards movement had begun.

Attention turned again to Title I. In late 1989 I received a call from Hayes Mizell. Mizell, a former southern civil rights worker, was currently the education program officer at the Edna McConnell Clark Foundation. He wanted to know if I would staff a commission to redesign Title I (then entitled Chapter 1) and have it housed at, but be independent of, CCSSO. I was excited, and my boss Gordon Ambach said okay.

The Commission on Chapter 1 was unique. It was chaired by David Hornbeck and had twenty-eight members who represented civil rights advocates, education researchers, state and local education officials, a business leader, and a parent advocate. Both teacher unions were represented. It met as a full group ten times, with no substitutes allowed, and held numerous subcommittee discussions. Early on the commission decided to write a model Chapter 1 statute, something no one had ever done.

The commission's effort was completely nonpartisan and was completed with unanimous agreement (and some partial dissents) before the 1992 presidential election. The report was released in December after the election of Bill Clinton. The commission called for the "same high standards for all children, performance-based assessment evaluating student progress toward standards . . . rich instruction and support in the classroom, generous investment in improving professional knowledge and skills, greater concentration of dollars in high-poverty schools, accountability for results, [and] rewards for successful schools [with] help—then sanctions—for schools that do not improve."[3]

As luck would have it, President Clinton appointed three commission members, including Stanford University's Marshall Smith, to high-level positions in the Department of Education. Smith was especially influential in the upcoming legislation. Indeed, key elements of the commission report were codified in the next two ESEA reauthorizations.

President Clinton had attended the 1989 governors' summit in Charlottesville. As president, he moved aggressively on the agenda established there. First he proposed Goals 2000, a new federal education program passed in Congress and signed into law in February 1994. Federal education assistance had always consisted mainly of categorical programs aimed at a particular problem or population of students. Goals 2000 intended to provide states and school districts with flexible funds to improve the quality of education for *all students*. It provided a framework for high standards by codifying eight national education goals. It placed the responsibility on states to define their standards and then to hold themselves accountable.

Next came the reauthorization of ESEA as the Improving America's Schools Act (IASA), signed into law in October 1994. IASA was aligned with Goals 2000, but more prescriptive about accountability and support for low performing schools. It required voluntary high standards, state assessments at three points in time to measure student performance against standards, and state accountability for student performance, including Adequate Yearly Progress and identification of schools in need of improvement. It looked similar to the Commission on Chapter 1's recommendations.

One very important new provision in IASA was a change to Title I fund distribution. Title I has always been very prescriptive about how districts funded schools. Prior to IASA, schools had to be sorted by grade spans and then ranked in order of poverty level. The largest amount of funds per pupil had to go to the highest-poverty schools. Per-pupil amounts could decrease as schools decreased in poverty, but district officials could skip over high-poverty schools where students on average performed well. If a Title I school successfully progressed, the next year it lost its Title I funds. This disincentive made no sense and thankfully was changed.

There was a second important change. Previously districts had the discretion to fund only certain grade spans. IASA required that all schools with over 75 percent poverty had to be funded. This was a way to be sure that high-poverty high schools, especially "dropout factories," would get Title I funds.

During consideration of Goals 2000 and IASA, vocal debates erupted over the concept of "opportunity-to-learn" standards. I was deeply invested in this controversy. Twenty years later, the debates still rage. Both Goals 2000 and IASA required states to develop opportunity-to-learn standards. Congress viewed these standards as necessary for high student performance. States had to submit to the Department of Education a school improvement plan that included strategies for providing an opportunity to learn for all students. But state proposals and implementation were voluntary, and states had little appetite to tackle inequitable resource issues.

Several organizations, including the National Governors Association, published reports on opportunity-to-learn standards. Though CCSSO never published a formal document, I was quite vocal about the issue and was given freedom to speak my mind.

Opportunity-to-learn standards are input, not outcome, standards. They include high-quality teachers, equitable funding based on student needs, challenging curriculum materials, and appropriate programs for English language learners and students with disabilities. The struggle over these standards is the same struggle over equal educational opportunity that has gone on for over a century. But with a new century on the horizon, a technological and data revolution was about to make the extent of school inequity much clearer. We've come to know so much. But resistance to correcting the inequities is as strong as ever.

THE LEAD-UP TO NCLB

As standards-based reforms took shape in every state, advocates and researchers alike searched for more effective ways to improve education for poor students. Several developed model school reforms, and in 1998

Congress enacted the Comprehensive School Reform Demonstration program to promote and expand "research-based" programs. The legislation listed nine required components for reforms to receive federal support. Good work ensued, but so did overblown claims of success. Much was learned, but the successful programs/schools never grew adequately in number. They were more expensive to operate than traditional school programs, and politicians, as usual, wouldn't or couldn't make the investments.

Meanwhile states were busy developing English and math standards and assessments. But oh, how these products ranged in quality! With the exceptions of Kentucky and Texas, states mostly went through the motions. Texas was especially unique because it began its reforms earlier than other states and was the only state that reported test results by subgroups of students—African American, Latino, and low-income. NAEP shows, then and now, that these Texas subgroups perform well above the national average. Texas's school reform leadership led to major political consequences, with the election of President George W. Bush and his proposal of the No Child Left Behind Act.

My CCSSO staff and I worked mightily to get state education agency staff to focus on low performing students. We raised significant funding to operate our High Poverty Schools Project. Through this project we held three-day conferences for state agencies and urban district staff to consider strategies employed by selected districts. We organized visits to high-performing high-poverty schools. We did this because I believed that state and district staff needed to witness successful schools and their students in order to convince them that low-income and minority students are able to learn at high levels.

The Clinton administration did little to enforce IASA, basically letting a thousand flowers bloom or wilt in the states. At the regular CCSSO meetings, Gordon Ambach pleaded with chiefs to pay attention to their agencies' administration of Title I. But his pleas were in vain and most agencies continued to operate Title I as a parallel program to other agency programs. Since states' Title I administrative costs were paid for by federal dollars, and of course focused on the least empowered schools and students, it was easy to ignore the program.

Ultimately, in 2001 Gordon Ambach decided to retire from CCSSO. After fifteen years there, I also decided to leave. The change in leadership was disastrous for CCSSO, at least from my perspective. The new leader eliminated the Resource Center on Educational Equity and the High

Poverty Schools Project. Since then, educational equity hasn't been a major focus of CCSSO.

ALONG COMES NCLB

Another ESEA reauthorization approached. For the new President Bush, with his compassionate conservatism, K–12 education was a priority. In Texas, he continued bipartisan reforms launched under Democrats, and was eager for a bipartisan reauthorization. He had two ready partners with Democratic leaders, Senator Ted Kennedy (D-MA) and Congressman George Miller (D-CA). They were disgusted with weak state IASA implementation, and were pleased to join with a Republican president who wholeheartedly embraced standards and accountability.

The advocacy community, also unhappy with IASA, was thrilled to have administration and congressional allies supporting its agenda. I participated in many discussions on the upcoming reauthorization while I was still at CCSSO. A key recommendation of advocates was that all students achieve academic proficiency by 2014. Advocates believed it should not take more than a generation to bring all students to proficiency. We knew that was optimistic, maybe impossible, but we believed there needed to be an end date and that it would be immoral to go out further than a generation of student schooling.

NCLB was enacted by Congress in late 2001 and signed by President Bush in January 2002. As Patrick McGuinn details in chapter 2, it went much further than IASA, requiring 100 percent student proficiency by 2014, annual assessments, subgroup reporting, and targeted school interventions.

Many Republicans grumbled about the law as they voted for it. A few years later Democrats began complaining also. As Robert Gordon explained in the *New Republic* after the 2004 presidential elections:

It matters whether we set high expectations for schools and teachers or accept mediocrity, and whether we impose consequences for failure or excuse it. That Republicans are fond of making these points—and unions and school officials are not fond of hearing them—does not make them less true. Progressives are misled by the logic of their own Bush-hatred: Bush is for NCLB, so NCLB must be bad. Never mind that President Clinton embraced accountability before President Bush, Governor Ann Richards before Governor Bush. As the demands of NCLB mount, and as resistance to those demands spreads into conservative strongholds like Texas and Utah, many progressives are joining the fun.[4]

The division among Democrats on education had begun, and this division is even greater today. It seems that advocates for disadvantaged students and advocates for adults employed in the education system are on very different sides. The forty-year bipartisan consensus on federal education programs began to fall apart.

In 2004, I joined the Center for American Progress (CAP), first as director of its task force on public education and ultimately as vice president for education policy. (I stayed for over nine years until I decided to retire from full-time work.) We built the CAP education program to advocate for low-income students and students of color and took on issues that progressive organizations had historically shied away from, including:

- restructuring the teaching workforce with differential compensation, serious evaluations with accountability for student performance, and revised tenure procedures;
- implementing school finance reform, including redesigning the Title I formula, closing the comparability loophole, and modifying the "supplement not supplant" provision;
- ensuring a return on investment of education expenditures;
- expanding school learning time; and
- enacting rigorous, common standards and assessments for all students.

CAP and organizations like the Thomas B. Fordham Institute did significant analyses comparing NAEP performance to state assessments. The phoniness of test results in many states became obvious and was one of the factors that led to governors promoting Common Core State Standards.

CAP, a multi-issue progressive think tank focused on action and communication, jumped into the new education wars on the left. Unhappiness with NCLB was constantly growing. It was time again to reauthorize ESEA/NCLB and the CAP Action Fund exerted its influence. We worked closely with the staff of Senator Kennedy and Congressman Miller. They tried mightily to reauthorize the law in 2008, but failed.

In late 2008, the country elected its first African American president, Barack Obama. The excitement among progressives over his election and their belief that major change would take place cannot be overstated. Of course, in retrospect we look mostly naïve, though some major advancements on education equity have taken place.

A NATIONAL RECESSION'S UNEXPECTED OPPORTUNITY FOR EDUCATION IMPROVEMENT

President Obama assumed office in the midst of the Great Recession. Amazingly, this crisis offered a rare opportunity to advance the federal education agenda beyond a focus on disadvantaged students. The ESEA/NCLB reauthorization was put on hold. The American Recovery and Reinvestment Act of 2009 (ARRA) pumped a one-time infusion of $100 billion in federal money into public education. The law contained four assurances that state and local education systems had to meet to receive the funds. These assurances covered increased teacher effectiveness and fairer distribution of highly qualified teachers, use of data systems to track progress and foster continuous improvement, progress toward rigorous college- and career-ready standards and high-quality assessments, and effective interventions to turn around the lowest performing schools. Advocates were ecstatic about the requirements, and educators went along because of their desperation for funds to at least partially offset the drastic cuts necessitated by the recession.

ARRA's most interesting provision was the Race to the Top (RTTT) program, a one-time $4.35 billion competitive grant program. RTTT triggered state progress on teacher evaluations, better data systems and assessments, and actions to turn around low performing schools. Most states changed their laws in order to meet the requirements of the competition, and most of those policy changes have remained. Arguably, it led to states coming together through the National Governors Association and CCSSO, with considerable philanthropic support, to develop the Common Core State Standards in 2009.

In the years following ARRA, control of Congress switched to Republicans. Moderates in both parties began disappearing and congressional gridlock ensued. Simultaneously, pressure mounted again to reauthorize ESEA/NCLB, but Congress reached no agreement. It was clear that the 2014 deadline for student proficiency was not even close to being met. The Department of Education had no choice but to establish an ESEA/NCLB waiver program. It established criteria for state waiver applications and seemed to make inconsistent judgments about what the department officials believed was acceptable. The waiver process became hugely unpopular, though I for one thought it was mostly okay. Secretary of Education Arne Duncan was widely attacked over implementation of the process.

In fairness to Duncan, his commitment to education equity cannot be questioned. In early 2011, he appointed a twenty-eight-member Equity and Excellence Commission. I was pleased to serve on it. But its membership was not politically balanced, and while it came out with a relatively strong report, it papered over divisions on the left. After its publication, several members walked away from its recommendations.

A NEW ESEA

By 2015, the backlash was in full swing. There was no longer bipartisan support for ESEA/NCLB, and both Republicans and Democrats were divided among themselves on how to go forward. In many places there were attacks on Common Core standards and standardized testing. Republicans had solid control of Congress and moved to reauthorize ESEA/NCLB. A bipartisan coalition of sorts agreed to support the Every Student Succeeds Act that was enacted in late 2015. President Obama signed the legislation.

Unfortunately, I believe ESSA is mostly a step backward. While many are celebrating the fact that ESEA was finally reauthorized after fourteen years, the new legislation just doesn't do what it's supposed to do: significantly assist educationally disadvantaged students.

Rather than sensibly redesign accountability, ESSA weakened it and placed unprecedented constraints on the secretary of education. ESSA looks more like IASA of 1994 than a forward-looking law for a new century. It virtually enshrines states' rights, a governance structure with negative history in guaranteeing equal educational opportunities. It also fails to address the inequitable school funding found throughout the country. With few exceptions, schools with the most low-income students receive the least amount of funding and the federal government looks the other way.

While ESSA offers some improvements, it's mostly a missed opportunity. It's weak on the training/assigning of quality teachers, ensuring meaningful on-the-job professional learning supports, and financing public schools equitably nationwide.

Bright spots are the data reporting requirements, which the law has strengthened. Especially important is the new requirement that actual federal, state, and local expenditures must be reported publicly at the school level. Hopefully researchers will dig into this data and document the stark inequity in resource expenditures that historically has plagued US schools and districts.

But all is not lost. There are very important lawsuits directed at improving education moving through several state and federal courts. Federal support for charter schools was reaffirmed in ESSA, and there is impressive growth in charters that are very successful with low-income and minority students. And since NCLB was enacted in 2002, over seventy state-level education advocacy organizations were founded in thirty-four states and the District of Columbia.

In theory, holding states responsible for providing high-quality education for all students makes sense. The United States is a huge country, and operating a national school system is not possible in practical terms. In population, US states resemble European countries, all of which have national systems of education, with some variation. But our country's size is no reason not to have national, enforceable standards for operating a fair system of public education.

WEAK STATE SYSTEMS OF PUBLIC EDUCATION

State education systems have always varied widely in capacity and commitment to quality and equity. Effectiveness depends on the quality of state leadership, and unfortunately there is very high turnover. Most state legislatures today are very conservative and uninterested in education equity. Technology advances, along with federal data collection requirements, provide state agencies and legislators with more knowledge about the makeup of their states' student bodies, teaching forces, and education finances. But despite this ready access to information that can and does reveal inequities, state efforts to correct even glaring problems are rare.

For at least two decades, most state legislatures have reduced funding for state education agencies (SEAs). Indeed, a well-kept secret—rarely documented because of the opaqueness of state education budgets—is that the federal government pays on average about 50 percent of SEA budgets.

So the frequently touted message of ESSA of returning decision making to the states is quite hollow. There is "no 'there' there," no capacity to fully implement ESSA except in a very few states like Massachusetts.

CONCLUSION AND THE FUTURE

Americans are quite comfortable with local control of education, and they don't really care that local control guarantees education inequity. Glaring achievement gaps in every state are frequently documented. And local control enshrines costly inefficiency. Surely, having almost 700 school districts in New Jersey, 1,200 in Texas, and over 850 in Illinois involves a lot of duplication of services.

Over the years I have tried to figure out why Americans are so resistant to pursuing truly equitable education for all students. I've concluded it has something to do with a belief system.

Americans historically have believed that there are limitless opportunities to succeed in this country, that hard work alone brings rewards, and that people are entitled to keep most of what they earn. They mostly distrust government except during economic calamities. Unlike Europeans, who pay higher taxes, they've never learned that taxes can result in better services for all—like universal health insurance and care, family leave and children's allowances, universal day care, and virtually free lower and postsecondary education. Yes, Europe is today experiencing financial stress and backlash, but most of its countries treat their citizens (and most immigrants) more fairly than the United States does.

While Americans are slowly coming to understand how interdependent our nation is economically with other nations, they don't yet seem to recognize interdependence within our own country. While our individualism and notions about freedom are valuable, they also hinder our understanding of interrelationships and the need to take a measure of responsibility for one another. I don't know how to convince affluent suburbanites to care about inner-city education, or parents of "gifted" students to care about the quality of education for "nongifted," or northerners to care about poor, mostly rural southern and western states with their weak tax bases and education systems.

Private-sector employers complain about the lack of enough qualified job applicants. This affects their companies' success. Closer to my current life, there is the example of baby boomers with health insurance not being able to get the care they can afford because of a shortage of adequately trained nurses and health technicians to operate fancy new medical machines. Even getting an appointment with one's primary care doctor has become difficult because of a shortage of such doctors, leading to the growth of concierge practices for the affluent. Given current demographics and income and achievement gaps, the workforce of the future is going to come from students of color and lower-income students who today are often getting a low-quality education.

Many Americans also have distorted views about the disadvantaged. They tend to believe that poor people are directly responsible for their conditions, or are "unlucky" and therefore should get some help, but not too much. They often put a racial twist on it, believing that low-income African Americans and Latinos are innately or culturally inferior and low-income whites mostly unlucky.

These views are harsh, I know, but how else can one explain national inaction? And what will move inaction to action? I frankly don't know. The documentation of immense achievement gaps and low performance of US students, regardless of income, on international tests seems not to raise alarms.

To prepare for writing this chapter I reviewed my writings and speeches over the past decades. One of the most interesting revelations was how I moved in the late 1980s from a focus on inequitable inputs to more equitable outcomes. Back then I seemed to assume that a focus on outcomes would force action on inequitable inputs, but it has not. Today I guess I believe we need to a return to a focus on inputs, though in a more sophisticated way.

Despite all my disappointment on progress toward equal educational opportunity, I must acknowledge progress made by researchers, educators, and some elected officials. There is no question that researchers have documented how high-poverty schools have been funded unfairly and inadequately. Others have made persuasive cases about what's needed to turn around low performing schools, and how to better support teachers. And there's growing attention to evidence-based solutions and system productivity. I also celebrate the adoption of much higher academic standards (with little backing down in the face of right-wing attacks), the development of much better tests, continuing attention to teacher evaluation in the face of backlash from many educators, the growth of charter schools, and the emergence of new organizations focused on better leadership. These have led to education success for many previously disadvantaged students and their entrance into the middle class.

But negatives offset the positives. There's been a drastic change in the US economy, especially with the decline in manufacturing and unmet demand for a better-educated workforce in an information age. There is continuing concentration of poverty with less socioeconomic integration in housing and schools. There is growing political hostility toward certain groups of immigrants and their children.

In the face of this, states maintain an ineffective and inefficient education structure and grossly underinvest in public education in most places, including not funding pension mandates or quality preschool. This results in low pay and bad working conditions that lead to high teacher and leadership turnover rates in high-poverty areas and a failure to attract talented young people to teaching. So, unsurprisingly, achievement gaps are not closing.

To return to ESEA/ESSA, I have a few recommendations if the climate ever changes and educational equity again becomes a national priority. Funding for Title I should be increased and its formula improved. Accountability provisions should be strengthened. The comparability loophole should be closed and the "supplement not supplant" provision fixed. ESEA/ESSA can never solve the education inequity challenges of the country—only major reform of state education systems can—but the federal government could at a minimum establish major financial incentives for states to change, as Race to the Top did.

There are many state-level reforms that could be undertaken. But to me the most important is changing state funding for public education. There should no longer be local funding of schools though property or other taxes.

As I have written elsewhere, I believe states should assume the entire cost of their public schools and adopt systems of weighted student funding where weights are assigned to students with extra educational needs—low-income students, English language learners, and students with disabilities. There should be extra weights for students in schools with large concentrations of low-income students. Each state should also develop a measure of return on investment and hold local educators accountable for the productivity of their organizations through public reporting of efficiency metrics. In addition, a wide variety of governance arrangements (traditional districts, charter schools, districts with noncontiguous schools sharing curricula and pedagogical approaches, virtual schools, districts organized to further economic integration of schools, state-operated districts of low performing schools, etc.) should be responsible for the design and operation of schooling using the dollars allocated under a state funding system. The state role in these matters would vary from state to state. The state funding mechanisms would also vary (state property tax, income tax, sales tax, etc.).

But for all the inequities within states, the greatest inequity in funding is actually between states. Addressing this would be very expensive. Federal funds should financially assist those states with insufficient wealth to generate necessary funds for schools as long as they meet a baseline level of tax effort. For this solution to be politically viable, federal funds will need to reach every state and support schools with high concentrations of low-income students as does the current ESEA/ESSA Title I. It has been estimated that this would mean the federal government assuming about 40 percent of the cost of public education. This of course is not likely any time soon, certainly not in my remaining lifetime.

But maybe change is on the horizon. Is a disgruntled electorate on both the left and right fed up with elected officials? Does it want a more activist federal government, at least in terms of providing basic supports including education at a significant level? Does it support new leaders, many of color? And most importantly, does it want state-level change? One can hope.

11

From ESEA to ESSA

Fifty Fast Years

Chester E. Finn, Jr.

Howdy however did we get from the Elementary and Secondary Education Act of 1965 to the Every Student Succeeds Act half a century later? It was quite a journey—and I had the privilege of traveling along much of it, sometimes doubling back on myself, sometimes with no clue as to where we were headed. Allow me to share a bit of history, some reminiscence, some confession, and a touch of belated self-criticism.

IN THE BEGINNING

ESEA arrived with birth defects. David Cohen and Susan Moffitt's indispensable 2009 book, *The Ordeal of Equality: Did Federal Regulation Fix the Schools?*, frames the mismatch between Lyndon Johnson's ambitious goals for this legislation and the flawed mechanisms that it relied on—that its architects had no choice but to rely on—in attempting to reach those goals. In LBJ's mind—and on his lips the day he signed the original ESEA into law—this was:

> the most sweeping educational bill ever to come before Congress. It represents a major new commitment of the federal government to quality and equality in the schooling that we offer our young people. I predict that all of those of both parties of Congress who supported the enactment of this legislation will be remembered in history as men and women who began a new day of greatness in American society . . . By passing this bill, *we bridge the gap between helplessness and hope for more than five million educationally deprived children*."[1] [Emphasis added.]

This aspiration had a powerful effect on me. A college senior that year, I was a budding social reformer and already a veteran of tutoring and social service programs for what we undergraduates thought of as "underprivileged kids." The War on Poverty was newly declared. I had read Michael Harrington's powerful 1962 book, *The Other America*, and I wanted to change the world, to uplift the poor and help the needy. President Johnson's conviction that this could best be done via education rang true, and so I headed off to ed school immediately after earning a BA. It's not much of an exaggeration to say that the onset of ESEA helped determine my career path.

My own path turned out to be somewhat smoother than ESEA's, for the actual means by which Uncle Sam undertook this ambitious project were no match for its aspiration. In fact, the mechanisms available to Washington were shaky and uneven. Even while terming the centerpiece Title I program a "breakthrough," "an expression of the old American idea, set down in Horace Mann's twelfth report, that public schools could be the 'balance wheel of the social machinery,' righting wrongs that the economy and society imposed on children," Cohen and Moffitt itemized the multiple barriers that it faced, including the following:

- "The aid was distributed in a way that greatly constrained federal influence."
- "The governance arrangements that favored local control and fragmentation persisted."
- "Though the formula decided how much money states and localities would get, it decided nothing about how that money would be spent." Those decisions would be made "by the same local educators whose schools had offered a thin educational diet to poor or black children."
- "Though Title I aimed to improve teaching and learning . . . it lacked the educational wherewithal . . . that would make it possible for governments to guide what happened in classrooms."
- The norm-referenced tests in common use were intentionally agnostic regarding curriculum, meaning that localities, states, and federal authorities had no way to determine whether students were learning what they were supposed to.

In sum, wrote Cohen and Moffitt, "Title I faced an extraordinary challenge: it was to improve instruction for children from poor families in a school system that lacked common instruments to influence instruction . . . Title

I's purpose was to improve education in a system that had been carefully designed to impede central political and educational influence on schools.'"[2]

And that's not all. Barely a year after LBJ signed this historic measure, the eminent sociologist James Coleman pulled the conceptual rug out from under it. His massive study, paid for by the federal government and known as *Equality of Educational Opportunity*, found no reliable relationship between the resources going into schools and the results they produce. In Coleman's words, "The major virtue of the study [was] shifting policy attention from . . . inputs (per pupil expenditure, class size, teacher salaries, and so on) to a focus on outputs."[3]

Consider the irony: as the Great Society was channeling federal dollars to public schools on the assumption that this would yield better results for poor kids, Coleman was raising profound questions about the efficacy of that strategy, indeed about the entire basis on which judgments of school quality had long rested. His findings were of course ignored for years by educators and government officials who didn't want to believe him. (It cannot have been coincidence that Washington released the Coleman Report over the Fourth of July weekend.) Yet his core findings were replicated by other scholars, and his central message—the weak link between school inputs and outcomes—has never been disproven.

Put all this together, and one ought not be surprised that evaluation after evaluation over the decades showed Title I to have scant impact on narrowing achievement gaps or boosting knowledge and skills among disadvantaged children. Its reach far exceeded its grasp; its resources were spread thin; the intermediaries that were responsible for its heavy lifting could not really be counted upon; and the fundamental paradigm on which it rested was, to put it gently, unproven.

HEAD VERSUS HEART

With the benefit of hindsight, I had every reason to expect these paltry outcomes and should have known better than to sign on, as I did, to several noble but doomed efforts to amend the law to overcome its inherent obstacles. But my heart didn't want to follow my head. (To some extent, that's still the case today.)

My head was being educated to doubt the efficacy of grand social engineering schemes. Even while getting credentialed as an educator, I was imbibing the cautionary views and findings of some of the nation's most intelligent and incisive policy skeptics, social scientists, and public intellectuals—people like Jim Wilson, Nat Glazer, Irving Kristol, and my own doctoral advisor and longtime mentor, the late Daniel P. Moynihan. Known as "neoconservatives" long before that term was linked to overseas adventurism, they watched the unfolding both of Great Society programs and of many earlier ventures, and showed how seldom such efforts yielded the desired results and how often they caused collateral damage.

I was even beginning myself to scribble away for publications such as *Commentary* and the *Public Interest*, the main outlets for such skeptical thinking. My head understood that large-scale reform initiatives undertaken by distant government can rarely overcome the forces of habit, tradition, culture, bureaucracy, and stubborn human nature, and that mighty efforts to overcome those forces were apt to produce all sorts of unintended consequences. For Pete's sake, as a graduate student I sat in on the Harvard faculty seminar, co-led by Moynihan and the statistician Frederick Mosteller, that was devoted to reanalysis of the Coleman data and its policy implications. My head understood that complex institutions are rarely moved to do things very differently—at least not moved rapidly and, when moved at all, not apt to do those different things with gusto and competence just because a law had been passed, a grant made, or a formula changed.

My head knew all that. But my heart was fighting the war on poverty, trying to teach social studies to bored (and semidisadvantaged) twelfth graders in a Boston suburb while volunteering for the Cambridge Economic Opportunity Committee; writing research-based papers for the late, great Martha Derthick, then a professor of government at Harvard; and coleading one of the country's first Upward Bound programs. It's so very easy to fall under the spell of a worthy end or noble cause, and, especially when fired with youthful idealism and career ambition, to seduce oneself into the expectation that somehow the experts and policy makers will find ways to overcome the constraints imposed by the available means to that end.

Hence I found myself cheering several of the numerous reauthorizations and amendments from 1965 through 2002 that sought in various ways not just to expand the Title I program (and its many companions under the ever-spreading ESEA Christmas tree) but also to target its funding (without narrowing political support for that funding). By stiffening federal regulation of many kinds, the essential project of those legislative repair jobs was to cajole, prod, tempt, frighten, embarrass, and coerce states and ultimately districts and schools to do more for educating disadvantaged kids.

ALTERNATIVE STRATEGIES

I still shared that aim, although time would prove that the means being pursued did not constitute a workable theory of action. Indeed, even while cheering some of the regulatory tightenings—especially the ultimate version that was embodied in No Child Left Behind—I was also party to several efforts to alter that approach and substitute different means, the kind my brain had reason to think might work better.

Those contrarian efforts, by and large, got nowhere on Capitol Hill. (Maybe the Democrats in charge of Congress weren't reading the *Public Interest*!) But try we did. I worked for both Presidents Nixon and Reagan (as well as Senator Moynihan) and did my bit to help them try to change the path of federal education policy in fundamental ways: turning prescriptive categorical programs into flexible block grants, mounting more rigorous evaluations and research initiatives, melding education aid into "revenue sharing," and even flirting with "voucherizing" Title I. I was at Moynihan's side in the White House when Nixon voiced doubt in 1970 that programs like Title I were effective and offered the country a National Institute of Education (NIE) to get under the hood and figure out what might work better. (Coleman's influence on Moynihan and ultimately on Nixon was palpable.) I was again at Moynihan's side on the Senate floor in 1978 when he and Senator Bob Packwood sought a sizable program of federal tuition tax credits so more kids could opt for private schools. (That was a tax code change, not a Title I change, but it surely would have altered the policy path!) Then I was at hand when Secretary of Education Bill Bennett brought forth in 1985 the Reagan administration's second attempt to persuade Congress that a market-based strategy—vouchers by which poor families could choose their own schools—would work better than top-down, Washington-knows-best programs like Title I.

Whatever one thought, or thinks, of such alternative approaches, in hindsight those proposing them weren't wrong about the ineffectuality of Title I as a mechanism for boosting academic achievement. Yet the screw-tighteners were ultimately in charge, and pretty much stayed in charge until December 2015. Yes, Congress did some block-granting, but not of Title I. Yes, the NIE came into being—for a time I served on its policy board—and launched an ambitious research agenda, including quests for better ways of educating disadvantaged children, but Title I itself remained intact (save for a name change between 1981 and 1994). Intermittent GOP pushes to contain or reshape it likely slowed its movement along the path, but the basic direction of that path remained fairly straight—and No Child Left Behind would be as far as it extended (at least as of today).

CHANGING CONTEXTS

While all this was happening to ESEA, much else was simultaneously occurring in and to American education—some of it involving federal policy, some not. Additional populations besides disadvantaged children came under Uncle Sam's protection and qualified for aid of various kinds: children with disabilities, non-English speakers, girls, Native Americans, homeless youngsters, and more. *A Nation at Risk* triggered widespread alarm about weak academic achievement, launching what became known as the "excellence movement" and—coupled with President George H. W. Bush's 1989 governors summit in Charlottesville—giving rise to "standards-based reform" as we know it.

Pressed by governors and many others for better state-level data than Ted Bell was able to deliver in the aftermath of *A Nation at Risk*, Bill Bennett and I—with the help of a commission chaired by Tennessee's Lamar Alexander—proposed a major overhaul of the National Assessment of Educational Progress (NAEP). With Ted Kennedy's help, the 1988 ESEA reauthorization incorporated those changes in NAEP, allowing for state-level results to be reported and keyed to "achievement levels" that NAEP's new governing board (which I chaired for a couple of years) dubbed "basic," "proficient," and "advanced." These functioned, in effect, as the first national education standards the United States had ever had.

NAEP wasn't the entire data story, either. The arrival of the Trends in International Mathematics and Science Study (TIMSS) and then the Program for International Student Assessment (PISA) enabled Americans to see how their students were doing compared with peers in other lands, and the picture was not pretty. Even uglier was the discovery—unveiled in 1987 by a self-publishing West Virginia psychiatrist named John Cannell—that states and districts all around the land were commonly reporting to their citizens that most of their pupils were "above average" according to the norm-referenced tests in common use. (This immediately became known as the "Lake Wobegon Report," after Garrison Keillor's mythical town where "all the women are strong, all the men are good-looking, and all the children are above average.") Secretary Bennett asked me—the research guy—if this could possibly be true, so we invited some well-known experts to investigate. It turned out that Dr. Cannell was essentially correct: US education leaders were giving people false good news.

Also during this period, school choice caught fire, burning in multiple directions. Public school choice, both intra- and interdistrict, spread to many states and communities. Charter schools launched in Minnesota in 1991, spread to California a year later, and qualified for federal aid in 1995. Even vouchers came to pass, with the Milwaukee program dating to 1989.

GOALS AND STANDARDS

The onset of "standards-based" reform in particular intersected with Title I, especially after President Bush and forty-nine governors, gathered in Charlottesville, established a set of "national education goals" meant to be achieved by the year 2000. These were arguably even more ambitious than Title I's goals but fully compatible with it. For example, one of the objectives spelled out under Goal 3 ("Student Achievement and Citizenship") declared, "The academic performance of elementary and secondary students will increase significantly in every quartile, and the distribution of minority students in each level will more closely reflect the student population as a whole."[4]

The goals, in retrospect, were pie-in-the-sky, both unrealistically ambitious and entirely lacking in means by which they might be achieved. Yet President Bush—host in Charlottesville and self-styled "education president"—earnestly wanted a strategy by which they might be realized. So incoming Secretary of Education Lamar Alexander set out to develop one, and I had the privilege of helping craft it (and got a charge from accompanying him to the Oval Office where Bush 41 dubbed it "the best thing I've seen").

Dubbed "America 2000," it was a multifaceted plan that didn't tighten the regulatory screws on federal dollars but rather proposed new, voluntary academic standards; new assessments by which to track student learning; a community-based program to get citizens around the nation fired up about prodding their own schools to attain higher standards; and a privately funded initiative called the New American Schools Development Corporation charged with reinventing the school itself.

The latter was launched because it did not require federal approval or funding, but Congress wanted no part of the rest of America 2000, so most of it didn't happen. (Alexander, however, barnstormed the land, doing his utmost to make the community part get traction.)

By 1993, a new president occupied the Oval Office. Bill Clinton had been centrally involved not only with multiple education reforms in Arkansas but also with the Charlottesville goal-setting process. He promptly sent Congress a pair of ambitious bills of his own. These emerged the following year as the "Goals 2000" and "Improving America's Schools" acts. The former picked up on the goals' theme and encouraged states to set academic standards and measure performance toward them. It was, in fact, frequently and justly confused with Bush's America 2000 scheme. But the latter (IASA) was a full-bore ESEA reauthorization of the screw-tightening sort. It essentially made a state's Title I funding contingent on its getting serious about academic standards and assessments for both schools and students.[5]

MOUNTING DOUBTS

I was wary. I knew there were problems with extant academic standards and tests. I sensed that, while "voluntary" might work in these realms, federal coercion was politically problematic and operationally challenging. I had served on a couple of commissions that wrestled fruitlessly with how to be national without being federal. At some point along the way, I'm pretty sure I was the first to quip that "the problem with national testing is that Republicans don't like 'national' and Democrats don't like testing."

Somewhat hyperbolically, Diane Ravitch and I wrote in 1995 that IASA was "the most meddlesome federal education law ever enacted," accused it of overreach and "hypercentralization," and suggested that this (plus other examples of federal excess) had contributed to the Republican electoral triumphs of 1994.

Unsurprisingly, implementation of IASA (and Goals 2000) once again proved fitful and challenging. While later evaluations reported modest achievement gains, it was impossible to know to what extent these were attributable to the revamped Title I program or to other developments in their cities and states. In any event, nobody could claim convincingly that much progress was being made in attaining Title I's principal objectives: the significant boosting of achievement and life prospects for poor kids and the narrowing of learning gaps between them and their more prosperous age mates.

TRYING AGAIN

Enter No Child Left Behind, another epic rewrite of ESEA that tightened the federal education screws more than ever before. Its "theory of action," to the extent that it had one, was that IASA had moved in the right direction but not far enough. Additionally, a number of states and cities—including new President George W. Bush's Texas—had done pretty well in boosting the achievement of poor and minority kids via reforms centered on standards, assessments, transparency, and some school choice.

I was pro-Bush, had given him some advice in Austin, and respected what he had accomplished, how he thought about education, and what he hoped to do. Maybe I was also a sucker. Maybe I just let heart overpower brain or, as is sometimes said, let hope vanquish experience. There was surely a touch of partisanship involved, as this was, finally, a Republican president's initiative with some hope of getting enacted. In any case, suspending my wariness of federal overreach, I applauded. Sitting in the East Room as the new president and Secretary of Education Rod Paige strode in to outline their grand plan in January 2001 (just days after Bush's inauguration), I beamed with optimism. Like Clinton, this president had been a formidable education reformer in his own state, and I was also wowed by Secretary Paige's knowledge, experience, and powerful track record as Houston superintendent (including launch of what became the Knowledge Is Power Program, or KIPP, network of charter schools). I allowed myself to share their confidence that these locally and state-generated reforms—relying once again on standards, assessments, accountability, and school choice—could be translated to the national level, and I somehow allowed myself once again to trust that Title I could yet become the principal vehicle for doing so.

Yes, I should have known better, should have forced mind to conquer heart and knowledge to overwhelm partisanship. But it's a fact that I beamed yet again in 2002 when this bold, sprawling, and by then bipartisan measure was signed into law. I convinced myself (and tried to convince others) that this federal screw-tightening, plus small advances on the choice front, would finally get the country's K–12 system to the point where it could help both to realize LBJ's 1965 vision and to vanquish what Bush 43 aptly termed the "soft bigotry of low expectations."

Sadly but again unsurprisingly, I was mostly wrong. Warier would have been wiser. My IASA instincts were sounder than my early NCLB expectations. This policy round didn't work very well, either. Yes, in combination with many other things going on at the national, state, and local levels, it contributed to some welcome upward blips in test scores for poor kids in the early grades, mainly in math. But it didn't really succeed. In a dozen important ways, it misfired. In some ways, it made things worse. It probably also made states and districts less responsible for their own actions and the fate of their own kids, even as they were held to account for those kids' achievement and their schools' performance. This mismatch between responsibility and authority, combined with clumsy, ill-fitting, federally dictated interventions into weak schools (and the identification of far too many schools as weak), gradually pissed off just about everyone, albeit in very different ways.

RUMBLINGS AND STIRRINGS

Meanwhile, much else continued to unfold in American politics and government. Ideological and partisan schisms widened. "Obamacare" worsened them, as did the advent of the Tea Party. The 2008 recession caused economic hardship, resentment toward the prosperous, and bitterness on the part of those left behind. The country experienced more anti-Washington sentiment than ever before.

In education, there was plenty of anger to go around, over testing, teacher evaluations, unreal expectations ("every child proficient by 2014"), Finland and Singapore envy, painful yet ineffectual school turnaround mandates, contentious Common Core standards, battles over vouchers and charters, curricular narrowing, resource shortfalls, and more. Much of this anger was directed toward Washington in general and NCLB in particular. NCLB, in fact, turned into what some came to refer to as a "tainted label." In time it was evident that this law's designers had overreached and caused problems that a divided and dysfunctional Congress now could not solve.

Nor was it entirely clear that the Obama administration really wanted Congress to solve them. Neither the White House nor the Education Department broke a sweat working to achieve legislative compromises that at several points looked attainable. Instead, the executive branch went its own way, first with the Race to the Top program, tucked within 2009's anti-recessionary "stimulus" act. This spread a lot of money across public education *and* across implementation of some of Secretary Arne Duncan's favorite policy initiatives, including the Common Core State Standards and allied assessments. Common Core had started outside Washington, but Duncan's embrace of it and use of federal funds to "incentivize" states to adopt it fed even more anti-Beltway sentiment, got the standards dubbed "Obamacore" (at least in places that didn't like either the Common Core or the fellow in the Oval Office), and generally threw sand in the gears of what had struck me as another worthwhile undertaking on the standards front.

Then came Duncan's unilateral decision to waive various NCLB provisions for states that agreed to do other things he wanted them to do, including things with no basis in statute. His explanation was that, if Congress was unable or unwilling to mend the flaws in NCLB and update the law, he would do it himself. His addition of new requirements and initiatives further exacerbated the sense that the executive branch was trampling on the Constitution and Uncle Sam was trying to run America's schools. The backlash against NCLB, Washington, and the federal role in education intensified.

Finally, way, way late, later than ever before, Congress bestirred itself to reauthorize ESEA yet again. Even though this move was sorely overdue, it still might not have happened, at least not in 2015, without the extraordinary bipartisan (and, by today's norms, marvelously old-fashioned) work of Senators Lamar Alexander and Patty Murray, chairman and ranking member, respectively, of the Senate Education Committee.

CHANGE OF DIRECTION

The thrust of this reauthorization (ESSA) was predictable, maybe even inevitable: a loosening of Washington's grip. This rollback, climb-down—call it what you like—eased the regulatory burden on states and districts on multiple fronts. All this was bipartisan but certainly not what everyone wanted. There were constituents in and out of Congress for further tightening of the federal education screws—Senator Elizabeth Warren tried hard in committee—but those folks couldn't muster the votes to turn this legislative cycle in their preferred direction. Republicans, now more heavily in thrall to the Tea Party and other anti-Obama types, were in charge of both chambers. The screw-tighteners did secure a host of provisions that preserve some of the spirit of NCLB and retain the metrics by which performance can be judged. (Indeed, ESSA made the reporting burden on states far weightier than before, even as the actual "must dos" were reduced.) Still, everybody acknowledges that ESSA amounts to a net diminution of federal control and a reempowerment of states to make their own decisions about K–12 education.

I cheered this shift, too. Yes, I can fairly be charged with cheering entirely too many different versions of ESEA over entirely too many years. Maybe I'm gullible, possibly an optimist (although I think of myself as a "glass half-empty" type), or perhaps just a naïf who assumes that doing something different has got to be better than what we've been doing. Grateful though I am for the opportunities I've had and proud of a few contributions that I think I've made, I cannot claim consistency. In hindsight, sticking with the Kristol-Wilson-Moynihan skepticism of big government reform schemes would have been wiser. But my heart just didn't want to do that. I'm an analyst, yes, but also still a reformer. Far too many kids are still poor, far too few of them are learning all that they should and could, and far too many schools are failing to do right by them. Sitting by the wayside and voicing doubt that anything could be done about these failures would simply have been wrong.

OVERREACH AND CLIMB-DOWN

Yes, NCLB was an overreach, and this could have been predicted by the failure of earlier moves along the same path, notably IASA. Yet this was not the only time in US history that Washington overreached in one realm or another, leading to things not working as intended, lots of people getting upset, much pushback, and eventually a climb-down, at least partway, by the feds (and, let's be honest, sometimes leading to things being worse, or at least not better, after the climb-down). Consider these three examples, none related to education, where the federal retreat was pretty dramatic:

- *The Alien and Sedition Acts.* Passed by Congress in 1798 and signed by President John Adams, these laws made it hard for immigrants to become citizens, made it easy for the president to imprison and deport noncitizens who were deemed dangerous or came from a hostile nation, and criminalized the making of false statements critical of the federal government.

   Three of the four measures were repealed under Thomas Jefferson. (The fourth lasted right through World War II.) But the aftermath brought its own carnage. The fracas pretty well destroyed the Federalist Party, delayed creation of a proper army, and sullied the cause of vigilant defense—and less than a dozen years later the British set fire to the White House!

- *Prohibition.* From ratification of the Eighteenth Amendment in 1920 until approval of the Twenty-First Amendment in 1933, the federal government attempted to ban the production, importation, transportation, and sale of alcoholic beverages. Highly unpopular and widely flouted, it was perhaps the most ineffectual overreach ever by the national government. It also encouraged smuggling, gangsterism, and disrespect for the law. Its repeal may not have done additional harm, but it left a legacy of organized crime.

- *The 55 mile-per-hour national speed limit.* Enacted in 1974 and nearly as feckless as Prohibition, the "National Maximum Speed" law sought to conserve fossil fuel during a time of economic stress and oil embargoes. But almost everyone hated it, plenty of people ignored it, and many states failed to enforce it. Twenty-one years later (1995), Congress returned full authority over speed limits to the states. Harm done? Maybe not, except further disrespect for Washington, for government, and, perhaps, for speed limits of every kind.

There's plenty more where those came from, including scads of regulations that were eased and deadlines extended when it became obvious that what Uncle Sam wanted just couldn't or wouldn't be done in the manner and on the timetable first envisioned.

Laws and regulations aren't the only things that strengthen, weaken, and sometimes strengthen again. Besides specific programs and policies, we're familiar with big cycles in our politics, akin to the business cycle and the movements of the outer planets. (It takes Uranus eighty-four "Earth years" to make a single circuit around the sun we share with it.) The big political cycles, obviously, have to do with whether the country is heading in a more "progressive" or "conservative" direction, and we've had multiple examples of both. Usually we head so far in one direction that the engine runs out of gas, even as more and more people get upset. So we begin to swing in the other direction. I don't know about after the 2016 election, but it's evident that, even as Barack Obama was getting elected and reelected, much of the rest of the country was heading in a more conservative direction.

CYCLING

That's certainly visible in ESSA. But that doesn't mean this direction is permanent. It is almost certainly just a phase. The thing about the Tenth Amendment, "states' rights," and congressional efforts to make states responsible for decisions is that states can be counted upon to make all manner of decisions with all sorts of consequences. Some will surely use their newly retrieved authority under ESSA to do wise and creative things, but others—you can bet on it—will be cowardly, foolhardy, and/or reactionary in ways that will appear to be, and maybe really are, bad for poor and minority kids. Whereupon there will be a mighty push to tighten the federal screws again so that states and districts will be compelled to stop doing bad things and rendered at least a little likelier to do what the savants in Washington think they should be doing.

Youthful idealists will surely join in that screw tightening, allowing heart to prevail over whatever they know about what might actually work. But such hopeful reforming doesn't always take the form of tighter screws. Arguably a bunch of today's young libertarians (including a number of school-choice supporters) are just as idealistic—and as naïve—about the worth of their end and what they see as the inevitable success of their chosen means.

Okay, by now I'm more experienced, certainly older, possibly wiser, and definitely less idealistic. Yet it still galls me that so many kids are getting a lousy education and have their futures blighted by circumstances entirely beyond their control; it's downright immoral. I'm still impatient and outraged that the problems identified by LBJ and so many others—up to and including Ted Kennedy and George W. Bush and Lamar Alexander and Patty Murray and millions of others—remain largely unsolved. Achievement gaps are still far too wide. Poor kids still learn far too little—so do most kids, for that matter—and that dims their prospects for a successful life and an escalation out of poverty.

CONSTRAINTS AND END RUNS

Even more frustrating is my awareness of the limited capacity of the formal education system as we know it to rectify this situation. This isn't just a limitation on what Washington can make happen. It's a limitation of the K–12 system itself. The tools that didn't work very well for Lyndon Johnson still don't work very well today, and while state leaders may wield them with somewhat greater effect than Uncle Sam, there are rigidities, constraints, and gaps in the enterprise itself that make it very difficult for it to yield markedly stronger outcomes.

That's much of the reason I've grown partial to "end runs" around the system itself, to charter schools and alternative pathways and marketplace strategies and "backpack funding" and other approaches for skirting the system's structural and attitudinal barriers and at least allowing people to do things differently if they want to and can—a very different thing from telling them that they must. End runs are arguably the opposite of "big government" and "social engineering." They are opportunities rather than mandates. They *can't* actually be mandated and, though they can obviously be encouraged by government (voucher programs, charter startup grants, etc.), every such encouragement invites its own regulatory overkill in the name of "government knows best how this should and shouldn't work." That's what governments do.

I don't expect governments to stop behaving like governments. I don't expect the cycle of overreach followed by rollback followed by overreach to quit suddenly. And I don't expect those involved to bridle their idealism or curb their hopes just because someone else says their chosen means may not be well matched to their undeniably worthy ends.

I wish ESSA well, of course, and will do what I can both to monitor its progress and to advise and assist those trying to make it work. But I felt that way in 1965, too, and again in 2001. And I'm probably not done with disappointment.

Conclusion

Frederick M. Hess and Max Eden

T he Every Student Succeeds Act was a rare bipartisan accomplishment in an era marked by gridlock and division. While President Obama called it a "Christmas miracle," in truth it wasn't miraculous. Rather, it reflected a broad shift in the national consensus on how best to balance the animating tensions in American education.

Our education debates are rife with shallow partisan rhetoric and obscure technocratic jargon. It often seems that politicians and policy makers stray too far afield from what really matters: what works. But as we argued in the introduction, there actually are fundamental differences in vision for how best to educate young citizens. As we've described, the debates reflect the tension between the Tenth and Fourteenth Amendments. Both have deep roots in the American experience, and the debate between them is central to who we are as a nation and how we govern ourselves.

Many Americans believe that children will be best served if their schools are a natural extension of their families and communities. The diversity of American life and the very personal nature of education are both compelling reasons why schools should be governed as close as possible to the children that they serve. Those who see wisdom in the Tenth Amendment intuition that education is a fundamentally local endeavor tend to be wary of top-down directives. They are skeptical that rules and regulations promulgated from a great distance will actually achieve their intended goals, and worry that they might actually work against the human dynamics of teaching and learning.

On the other hand, many Americans also worry that states and communities can't be totally trusted to serve historically disadvantaged students, so a strong federal role is essential for ensuring that no child is left behind. Those who see a necessity for the federal government to make good on the Fourteenth Amendment's promise of equal protection tend to be more optimistic about the ability of policy makers to drive meaningful change, and are willing to accept disruption in the hope that the long arc of federal policy will bend toward justice.

Americans bring these intuitions to bear on more than just education, of course. The question of how best to balance these tensions goes to the core of American political life. Broadly speaking, adherents of the Tenth Amendment favor a limited government that allows for the mediating institutions of civil society to flourish. Adherents of the Fourteenth Amendment favor an energetic central government to secure the status of vulnerable minorities.

For a generation, as every other element of American politics grew increasingly polarized, education was a notable redoubt of bipartisanship. But the apparent consensus merely reflected the fact that the Tenth and Fourteenth Amendment intuitions don't fall neatly across party lines. An alliance between the right-leaning business community and the left-leaning civil rights community pushed an ever-expanding federal role. Civil rights activists thought it a moral necessity; business leaders thought it an economic imperative; and both were confident that enacting the right policies would achieve their goals.

No Child Left Behind extended the legacy of President Lyndon B. Johnson's original Elementary and Secondary Education Act, but with a scope and ambition that the architect of the Great Society could have hardly imagined. Rather than merely targeting aid toward disadvantaged groups, the federal government set state policy. States had to test students and hold schools that weren't improving accountable by implementing a set of federally prescribed school interventions. President Obama extended NCLB further, but not through the legislative process. Rather, he used the carrots and sticks of executive power to incent states to adopt policies around college- and career-ready standards, test-based teacher evaluation, and charter schooling.

Much of the substance of this agenda had bipartisan support when it was enacted at the state level. But when the decisions started being made from

Washington, many small-government conservatives veered off and teacher unions grew uneasy, creating a new bipartisan alliance.

Those skeptical of federal involvement found their concerns confirmed by No Child Left Behind and the Obama administration. Under Bush and Obama, federal involvement started directly affecting teaching and learning; it was no longer merely a concern for back-office school administrators. Parents were alarmed by the heightened focus on federal testing, fearing that it was narrowing the curriculum and doing nothing to help their kids. There were many who applauded the federal government's involvement in encouraging states to adopt new academic standards and test-based teacher evaluation. But many parents were perplexed at exactly how these changes were decided and upset that large-scale changes in education were taking place with little discussion or debate in their communities. Political conservatives, who had only ever given NCLB tepid approval, capitalized on these parental concerns and clamored for a smaller federal footprint.

Teachers, too, were concerned; in response to their worries, teacher unions began to embrace the notion of a more limited federal role. Unions had long argued that educational justice required the federal government to steer more money to schools that taught disadvantaged students. But when the role of the federal government shifted from directing money to dictating policy, unions had second thoughts. They worried that wave after wave of policy was doing more harm than good. Many teachers thought it was unfair and counterproductive to be evaluated by tests tied to standards that they barely had time to master.

This new left-right alliance between teacher unions and small-government conservatives supplanted the old alliance between civil rights groups and business leaders, and the Every Student Succeeds Act was the first time in a generation that federal education law was shaped and passed with an eye toward a more limited federal role. Now, this compromise didn't satisfy everyone. But it gave both sides a reason to claim victory.

ESSA'S THREE KEY BALANCING ACTS

As several contributors have noted, Republicans and Democrats saw the same law quite differently. As Alyson Klein reports in chapter 3, House Education and Workforce Committee chairman John Kline (R-MN) saw ESSA as "a new approach to K–12 education [where] classrooms will no longer be micromanaged by the US Department of Education." On the other hand, President Obama declared that ESSA "build(s) on the momentum that has already been established" and gives the Department of Education the "oversight to make sure state plans are sound."

Remarkably, both views make sense depending on how you look at ESSA, giving the compromise a certain Rorschach-esque quality. ESSA attempted to strike a balance that maintained the basic parameters of No Child Left Behind while allowing states more flexibility to maneuver within them. ESSA's three key balancing acts on testing, school evaluation, and school intervention gave both sides cause for satisfaction.

On testing, ESSA maintained NCLB's requirement that schools administer seventeen federally mandated standardized tests. But states were given the freedom to pare back the additional tests that went above and beyond the letter of federal law, such as the tests many states had adopted to comply with the Obama administration's policies on test-based teacher evaluation. Under ESSA, states can set their own course on teacher evaluation. Similarly, the pressure to make Adequate Yearly Progress under NCLB had led states and districts to implement tests around the federally required tests. ESSA's architects hoped that the new balance on school evaluation and intervention could help states rebalance their standardized testing.

On school evaluation, ESSA maintained NCLB's requirement that states evaluate schools and publicly report school performance. But states were given the freedom to develop more nuanced, robust evaluation metrics. Under NCLB, schools had primarily been evaluated on students' proficiency on standardized tests. Parents and teachers had complained that the focus on "proficiency" had hollowed out the curriculum and caused teachers to focus on the "bubble kids" hovering around the cutoff score to the exclusion of students who were well ahead or behind. What's more, the public couldn't make heads or tails of what "proficiency" actually meant. ESSA's architects hoped that, by encouraging states to evaluate schools on factors such as student growth and school climate, states could develop school performance systems that helped inform parents while encouraging, rather than hindering, a well-rounded education.

On school intervention, ESSA maintained NCLB's requirement that states intervene in persistently low performing schools. But states were given more freedom in identifying those schools and prescribing interventions. Under NCLB, every school that failed to make AYP on standardized tests had been subject to a federal "remedy cascade" of school interventions. Under ESSA, states must identify the lowest performing 5 percent of schools, and all high schools with graduation rates below 67 percent, for intervention. But schools and districts may develop their own school improvement plans, and states will have the flexibility to pursue a wide range of options if the district-based interventions don't bear fruit. ESSA's architects hoped that this added flexibility would help foster community buy-in for school improvement and give states the freedom to act decisively if that approach fails.

WILL THE NEW CENTER HOLD?

Will this new balance provide a lasting and stable base for public education? As we recounted in the introduction, Senator Lamar Alexander, an architect of ESSA, guessed that it would. He declared, "We've got a law that will govern the federal role in K–12 education for ten or twenty years" that "recognizes that the path to higher standards, better teaching and real accountability is classroom by classroom, community by community, and state by state—and not through Washington, DC."

Perhaps ESSA has struck a lasting balance, but it seems unlikely. As Patrick McGuinn details in chapter 1, federal education policy has exhibited a cyclical pattern over the past half century: new ambitions lead to a period of expansion, that expansion faces friction and calls for reevaluation, a period of retrenchment follows, then new ambitions lead to another period of expansion that again faces friction and calls for reevaluation. ESSA can be understood as fitting into this cycle, no stage of which has lasted longer than a decade.

Even before ESSA hit President Obama's desk, though, two things seemed fairly certain. The first was that the era of bipartisan comity would prove limited. As Alyson Klein reports in chapter 3, ESSA's bipartisan glow dimmed the spring after it was passed, as Senator Alexander grilled Secretary of Education John King on what Alexander saw as federal overreach that violated the intent, and even at times the letter, of the law. For his part, Secretary King thought he was fulfilling an expected, and vital, role.

Klein points out that while ESSA commanded the assent of majorities of both parties, majorities in each also made clear that their ideal law would look quite different. In the Senate, 43 Democrats voted for a failed amendment for a much stronger federal role; in the House, 195 Republicans voted for a failed amendment to allow states to opt out entirely from federal requirements. These tectonic divides are not going anywhere. As Jeffrey

Henig, David M. Houston, and Melissa Arnold Lyon relate in chapter 2, it's easy enough for strange bedfellows to come together and agree on a bill when it's merely words on paper. People and parties who want mutually exclusive things can all convince themselves that a law actually reflects *their* ideological priors. But when the rubber hits the road, many find themselves unpleasantly surprised.

The second safe prediction is that many states will miss the "Goldilocks zone" in implementation. Chad Aldeman argues in chapter 6 that ESSA places all the burden of school reform on state and local leaders, giving them no cover for taking strong action and providing little backstop against backsliding or intentional obfuscation. The explicit prohibitions on the secretary of education's powers will make attempts at federal oversight fraught with political and judicial difficulties. We suspect that Aldeman's concern will be borne out in some states, but that others will end up on the other side of the Goldilocks zone, moving aggressively to implement policies that aren't ready for primetime. For example, ESSA allows states to evaluate schools on nonacademic factors such as school climate and social-emotional learning. If this is done right, schools may be encouraged to focus on providing a robust and well-rounded education. But if policy makers get carried away by the fad of the hour, such as student "grit," the scope and scale of high-stakes micromanagement could be extended well past reading and math.

THREE POTENTIAL PITFALLS

No Child Left Behind had its fair share of unintended consequences that seem like they should have been obvious right from the start. It seems only logical that NCLB's emphasis on high-stakes standardized testing would lead to a broad public fear that a rich, well-rounded education was being cast aside in favor of "teaching to the test"; that not all students would reach proficiency by 2014; that the AYP system built on that assumption would lose its credibility; and that when states and schools rushed to implement teacher evaluation systems based on brand-new tests aligned to brand-new standards, the result would produce more indignity than insight. But neither NCLB's architects in Congress nor Race to the Top's maestros in the Department of Education quite saw these things coming.

No doubt that ESSA, too, will have its fair share of unintended consequences. Now, second-guessing policy makers with the benefit of years of hindsight is always an easy game, and predicting the future is often a fool's

errand. But the contributors have illuminated the prospect of three potential pitfalls, any one of which may come to define ESSA's legacy.

One concern is that some of ESSA's compromises may end up splitting
the proverbial baby. As Michael Casserly notes in chapter 9, this risk is especially pronounced for students with severe cognitive disabilities. States must
test all students by the same standards, and are allowed to exempt only 1
percent of students who have "severe cognitive disabilities." But twenty-
seven states already identify more than 1.14 percent with that level of disability. What's more, states are not allowed to directly limit the number of
such students that districts may identify, so they lack the leverage to meet
the federal requirement. As Casserly argues, clumsy implementation seems
virtually assured. States may find ways to encourage districts to underdiag-
nose disabled students. Or state policy makers may use students with cognitive disabilities to justify lowering standards across the board.

A second worry is that the data transparency requirements might end
up stunting rather than spurring state policy initiatives. As Charles Barone
relates in chapter 4, schools and districts will now be required to report new
data on student achievement for homeless students, students in foster care,
and students in active-duty military families. This is along with the previously required disaggregation by race, language status, poverty status, and
disability; indicators of school quality, including data on in-school suspensions, out-of-school suspensions, expulsions, school-related arrests, referrals to law enforcement, chronic absenteeism, and incidents of violence
(including bullying and harassment); per-pupil expenditures of federal,
state, and local funds including actual personnel expenditures and nonpersonnel expenditures disaggregated by source for each school system
and school (Title I and non–Title I); and much, much more. That's a lot to
ask of schools and systems. ESSA's operating assumption was that states are
fit to design, implement, and monitor policies on their own initiative. But
the costs of compliance may go well beyond the time and energy it takes
to reliably collect and report these statistics. The more that state education
agencies need to comply with, the less likely it is that they'll make the transition from being passive paperwork monitoring organizations to active
agents of reform.

Finally, ESSA's data requirements and more holistic approach to school
evaluation may not merely stunt policy but could also fundamentally shift
the locus of control from state legislatures and education agencies to the
judiciary. There is a long tradition of state lawsuits being used to remedy

educational inequities. NCLB's proficiency data provided "dynamite" for plaintiffs, allowing them to sue on academic disparities even when funding seemed fair on its face. As Arnold Shober notes in chapter 7, ESSA's architects might "discover that they have created a measure—classroom climate, parental involvement, or student perseverance—for courts to require equity. The push for standards, accountability, and transparency was meant to empower parents, teachers, [and] districts," but it could place state policy "even more firmly in the hands of state judges. The result would not be innovation, creativity, or even local democracy; ESSA could instead paralyze state education policy."

A law designed to empower local problem solvers with the data and responsibility to make smart decisions for the students they serve might well become a cudgel for state judiciaries or the federal government. This is especially problematic because the judiciary is simply not well suited to govern public policy. Courts are places where rights are secured and defended; they're not venues for finding compromise and can't return to former decisions if things go awry. They also have the unfortunate habit of imposing unworkable, bureaucratic requirements; failing to weigh costs and benefits; and short-changing practical considerations. What's more, when judges tell legislators they must rewrite a law, policy becomes a game of ping-pong rather than a matter of deliberation.

This is not what many congresspeople thought they were signing up for. If a bill designed to empower states and districts empowers judges instead, then the political backlash may be severe—especially if the Department of Education puts its thumb on the scale. Many Democrats wanted a much stronger federal role; many Republicans wanted no federal role. ESSA's common ground might well be undone by activist courts or federal overreach. And if so, ESSA may be the last bipartisan compromise on education for a long while.

ESSA AND BEYOND

We obviously hope that these unintended consequences don't materialize and ESSA works out broadly as intended. We also hope that this book has helped make sense of the tensions and trade-offs in ESSA's balancing act. We recruited a set of contributors with deep expertise and diverse perspectives to show how thoughtful and experienced analysts can come to different conclusions about the merits of ESSA and the proper role of the federal government in K–12 education.

Since No Child Left Behind was passed in 2001, much of the debate in K–12 education has taken the necessity of a strong federal role for granted. Arguments tended to be about what more the federal government should do to ensure equity and improve education. Advocates sincerely believed that education was "the civil rights issue of our time" and were impatient and dismissive of anyone who expressed doubts about the efficacy of federal policies. It was an understandable sentiment; today's education reform efforts have a lot in common, in aspirations and ambitions, with reform efforts in the civil rights era. Back then, doubts about the federal role were often thinly veiled arguments to maintain an unjust status quo.

Now, we know this might be a controversial assertion, but: 2015 was not 1965. Advocates often assume that disagreements with their proposed *means* must really be a pretext for rejecting the *end* of promoting educational equity. But it's more useful, and more accurate, to divide education debates into three tiers: principle, process, and practice. There are real, principled disagreements over whether equity requires certain policies. For instance, some advocates believe that the government ought to transfer high performing teachers to low performing schools; others don't think such a policy is necessary, much less prudent.

Even when there is agreement on principle, there are often process disagreements on whether Washington should be making these decisions. Some advocates view federal involvement in teacher evaluation as necessary and proper; others believe that the states are better positioned to determine their own policies.

And even when there is agreement on principle and process, fair-minded citizens can still wonder whether in practice a policy was actually prudent and worth the costs. Twenty-first-century debates over education policy have taken place on all three tiers. It is easy, and often tempting, to reduce these complex and nuanced debates to a simple black-and-white frame. But that misses the point that carefully sorting through these complex difficulties and trade-offs is what a free people do in a large, diverse, and complicated nation.

There tends to be a lot of certitude in education policy, but it's far better to proceed with humility and to be wary of assuming that more policy means that schools are getting better. Even a seasoned expert like Chester E. Finn, Jr., who, as he says in chapter 11, was "educated to doubt the efficacy of grand social engineering schemes," found himself siding with his heart over his head and applauding expansions in the federal role. It's easy to cheer the adoption of school accountability systems, new models of school intervention, teacher evaluation systems, and college- and career-ready academic standards as markers of progress. What really matters is what they all mean in practice.

Perhaps it struck you, as it struck us, that the contributors rarely touched on what ESSA means for classrooms. That might seem like an oversight, but it's actually more of a revelation. For all the high-minded talk about tackling national challenges, it's easy for advocates in Washington to lose sight of the fact that education happens in a classroom, between a teacher and a student. It's exceedingly difficult to project how a law passed by Congress will filter down to the classroom.

There is, and will always be, a wide chasm between the noble aims of federal policy makers and the actual consequences of their policies. In education, it matters far more how well a policy is executed than simply whether it's adopted. In theory, we'd love for a good idea to be implemented faithfully and simply work. But the complex game of telephone involved in any attempt at federal policy makes that unlikely. In general, here is how it works.

Policy makers and advocates in Washington see things that they find troublesome and suggest a potential solution. Elements of that idea get enacted into federal law, though much will be compromised in the legislative process. Then the Department of Education interprets the law, often differently from what its legislators had in mind. After that, state education agencies are tasked with further interpreting, implementing, and monitoring the policy directives they receive. And so on from superintendents, to school district administrators, to principals, and finally to teachers.

Now, federal policy certainly does matter. No Child Left Behind did shift the dynamic between teacher and student, just not quite in the way that advocates hoped. Given the nature of American education, the assumption that any given policy initiative will achieve the ends that its advocates hope is more a leap of faith than a product of reason.

That's why, for our part, we tend to see wisdom in ESSA's efforts to recalibrate and devolve authority. Policy can make people do things, but it can't make them do those things *well*. We believe that the more autonomy teachers and principals have to build communities of learning and professional practice, the more progress we'll see. And we fear that top-down policy directives can hinder that by turning teachers and leaders into creatures of compliance rather than empowered entrepreneurs.

Not everyone sees things the way we do, including many of the contributors to this volume. And that's for the best. Grappling with the tension between maintaining a flexible, diverse education system and ensuring that disadvantaged students aren't left behind is what citizens in a free country do. ESSA is the latest attempt to strike a constructive balance. It won't, and shouldn't, be the last.

Afterword

Anticipating the Outcome of ESSA's Rorschach Test

The Every Student Succeeds Act is an opportunity to reflect on the federal role in education. As I listen to the various commentaries on ESSA, it strikes me that folks are reacting to an education policy Rorschach test. Those who viewed the No Child Left Behind Act and Race to the Top program as unwarranted federal intrusions that tipped the scales toward unduly harsh accountability are now welcoming ESSA as a rebalancing of federal and state authority and a tempering of accountability. Those who believe that a strong federal presence is essential for equity tout the ESSA provisions that maintain accountability for serving the least well-served students.

I propose that in an era when political boundaries—state and national—bear decreasing relevance to economic and social opportunity, we can't afford to pin our hopes on a balkanized education system. For our students to succeed, we must be ambitious in our aspirations for achievement and aggressive in our efforts to address low performance. Without a strong, tactical federal presence, our nation increasingly will be handicapped by uneven educational opportunity and attainment.

I write this essay in anticipation of the 2016 presidential election. You are reading it after it's been settled. The next administration, whoever leads it, will have substantial room to err on the side of too much leeway (by intervening only in cases of the most blatant disregard for state obligations under ESSA) or too much stringency (constraining state policy by aggressive regulation). Hopefully it will strike the right balance. This, to me, is the opportunity and challenge of ESSA. I am optimistic about ESSA's potential to promote more effective policies and practices that advance the education of the most underserved. At the same time, I worry about ESSA's potential to condone complacency.

As I lead the Massachusetts elementary and secondary education system, we are preparing to transition to the ESSA era. Looking back, I can see how my four decades as an educator and leader were influenced by the evolution of federal law in ways that were mostly for the better. In this essay, I provide my reflections on the Elementary and Secondary Education Act, signed into law by President Lyndon B. Johnson, and its most recent reauthorization as ESSA, signed into law by President Barack Obama. ESEA's evolution reflects evolving national interests and aspirations for our state-by-state system of public education.

THE PUBLIC EDUCATION MISSION EVOLVES, CIVIL RIGHTS EMERGE, AND ESEA IS BORN

Historian Patricia Graham concludes that the history of American education is one of improvement and responsiveness to an evolving mission.[1] In the early part of the twentieth century, the mission focused primarily on assimilation as the nation's population grew through immigration. During this period, the Massachusetts state education agency included a "Division of Americanism" with staff who traveled the Commonwealth to provide civics and English language instruction.

As the nation's wealth grew from the 1920s through World War II, the education system shifted its attention to a more progressive curriculum and pedagogy, designed in part to support the individual needs of students. Post–World War II, the dominant mission of our schools became access. Schools were asked to desegregate, educate disabled students, and establish a high school education as the default education credential. The GI Bill placed higher education within the grasp of a growing number of citizens.

With the nation's attention drawn to our history of racial animus and both de facto and de jure segregation, the 1960s witnessed a flurry of civil rights legislation. Under the leadership and political acumen of President Lyndon B. Johnson, the legislation included the 1965 passage of ESEA. Since the 1983 *A Nation at Risk* report, attainment and excellence have moved to the forefront of education policy.[2] ESEA has bridged the policy shift that has evolved from access and opportunity to attainment.

The relationship between states and the federal government is bidirectional, and the histories of state education agencies and ESEA are intertwined.

Each ESEA reauthorization was informed by state and district policies and practices.

ESEA'S EARLY YEARS AND MINE

ESEA established a robust federal presence in K–12 education and represented a substantial policy shift in the locus of influence, with Congress and the federal government more actively steering programs and priorities. At birth, ESEA's focus was on compensating "disadvantaged" children for inadequate schooling.

The Migratory Children's Program of ESEA underwrote my first teaching job, in the mid-1970s in Connecticut. Connecticut used the funds to provide six-week summer programs to boost the schooling of children who fell behind, in large part because of instability in school enrollment. Many of my students' families migrated annually in search of seasonal employment—with work in the shade-grown tobacco farms of the Connecticut River Valley a yearly draw.

ESEA's compensatory focus enabled programs for students that states often lacked an incentive to serve. Migrant children are a prime example. Since they were not stable residents, it is unlikely that Connecticut would have prioritized compensation for the circumstances that migrants faced. Congress, through ESEA, addressed an underserved population and, in the process, my career began by helping to deliver on this policy goal.

IASA, STANDARDS, ASSESSMENTS, AND CONNECTICUT

The early focus on compensatory education evolved through successive ESEA reauthorizations. ESEA's initial focus on inputs shifted to a greater emphasis on outputs. The 1994 Improving America's Schools Act (IASA) adopted the standards-based policy framework that defined a growing number of state reforms. This outcome-driven policy framework required states to develop academic content standards, administer English and mathematics assessments based on the standards (at least once in elementary, middle, and high school grade spans), and report publicly on the productivity of schools and districts.

The movement toward standards-based reform started in the states and was propelled by the federal government. In the 1980s, Connecticut launched standards-based reform, but in hindsight the state got it backward.

Connecticut first developed and implemented assessments in English/language arts and math in grades 4, 6, and 8, based on test blueprints, but without prior content standards.

From 1993 to 1997, I ran the curriculum bureau for the Connecticut Department of Education. My responsibilities included developing Connecticut's first set of academic content standards. IASA encouraged states to develop academic content standards first, and then align assessments to those standards. Thus, federal law not only catalyzed state action, but also helped to guide it.

ACCOUNTABILITY'S BOTTOM-UP EVOLUTION AND PHILADELPHIA

By the late 1990s, the majority of states and many larger school districts had developed systems for rating schools. The next reauthorization of ESEA, the No Child Left Behind Act, drew strongly from state and local implementation of test-based accountability systems.

I served as Executive Director of Assessment and Accountability in Philadelphia from 1997 to 2001, where my responsibilities included developing and implementing the system for evaluating the performance of 265 district schools. The district established a set of principles to guide the development of the accountability system: setting worthwhile targets for performance, ensuring that adults and students share responsibility for performance, and ensuring reciprocal accountability, wherein students and schools could count on support in return for expectations for performance.[3]

The assessment and accountability requirements in NCLB clearly were influenced by state and district experiences. In particular, achievement gains by North Carolina and Texas under their accountability systems drew considerable attention. It is no coincidence that President George W. Bush drew from the system that he knew best for the 2001 reauthorization of ESEA.

NCLB, ACCOUNTABILITY, AND OHIO

No Child Left Behind extended the outcome focus of IASA. In my role as Senior Associate Commissioner for the Ohio Department of Education, I assumed responsibility for aligning Ohio policies with the NCLB requirements.

NCLB expanded the assessment requirement in English and mathematics to grades 3–8, as well as to grade-span assessments in science. NCLB also required that states set learning targets and establish trajectories to achieve 100 percent proficiency within twelve years, disaggregate student test results, and hold schools and districts accountable for failure to meet the targets. Further, NCLB introduced a focus on the educator workforce through the Highly Qualified Teacher standard.

Ohio capitalized on the federal mandate by refining and updating the state assessment and accountability system. Annual testing enabled us to calculate year-to-year individual growth scores, which became a component of our school and district accountability system. This added dimensionality allowed us to distinguish, for example, between two schools of similar achievement levels, one of which demonstrated strong and the other weak year-to-year student learning gains.

Annual testing gave us more data than we ever had before. As a result, information reporting, transparency, and accessibility increased substantially. Ohio and many other states developed longitudinal data systems that allow analyses and insights into the relationship among programs, practices, personnel, and student achievement.

Prior to NCLB, Ohio state law actually forbade data disaggregation. What's more, Ohio had permitted districts to determine which students with disabilities they were to assess, and whether to even report those students' scores. At the time, educators were split on the NCLB disaggregation requirement—particularly as it related to students with disabilities. Many teachers and administrators thought it was unfair and unrealistic to ask students with disabilities to master the general curriculum. Others thought that failing to count them contributed to low expectations. NCLB settled the question: students with disabilities now were firmly on each district's radar, and a period of reflection on appropriate practices and policies was launched.

NCLB has come to be viewed widely as a rigid, top-down, federal straitjacket. Some commentators have gone as far as to assert that nothing worthwhile came from it. I disagree. NCLB's focus on achievement gaps and robust data use represents lasting and positive policy progress.

RACING TO THE TOP IN MASSACHUSETTS

With NCLB extended well beyond the customary reauthorization period, the limitations of its rigid Adequate Yearly Progress (AYP) requirement were amplified. One illustration of NCLB's limitations is that by 2010, more than 80 percent of Massachusetts schools were failing AYP, thus undermining the credibility of the law. Some states lowered performance standards on their tests in an effort to blunt the impact of NCLB.

Race to the Top (RTTT) pushed federal policy forward, even as Congress failed to reauthorize NCLB. By building on the widely regarded strengths and weaknesses of NCLB, RTTT continued federal attention to accountability for results while requiring that educator standards be grounded in effectiveness, not simply paper qualifications. With NCLB sometimes characterized as a "race to the bottom," it is no coincidence that the Obama administration chose "Race to the Top" as the brand for an initiative that required states to aim for academic performance targets that signal college and career readiness.

While RTTT was seen as federal intrusion in many quarters, in Massachusetts it solidified a set of initiatives that we initially undertook in 2008, including a more nuanced accountability system than NCLB's AYP provided, a more aggressive and staged approach to support and intervention with low performing schools and districts, an upgrading of English/language arts and mathematics academic content standards, a new-generation student assessment system, and a focus on educator development informed by an evaluation system that includes attention to student learning impact.

In Massachusetts, then, as in a number of other states, RTTT propelled a set of reforms that we already had undertaken. RTTT helped motivate the legislature to codify in statute upgrades to our emerging accountability and assistance program. Further, RTTT's funding allowed us to boost execution of the reforms during the recession, when the resulting fiscal austerity would have slowed down implementation.

LEADING A STATE AND LOOKING AHEAD

As I compose this essay from the vantage point of six months into the Every Student Succeeds Act, it is clear that the law is promoting substantial discussion about innovative assessment approaches and the architecture of accountability systems. Much of the discussion concerns broadening the inputs and outputs of accountability systems beyond test scores. I anticipate that this activity will yield worthwhile advances in codifying elements of quality that are important barometers of school and district efficacy. At the same time, incorporating a broad array of variables to infer school health has the potential to mask the bottom line: are students learning, and are they learning what matters to be prepared for opportunities in the twenty-first century?

ESSA clearly gives Massachusetts flexibility to run our current system and incorporate refinements that we could not have implemented under NCLB. The system we have been implementing for the past several years is much more nuanced than was AYP. We incorporate growth and status achievement measures and we classify schools and districts into five categories, with varying levels of intervention and support tied to those categories. Until ESSA, we have been operating this system under a waiver from the US Department of Education. Now, we can do so under the auspices of the statute.

AN APPEAL TO THE NEXT ADMINISTRATION

Evidence abounds that America has lost its educational standing. On the Program for International Student Assessment (PISA), the United States performs in the middle of the pack internationally. According to the Organization for Economic Cooperation and Development (OECD), whereas the United States led the world in college attainment two or three decades ago, at least a dozen nations have surpassed us at this point.

It can be argued that in the United States, we are doing no worse than we were twenty or thirty years ago. But this means that we have plateaued while many of the world's nations have doubled down, invested smartly, and aimed higher, and now surpass us. In short, many nations are "upping their educational game" in pursuit of a brighter future for their citizens.

If we believe that our nation's future is as tied to education as it is to energy, health care, technology, transportation, and the environment, then we should be alarmed. It is particularly sobering to realize that stagnation of US educational attainment cannot be attributed to lack of investment. Over the past four decades, holding the value of the dollar constant, the United States has effectively doubled real per-pupil spending. Some, but not all, of the increase can be explained by the fact that we have gone the extra mile to serve all students, including those with disabilities. While this helps explain the increased investment, it does not explain the lack of improved educational attainment over the same period.

I believe that securing a sound future for the United States demands a coherent federal approach to education. We must continue to refine the relationship among state, local, and federal government. The fragmentation of our state-by-state approach, and the resulting disparities in educational attainment within and among states, bodes poorly for us. The federal government can and should play the role of promoting, investing in, and demanding excellence and equity.

We must be ambitious and aggressive in our efforts to address low academic performance. The Every Student Succeeds Act can be the catalyst for this role, but it will depend on what the next administration sees in this Rorschach test. ESSA can help foster a productive mix of federal, state, and local direction, but does not guarantee it. The next administration will have to exercise the resolute leadership that ESSA permits if we are to eliminate the uneven educational opportunity and attainment that increasingly handicap our nation's future.

Mitchell D. Chester
Commissioner of Elementary and Secondary Education,
Massachusetts Department of Elementary and
Secondary Education

Notes

Introduction

1. "No Child Left Behind's Successor," *Wall Street Journal*, November 29, 2015, http://www.wsj
.com/articles/no-child-left-behinds-successor-1448838727.
2. Washington Research Project and NAACP Legal Defense Fund, Inc., *ESEA Title I: Is It Helping
Poor Children?* (Washington, DC: US Department of Health, Education & Welfare, Office of
Education, 1969), http://files.eric.ed.gov/fulltext/ED036600.pdf.
3. "The PDK/Gallup Poll of the Public's Attitudes Toward Public Schools," http://pdkpoll.pdkintl
.org/october.
4. David Brooks, "Race to Sanity," *New York Times*, June 3, 2010, http://www.nytimes.com/2010
/06/04/opinion/04brooks.html.
5. Alyson Klein, "Alexander: Federal Role on K–12 Will Be 'Very Different' Under ESSA,"
Education Week, December 17, 2015, http://blogs.edweek.org/edweek/campaign-k-12/2015/12
/alexander_senate_will_hold_thr.html?print=1.

Chapter 1

1. For a detailed historical analysis of the evolution of federal education policy, see Patrick
McGuinn, *No Child Left Behind and the Transformation of Federal Education Policy 1965–2005*
(Lawrence: University Press of Kansas, 2006).
2. As cited in Julie Roy Jeffrey, *Education for Children of the Poor: A Study of the Origins and
Implementation of the Elementary and Secondary Education Act of 1965* (Columbus: Ohio
State University Press, 1978), 3.
3. "Remarks in Johnson City, Texas, Upon Signing the Elementary and Secondary Education
Bill, April 11, 1965," *Public Papers of the Presidents of the United States: Lyndon B. Johnson,
1965*, volume I, entry 181 (Washington, DC: Government Printing Office, 1966), 412–414.
4. For a thorough discussion of the political context surrounding the passage of ESEA, see
Phillip Meranto, *The Politics of Federal Aid to Education in 1965* (Syracuse: Syracuse
University Press, 1967); Eugene Eidenberg and Roy D. Morey, *An Act of Congress: The
Legislative Process and the Making of Education Policy* (New York: W.W. Norton and Co.,
1969); and Hugh Davis Graham, *The Uncertain Triumph* (Chapel Hill: The University of North
Carolina Press, 1984).
5. The legislation contained four additional titles. Title II of the ESEA created a five-year
program (funded at $100 million for the first year) to fund the purchase of library resources,
instructional materials, and textbooks by state educational agencies (which were then to loan
them out to local public and private school students). Title III created a five-year program
of matching grants to local educational agencies to finance supplemental education centers
and services. (It was also allocated $100 million for the first year.) Title IV gave the US Com-

missioner of Education the authority to enter into contracts with universities and state educational agencies to conduct educational research, surveys, and demonstrations. This title received $100 million in funding for the five-year period. Finally, Title V provided $25 million over five years to strengthen state departments of education.

6. As cited in Joel Spring, *The Sorting Machine: National Educational Policy Since 1945* (New York: David McKay Company, Inc., 1976), 225.

7. Title II provided financial assistance to local education agencies (districts) to help them develop the capacity to support reform efforts as well as aid for libraries and instructional materials. Title III provided matching grants for the creation of supplementary educational centers and services to promote innovation, while Title IV funded university-based educational research and training. Title V provided support for state education agencies, and Title VI was entitled "general provisions."

8. As quoted in James Sundquist, *Politics and Policy: The Eisenhower, Kennedy, and Johnson Years* (Washington, DC: The Brookings Institution, 1968), 215.

9. Eugene Eidenberg and Roy Morey, *An Act of Congress: The Legislative Process and the Making of Education Policy*, 247.

10. Graham, *The Uncertain Triumph*, 193.

11. See Paul Peterson et al., *When Federalism Works* (Washington, DC: Brookings Institution Press, 1986), 136–140 for a more detailed discussion of the local tendency to shift federal funds from redistributive programs to other purposes.

12. The USOE was ill suited to a compliance role—it had long been a small, passive organization that focused on collecting and disseminating statistical data on education and did little else. The result, as John and Anne Hughes noted, was that "if USOE had limitations on its policy-making authority and capability—and these have been legion—its ability to enforce its policies has been even more limited. The state agencies and the local districts, by and large, were used to going their own ways, which often meant disregarding federal requirements." John Hughes and Anne Hughes, *Equal Education: A New National Strategy* (Bloomington: Indiana University Press, 1972), 50.

13. John E. Chubb, "Excessive Regulation: The Case of Federal Aid to Education," *Political Science Quarterly* 100, no. 2 (Summer 1985): 287.

14. Diane Ravitch, *The Troubled Crusade: American Education 1945–1980* (New York: Basic Books, 1983), 312.

15. Michael Newman, *America's Teachers* (New York: Longman, 1994), 166.

16. Ravitch, *The Troubled Crusade*, 267.

17. The move was widely regarded as a political payback for the endorsement and support of the National Education Association and the American Federation of Teachers during the 1976 election. Legislation to create a new federal department for education had been introduced 130 times between 1908 and 1975, but the idea had always generated a great deal of political opposition from a variety of interests. D. T. Stallings, "A Brief History of the U.S. Department of Education, 1979–2002," *Phi Delta Kappan* 83, no. 9 (May 2002): 677.

18. For an extended discussion of the expansion of federal compensatory education programs and the accompanying increase in federal education regulations, see Paul Paterson's "Background Paper" in *Making the Grade: Report of the Twentieth Century Fund Task Force on Federal Elementary and Secondary Education Policy* (New York: Twentieth Century Fund, 1983).

19. *Historic Documents of 1980* (Washington, DC: Congressional Quarterly, Inc., 1981), 583–584.

20. Parris N. Glendening and Mavis Mann Reeves, *Pragmatic Federalism* (Pacific Palisades, CA: Palisades Publishers, 1984), 243.

21. As D. T. Stallings has noted, "The new administration planned to move the Department of Education away from awarding categorical grants and toward the awarding of block grants, with the goal of eventually eliminating federal grants entirely, which would cause the federal role to revert to what it had been in 1838—nothing more than collecting statistics." Stallings, "A Brief History," 678.

22. Deborah A. Verstegen and David L. Clark, "The Diminution in Federal Expenditures for Education During the Reagan Administration," *Phi Delta Kappan* 70, no. 2 (October 1988): 137.

23. The National Commission on Excellence in Education, *A Nation At Risk: The Imperative for Educational Reform* (Washington, DC: Government Printing Office, 1983).

24. Thomas Toch, *In the Name of Excellence* (Oxford, UK: Oxford University Press, 1991), 36.

25. Paul Manna, "Federalism, Agenda Setting, and the Dynamics of Federal Education Policy" (presented at the annual meeting of the American Political Science Association, August 29 through September 1, 2002).

26. "White House Fact Sheet on the President's Education Strategy," *bushlibrary.tamu.edu*, April 18, 1991, http://bushlibrary.tamu.edu/papers/1991/91041807.html.

27. Heather Bodell, *Goals 2000: A National Framework For America's Schools* (Arlington, VA: Education Funding Research Council, 1994), 8.

28. Richard Riley, "Reflections on Goals 2000," *Teachers College Record* 96, no. 3 (Spring 1995): 1.

29. Marshall Smith, Brett Scoll, and Valena Pliskp, "The Improving America's Schools Act: A New Partnership," in Jack Jennings, ed., *National Issues in Education: Elementary and Secondary Education Act* (Washington, DC: Phi Delta Kappa, 1995), 7.

30. The legislation also contained an important boost to public school choice by allowing school districts to use federal Title I funds to enable eligible students to transfer to another public school within that system and by providing a small amount ($15 million in the first year) of federal start-up funds for charter schools.

31. Interview with author, March 23, 2003.

32. Jack Jennings, *Why National Standards and Tests?* (Thousand Oaks, CA: Sage Publications, 1998), 127–128.

33. Elizabeth Harrington, "Education Spending Up 64% Under No Child Left Behind But Test Scores Improve Little," *U.S. News and World Report*, September 26, 2011, http://www.cnsnews.com/news/article/ education-spending-64-under-no-child-left-behind-test-scores-improve-little.

34. For detailed analyses of the NCLB from the viewpoint of state implementers, see "State Requirements Under NCLB," Education Commission of the States, January 2003, www.ecs .org; and "NGA Summary of the Timeline Requirements of NCLB," National Governors Association, www.nga.org.

35. A school that failed to meet state performance targets for two consecutive years must be given technical assistance from the district to help it improve, and students in that school had to be given the option to transfer to another public school in the district. If a school did not improve in the third year, students had to be given the option of using their share of Title I funds to pay for tutoring or other supplemental educational services. Schools that failed for four consecutive years had to implement corrective actions, such as replacing staff or adopting a new curriculum, and in the fifth year the failing school had to be reconstituted with a new governance structure (such as by reopening as a charter school).

36. In March 2003, for example, the Bush Department of Education threatened to withhold $783,000 in federal funds from Georgia for the state's failure to meet the testing requirements

of the 1994 law. For more information on this, see Erik W. Robelen, "Department Levies $783,000 Title I Penalty on GA," *Education Week*, May 28, 2003, http://www.edweek.org/ew/articles/2003/05/28/38hea.h22.html.

37. While improving educational "equity" clearly remains a central goal of federal education policy, NCLD defines this goal very differently from the original ESEA. The old "equity regime" had equalization of school resources and access as its central objectives. NCLB, meanwhile, defines equity in terms of closing racial and socioeconomic achievement gaps as measured on standardized tests. It also supplements this goal with a concern for improving the educational performance of all students in America.

38. Ironically, however, even as federal accountability for K–12 education reform is being scaled back somewhat, the pressure is increasing to hold the higher education sector accountable for better and more efficient student learning outcomes. For more on this development, see Christopher Loss and Patrick McGuinn, eds., *The Convergence of K–12 and Higher Education: Policies and Programs in a Changing Era* (Cambridge, MA: Harvard Education Press, 2016).

Chapter 2

1. Patrick J. McGuinn, *No Child Left Behind and the Transformation of Federal Education Policy, 1965–2005* (Lawrence: University Press of Kansas, 2006).

2. Ibid.

3. Frederick M. Hess and Michael J. Petrilli, *No Child Left Behind: A Primer* (New York: Peter Lang, 2006).

4. McGuinn, *No Child Left Behind*, 9.

5. Jesse H. Rhodes, *An Education in Politics: The Origin and Evolution of No Child Left Behind* (Ithaca, NY: Cornell University Press, 2012).

6. McGuinn, *No Child Left Behind*.

7. Ibid.

8. Rhodes, *An Education in Politics*.

9. Peter Baker, "An Unlikely Partnership Left Behind," *Washington Post*, November 5, 2007, http://www.washingtonpost.com/wp-dyn/content/article/2007/11/04/AR2007110401450.html.

10. United States Department of Education, *Title I Accountability and School Improvement from 2001 to 2004* (Washington, DC: US Department of Education, 2006), https://www2.ed.gov/rschstat/eval/.../tassie3.doc; Paul Manna, *Collision Course: Federal Education Policy Meets State and Local Realities* (Washington, DC: CQ Press, 2010).

11. Doug Mesecar, "The Rise and Fall of Supplemental Educational Services: Policy Implication for Government Markets," American Enterprise Institute, January 15, 2015, https://www.aei.org/wp-content/uploads/2015/01/The-Rise-and-Fall-of-Supplemental-Educational-Services.pdf.

12. Phi Delta Kappan/Gallup Poll, "The PDK/Gallup Poll of the Public's Attitudes Toward Public Schools," http://pdkpoll.org.

13. Education Commission of the States, *ECS Report to the Nation: State Implementation of the No Child Left Behind Act* (Denver: Education Commission of the States, 2004).

14. Manna, *Collision Course*.

15. Alex Usher, "AYP Results for 2010–11" (Washington, DC: Center on Education Policy, 2012), http://cep-dc.org/displayDocument.cfm?DocumentID=414.

16. Rhodes, *An Education in Politics*.

17. McGuinn, *No Child Left Behind*.

18. David J. Hoff, "Education Department Announces More Flexible Approach to NCLB Law,"

Education Week, April 7, 2005, http://www.edweek.org/ew/articles/2005/04/07/31spellings
_web.h24.html.

19. Rhodes, *An Education in Politics.*

20. Manna, *Collision Course.*

21. Rhodes, *An Education in Politics.*

22. Sam Dillon, "For a Key Education Law, Reauthorization Stalls," *New York Times*, November 6, 2007, http://www.nytimes.com/2007/11/06/washington/06child.html.

23. Henry Giroux, "Obama's Dilemma: Postpartisan Politics and the Crisis of American Education," *Harvard Educational Review* 79, no. 2 (2009): 250–266.

24. John W. Kingdon, *Agendas, Alternatives, and Public Policies*, 2nd ed. (Boston: Little, Brown & Company, 1995).

25. Alyson Klein, "Was Race to the Top Authorized?" *Education Week*, May 6, 2010, http://blogs.edweek.org/edweek/campaign-k-12/2010/05/was_race_to_the_top_authorized.html; Patrick J. McGuinn, "Presidential Policymaking: Race to the Top, Executive Power, and the Obama Education Agenda," *The Forum* 12, no. 1 (2014): 61–79.

26. United States Department of Education, *Race to the Top Program Executive Summary* (Washington, DC: United States Department of Education, 2009), http://www2.ed.gov/programs/racetothetop/executive-summary.pdf. The four core areas involved college ready standards, data systems, effective teachers, and turning around low achieving schools.

27. McGuinn, "Presidential Policymaking."

28. Sam Dillon, "States Receive a Reading List: New Standards for Education," *New York Times*, June 2, 2010, http://www.nytimes.com/2010/06/03/education/03standards.html.

29. Stephen Sawchuck, "NEA's Delegates Vote 'No Confidence' in Race to the Top," *Education Week*, July 4, 2010, http://blogs.edweek.org/edweek/teacherbeat/2010/07/neas_delegates_vote _no_confide_2.html.

30. Tamar Lewin, "Many States Adopt National Standards for Their Schools," *New York Times*, July 20, 2010, http://www.nytimes.com/2010/07/21/education/21standards.html.

31. Alexis Simendinger, "Feeling Legislative Chill, Obama Flexes Executive Muscles," *Real Clear Politics*, September 26, 2011, http://www.realclearpolitics.com/articles/2011/09/26/feeling _legislative_chill_obama_flexes_executive_muscles_111471.html; Joseph P. Viteritti, "The Federal Role in School Reform: Obama's Race to the Top," *Notre Dame Law Review* 87 (2011): 2087.

32. Chester E. Finn and Frederick M. Hess, "On Leaving No Child Behind," *Public Interest* 157 (2004): 35; Lewin, "Many States"; Sawchuck, "NEA's Delegates"; Viteritti, "The Federal Role in School Reform"; Lawrence A. Uzzell, "No Child Left Behind: The Dangers of Centralized Education Policy," Cato Institute, May 31, 2005, http://www.cato.org/pubs/pas/pa544.pdf.

33. Viteritti, "The Federal Role in School Reform."

34. The four states that did not apply for RTTT are Alaska, North Dakota, Texas, and Vermont.

35. William G. Howell, "Results of President Obama's Race to the Top," *Education Next* 15, no. 4 (2015), http://educationnext.org/results-president-obama-race-to-the-top-reform/.

36. McGuinn, "Presidential Policymaking."

37. Simendinger, "Feeling Legislative Chill, Obama Flexes Executive Muscles."

38. Wayne Riddle, "Major Accountability Themes of Approved State Applications for NCLB Waivers," Center on Education Policy, March 2012, https://www.cep-dc.org/cfcontent_file .cfm?Attachment/Riddle_Paper_WaiverApp_030812.pdf.

39. The White House, "Obama Administration Approves NCLB Flexibility Request for Maine (Washington, DC: The White House, 2013), http://www.ed.gov/news/press-releases/obama-administration-approves-nclb-flexibility-request-maine.

40. Lyndsey Layton, "Christie Goes from Common Core Supporter to Critic, Blames Obama," *Washington Post*, https://www.washingtonpost.com/local/education/christie-goes-from-common-core-supporter-to-critic-blames-obama/2015/02/17/5e80e66a-b6c4-11e4-aa05-1ce812b3fdd2_story.html

41. David Whitman, "The Surprising Roots of the Common Core: How Conservatives Gave Rise to 'Obamacore,'" The Brookings Institution, September 2015, http://www.brookings.edu/~/media/research/files/papers/2015/09/08-conservative-roots-of-the-common-core-whitman/surprising-conservative-roots-of-the-common-core_final.pdf, 2.

42. McGuinn, "Presidential Policymaking."

43. Ibid.

44. Mike Rose, "AFT Calls for Moratorium on Common Core Consequences," American Federation of Teachers, May 1, 2013, http://www.aft.org/news/aft-calls-moratorium-common-core-consequences#sthash.sf6sx0t1.dpuf.

45. Kevin Carey, "Why G.O.P. and Teachers Are Uniting to Stop Obama Effort to Help Poor Schools," *New York Times*, May 17, 2016, http://www.nytimes.com/2016/05/18/upshot/why-poor-districts-receive-less-government-school-funding-than-rich-ones.html; Whitman, "The Surprising Roots of the Common Core."

46. Valerie Strauss, "Arne Duncan: 'White Suburban Moms' Upset That Common Core Shows Their Kids Aren't 'Brilliant,'" *Washington Post*, November 16, 2013, https://www.washingtonpost.com/news/answer-sheet/wp/2013/11/16/arne-duncan-white-surburban-moms-upset-that-common-core-shows-their-kids-arent-brilliant/.

47. William J. Crotty, *The Obama Presidency: Promise and Performance* (Plymouth, UK: Lexington Books, 2012), 76.

48. Jeffrey R. Henig, "The Politics of Data Use," *Teachers College Record* 114, no. 11 (2012); Kenneth Prewitt, Thomas A. Schwandt, and Miren L. Straf, eds., *Using Science as Evidence in Public Policy* (Washington, DC: The National Academies Press, 2012).

Chapter 3

1. Rep. John Kline (R-MN), chairman of the House Education Committee, personal communication, June 9, 2016.

2. Sen. Patty Murray (D-WA), personal communication, April 20, 2016.

3. Sen. Lamar Alexander (R-TN), personal communication, June 6, 2016.

4. Kline, interview with author, June 9, 2016.

5. Alexander, interview with author, June 6, 2016.

6. Rep. Robert C. "Bobby" Scott, personal communication, April 20, 2016.

7. Kline, personal communication, June 9, 2016.

8. Alexander, personal communication, June 6, 2016.

Chapter 4

1. US Department of Education, January 11, 2016, http://www2.ed.gov/about/overview/budget/budget16/16action.pdf.

2. Amy Golod, "Common Core: Myths and Facts," *U.S. News and World Report*, March 4, 2014,

3. http://www.usnews.com/news/special-reports/a-guide-to-common-core/articles/2014/03/04/common-core-myths-and-facts.

4. Association of University Centers on Disabilities, "Every Student Achieves Act (S. 1177) Preliminary Summary of Provisions That Directly Impact Students with Disabilities," December 10, 2015, https://www.aucd.org/docs/policy/education/2015_1210_essa_provisions.pdf.

5. American Educational Research Association, American Psychological Association, and National Council on Measurement in Education, *The Standards for Educational and Psychological Testing* (Washington, DC: American Psychological Association 2014), http://www.apa .org/science/programs/testing/standards.aspx.

6. Data Quality Campaign, "Empowering Parents and Communities Through Quality Public Reporting," April 2014, http://dataqualitycampaign.org/wp-content/uploads/2016/03/ Empowering-Parents-and-Communities-Through-Quality-Public-Reporting-Primer_1.pdf.

7. Vernon G. Smith and Antonia Szymanski, "Critical Thinking: More Than Test Scores," *NCPEA International Journal of Educational Leadership Preparation* 8, no. 2 (2013): 16–26, http://files.eric.ed.gov/fulltext/EJ1016160.pdf.

8. John Larmer and John R. Mergendoller, "Seven Essentials for Project-Based Learning," *ASCD* 1, no. 6 (2010): 34–37, http://www.ascd.org/publications/educational_leadership/sept10/vol68 /num01/Seven_Essentials_for_Project-Based_Learning.aspx.

9. Daniel Koretz et al., *The Reliability of Scores from the 1992 Vermont Portfolio Assessment Program* (CSE Report 355) (Los Angeles: University of California, Los Angeles, National Center for Research on Evaluation, Standards, and Student Testing, 1993), http://cresst.org /publications/cresst-publication-2727/.

10. Catherine Gewertz, "ESSA's Flexibility on Assessment Elicits Qualms from Testing Experts," *Education Week*, December 8, 2015, http://www.edweek.org/ew/articles/2015/12/21/essas-flexibility-on-assessment-elicits-qualms-from.html.

11. Ibid.

12. Brian Gill et al., *State and Local Implementation of the No Child Left Behind Act, Volume IV— Title I School Choice and Supplemental Educational Services: Interim Report* (Santa Monica, CA: RAND Corporation, 2008), http://www.rand.org/pubs/reprints/RP1332.html.

13. Ibid.

14. US Government Accountability Office, *No Child Left Behind: Education Should Clarify Guidance and Address Potential Compliance Issue for Schools in Corrective Action and Restructuring Status* (GAO-07-1035) (Washington, DC: US Government Accountability Office, 2007), http://www.gao.gov/assets/270/266037.pdf.

15. Morgan S. Polikoff and Stephani L. Wrabel, "When Is 100% Not 100%? The Use of Safe Harbor to Make Adequate Yearly Progress," *Education Finance and Policy* 8, no. 2 (Spring 2013): 251–270.

16. Drew H. Gitomer, *Teacher Quality in a Changing Policy Landscape: Improvements in the Teacher Pool* (Princeton, NJ: Educational Testing Services, 2007).

Chapter 5

1. National Governors Association, "Nation's Governors Endorse Every Student Succeeds Act," November 30, 2015, http://www.nga.org/cms/home/news-room/news-releases/2015--news-releases/col2-content/nations-governors-endorse-esea.html.

2. Raegan Miller, "Secret Recipes Revealed: Demystifying the Title I, Part A Funding Formulas," Center for American Progress, August 17, 2009, http://www.americanprogress.org/issues /education/report/2009/08/17/6544/secret-recipes-revealed-demystifying-the-title-i-part-a-funding-formulas; Gareth Davies, *See Government Grow: Education Politics from Johnson to Reagan* (Lawrence: University of Kansas Press, 2007).

3. See, for example, Raj Chetty et al., "How Does Your Kindergarten Classroom Affect Your Earnings? Evidence from Project STAR," *Quarterly Journal of Economics* 126, no. 4 (November 2011): 1593–1660. More recent research also confirms that gains in test scores that result from interventions, such as being assigned to a particularly effective teacher or attending a school

facing accountability pressure, also predict improvements in adult outcomes. Raj Chetty, John Friedman, and Jonah Rockoff, "Measuring the Impacts of Teachers II: Teacher Value-Added and Student Outcomes in Adulthood," *American Economic Review* 104, no. 9 (September 2014): 2633–2799; David J. Deming et al., "School Accountability, Postsecondary Attainment, and Earnings," *Review of Economics and Statistics*, forthcoming (doi:10.1162/REST_a_00598).

4. C. Kirabo Jackson, "Non-Cognitive Ability, Test Scores, and Teacher Quality: Evidence from 9th Grade Teachers in North Carolina" (NBER working paper no. 18624, National Bureau of Economic Research, 2012).

5. Ohio Department of Education, "Testing Report and Recommendations," January 2015, http:// education.ohio.gov/getattachment/Topics/Testing/Sections/Related-Information/Testing-Report-and-Recommendations-2015-1.pdf.aspx.

6. David Deming et al., "School Choice, School Quality and Postsecondary Attainment," *American Economic Review* 104, no. 3 (2014): 991–1014.

7. Grover Whitehurst and Katherine Lindquist, "Test More, Not Less," Brown Center Chalkboard, Brookings Institution, January 22, 2014, https://www.brookings.edu/research /test-more-not-less/.

8. The indicators based on academic achievement, graduation rates, and the progress of English language learners toward proficiency must simply all receive "substantial" weight and, in the aggregate, "much greater weight" than whatever states use as their additional indicator of school quality or student success.

9. Thomas S. Dee and Brian Jacob, "The Impact of No Child Left Behind on Student Achievement," *Journal of Policy Analysis and Management* 30, no. 3 (2011): 418–446; Manyee Wong, Thomas D. Cook, and Peter M. Steiner, "Adding Design Elements to Improve Time Series Designs: No Child Left Behind as an Example of Causal Pattern-Matching," *Journal of Research on Educational Effectiveness* 8, no. 2 (2015): 245–279.

10. Thomas Dee, "School Turnarounds: Evidence from the 2009 Stimulus" (NBER working paper no. 17990, National Bureau of Economic Research, 2012).

11. Michael J. Petrilli, "The Problem with "Implementation Is the Problem," in Frederick M. Hess and Chester E. Finn, Jr., eds., *No Remedy Left Behind: Lessons from a Half-Decade of NCLB* (Washington, DC: AEI Press, 2007), 96–117.

12. Paul Manna, *Collision Course: Federal Education Policy Meets State and Local Realities* (Washington, DC: Congressional Quarterly Press, 2011), 76–81.

13. Nora Gordon, "The Best Part of NCLB Reauthorization You Haven't Heard Of," EdNext Blog, *Education Next*, April 23, 2015, http://educationnext.org/best-part-nclb-reauthorization-youve-never-heard/.

14. Marguerite Roza et al., "How Within-District Spending Inequities Help Some Schools to Fail," *Brookings Papers on Education Policy*, no. 7 (2004): 201–227.

15. Paul Manna and Michael J. Petrilli, "Double Standard? 'Scientifically Based Research' and the No Child Left Behind Act," in *When Research Matters: How Scholarship Influences Education Policy*, ed. F. M. Hess (Cambridge, MA: Harvard Education Press, 2008).

Chapter 6

1. David V. Anderson et al., "Heartland Institute Education Experts React to House Approval of the Every Student Succeeds Act," Heartland Institute, December 3, 2015, https://www .heartland.org/news-opinion/news/heartland-institute-education-experts-react-to-house-approval-of-the-every-student-succeeds-act.

2. Conor Williams, "Williams: Why Progressives Should Fear, Conservatives Should Hate and Obama Should Veto the NCLB Rewrite," The 74 Million, December 2, 2015, https://www

.the74million.org/article/williams-why-progressives-should-fear-conservatives-should-hate-and-obama-should-veto-the-nclb-rewrite.

3. The Education Trust, "The Education Trust Statement on the Every Student Succeeds Act of 2015,"December2,2015,https://edtrust.org/press_release/the-education-trust-statement-on-the-every-student-succeeds-act-of-2015/.

4. Office of the Press Secretary, "Remarks by the President at Every Student Succeeds Act Signing Ceremony," *The White House*, https://www.whitehouse.gov/the-press-office/2015/12/10/remarks-president-every-student-succeeds-act-signing-ceremony.

5. Emmett McGroarty, "Obama Administration Reveals GOP Leaders' Betrayal on Common Core in Ed Bill," The Pulse 2016, December 21, 2015, http://www.educationviews.org/obama-administration-reveals-gop-leaders-betrayal-common-core-ed-bill/.

6. Elizabeth Davidson et al., "Fifty Ways to Leave a Child Behind: Idiosyncrasies and Discrepancies in States' Implementation of NCLB," *Educational Researcher* 44, no. 6 (2015), http://edr.sagepub.com/content/44/6/347.full?keytype=ref&siteid=spedr&ijkey=zSQ1%2FxVmCgEcA#xref-fn-25-1.

7. Matthew M. Chingos, "Breaking the Curve: Promises and Pitfalls of Using NAEP Data to Assess the State of Student Achievement," Urban Institute, October 2015, http://www.urban.org/sites/default/files/alfresco/publication-pdfs/2000484-Breaking-the-Curve-Promises-and-Pitfalls-of-Using-NAEP-Data-to-Assess-the-State-Role-in-Student-Achievement.pdf.

8. John Chubb and Constance Clark," The New State Achievement Gap: How Federal Waivers Could Make It Worse—Or Better," Education Sector, 2013, http://www.educationsector.org/sites/default/files/publications/NewStateAchieveGap-RELEASED.pdf.

9. US Department of Education, "ED Data Express: Data about Elementary & Secondary Schools in the U.S.--Custom Reports," http://eddataexpress.ed.gov/state-tables-main.cfm.

10. Chad Aldeman, "New K–12 Education Law Leaves Schools Behind," *Washington Post*, December 11, 2015, https://www.washingtonpost.com/opinions/new-k-12-education-law-leaves-schools-behind/2015/12/11/e0ffb894-9f73-11e5-a3c5-c77f2cc5a43c_story.html.

11. Thomas Ahn and Jacob Vigdor, "The Impact of No Child Left Behind's Accountability Sanctions on School Performance: Regression Discontinuity Evidence from North Carolina" (preliminary draft, February 2013), http://econ.msu.edu/seminars/docs/ahnvigdornclb_uva.pdf.

12. David J. Deming et al., "When Does Accountability Work?" *Education Next* 16, no.1 (winter 2016), http://educationnext.org/when-does-accountability-work-texas-system/.

13. US Department of Education, "Fiscal Year 2017 President's Budget," February 9, 2016, http://www2.ed.gov/about/overview/budget/budget17/17pbapt.pdf.

14. Paul Manna and Jennifer Wallner, "Stepping-Stones to Success or a Bridge Too Far?" in *Carrots, Sticks, and the Bully Pulpit*, eds. Frederick M. Hess and Andrew P. Kelly (Cambridge, MA: Harvard Education Press, 2011).

15. EdFacts accountability data, http://www2.ed.gov/about/inits/ed/edfacts/index.html.

16. NCTQ, "State of the States 2012: Teacher Effectiveness Policies," 2012, http://www.nctq.org/dmsView/State_of_the_ States_2012_Teacher_Effectiveness_Policies_NCTQ_Report.

17. Chad Aldeman and Carolyn Chuong, "Teacher Evaluations in an Era of Rapid Change: From 'Unsatisfactory' to 'Needs Improvement,'" Bellwether Education Partners, August 2014, http://bellwethereducation.org/sites/default/files/Bellwether_TeacherEval_Final_Web.pdf.

18. Martin R. West, "From Evidence-Based Programs to an Evidence-Based System: Opportunitites Under the Every Student Succeeds Act," Brookings Institute, February 5, 2016, http://www.brookings.edu/research/papers/2016/02/05-evidence-based-system-opportunities-under-essa-west.

19. Matthew M. Chingos and Grover J. "Russ" Whitehurst, "Class Size: What Research Says and What It Means for State Policy," Brookings Institute, May 11, 2011, http://www.brookings.edu /research/papers/2011/05/11-class-size-whitehurst-chingos.

20. Tables 1 and 3 from National Center for Education Statistics, "Projections of Education Statistics to 2022," 41st ed., https://nces.ed.gov/pubs2014/2014051.pdf.

21. US Department of Education, Institute of Education Sciences, "Fiscal Year 2016 Budget Request," https://www2.ed.gov/about/overview/budget/budget16/justifications/w-ies.pdf. Inflation adjustment from Bureau of Labor Statistics, "CPI Inflation Calculator," http://data .bls.gov/cgi-bin/cpicalc.pl?cost1=517.00&year1=2006&year2=2015.

22. Democrats for Education Reform, "[Release] New Grants for Public Charters Are Latest Milestone in Obama's Ed Reform Legacy," September 28, 2015, http://dfer.org/ release-new-grants-for-public-charter-schools-are-latest-milestone-in-obamas-education-reform-legacy/.

23. For more on the performance compact idea, see Chad Aldeman, Kelly Robson, and Andy Smarick, "Pacts Americana: Balancing National Interests, State Autonomy, and Education Accountability," Bellwether Education Partners, June 2015, http://bellwethereducation.org /sites/default/files/Bellwether_ESEA_June2015.pdf.

Chapter 7

1. The Education Gadfly, "ESSA Oversight Hearing: Full Transcript," Thomas B. Fordham Institute, April 13, 2016, http://edexcellence.net/articles/ essa-oversight-hearing-full-transcript.

2. See Paul Manna, *Collision Course: Federal Education Policy Meets State and Local Realities* (Washington, DC: CQ Press, 2011); Edgar L. Morphet and David L. Jesser, *Emerging State Responsibilities for Education* (Denver: Improving State Leadership in Education, 1970).

3. Arnold F. Shober, *In Common No More: The Politics of the Common Core State Standards* (Boulder, CO: Praeger Publishers, 2016).

4. Aimee Rogstad Guidera, "From Building Systems to Using Their Data," in *A Byte at the Apple*, eds. Marci Kanstoroom and Eric C. Osberg (Washington, DC: Thomas B. Fordham Institute, 2008), 248–65.

5. §200.2(b)(4)(i).

6. Kevin Carey, "Hot Air: How States Inflate Their Educational Progress Under NCLB," *Education Sector* (May 2006), http://educationpolicy.air.org/sites/default/files/publications /Hot_Air_NCLB.pdf.

7. Alyson Klein, "ESEA Reauthorization: Four Ways a New Law Would Differ from NCLB Waivers," *Education Week*, December 7, 2015, http://blogs.edweek.org/edweek/campaign-k-12/2015/12/esea_reauthorization_four_big_.html; Wisconsin Center for Education Research, "ASSETS: Member States," April 26, 2016, http://assets.wceruw.org/aboutus/memberStates .aspx.

8. Tony Evers, "State of the State Address" (Council of Chief State School Officers Legislative Conference, Washington, DC, April 6, 2016), http://www.ccsso.org/Documents/2016/CCS-SOStateoftheStateSpeechPreparedRemarks04042016.pdf, 5.

9. Michele McNeil, "Many States Left Key NCLB Flexibility on the Table," *Education Week*, April 16, 2014, http://www.edweek.org/ew/articles/2014/04/10/28multiple.h33.html.

10. Kevin Haggerty, Jenna Elgin, and Andrew Woolley, "Social-Emotional Learning Assessment Measures for Middle School Youth" (Seattle: Social Development Research Group, University of Washington, 2011), https://audition.prevention.org/Resources/documents/SELTools.pdf.

11. Michele McNeil, "U.S. Department of Education Grants California Districts' CORE Waiver," *Politics K–12*, August 6, 2013, http://blogs.edweek.org/edweek/campaign-k-12/2013/08/us _education_department_grants.html.

12. Interview with the author, April 20, 2016.

13. Maine Department of Education, "Data Quality Recertification Training Starts Nov. 7," *Maine DOE Newsroom*, October 26, 2011, http://mainedoenews.net/2011/10/26/ data-quality-recertification/.

14. Data Quality Campaign, "10 State Actions," *State Analysis by State Action* (2014), http:// dataqualitycampaign.org/your-states-progress/10-state-actions/.

15. Martin R. West and Paul E. Peterson, "The Adequacy Lawsuit: A Critical Appraisal," in *School Money Trials: The Legal Pursuit of Educational Adequacy*, eds. Martin R. West and Paul E. Peterson (Washington, DC: Brookings Institution Press, 2007), 1–22, http://www.jstor.org /stable/10.7864/j.ctt1261zg.

16. Michael Rebell, quoted in Robert M. Costrell, "The Winning Defense in Massachusetts," in *School Money Trials*, 278–304, http://www.jstor.org/stable/10.7864/j.ctt1261zg.

17. Christopher Berry and Charles Wysong, "Making Courts Matter: Politics and the Implementation of State Supreme Court Decisions," *The University of Chicago Law Review* 79, no. 1 (2012): 1–29, http://www.jstor.org/stable/41552893.

18. Alyson Klein, "Ed. Dept.'s Plan for Remaking Turnaround Grants Not Flexible, Educators Say," *Education Week*, October 9, 2014, http://blogs.edweek.org/edweek/campaign-k-12/2014/10/ed_depts_proposal_for_remaking.html.

19. Interview with the author, April 20, 2016.

20. Alyson Klein, "New SIG Data Serve Up Same Old Conclusion: Mixed Results," *Education Week*, November 12, 2015, http://blogs.edweek.org/edweek/campaign-k-12/2015/11/new_ sig_data_serves_up_same_ol.html.

21. Greg Anrig, "Five Things Successful Turnaround Schools Have in Common," *Education Week*, August 19, 2015, http://www.edweek.org/ew/articles/2015/08/19/five-things-successful-turn-around-schools-have-in.html; Nelson Smith, "Redefining the School District in America" (Washington, DC: Thomas B. Fordham Institute, 2015), http://eric.ed.gov/?id=ED559998.

22. Anrig, "Five Things."

23. Arnold Shober, *Splintered Accountability: State Governance and Education Reform* (Albany, NY: SUNY Press, 2011).

24. Suzanne Perez Tobias, "New Vision for Kansas Education Stresses Individual Students, Soft Skills," *Wichita Eagle*, October 27, 2015, http://www.kansas.com/news/local/education/ article41527896.html.

25. ESSA Implementation: Perspectives from Education Stakeholders Senate Health Education Labor and Pensions (HELP) Committee, Washington, DC, May 18, 2016 (testimony of Dr. Tony Evers, State Superintendent of Public Instruction, Wisconsin), http://www.help.senate. gov/download/testimony/evers-testimony.

26. Daarel Burnette II, "States Rush to Retool Accountability Following ESSA Passage," *Education Week*, March 16, 2016, http://www.edweek.org/ew/articles/2016/03/16/states-rush-to-retool-accountability-following-essa.html, 16.

27. Andy Smarick, "States v. Districts in the Every Student Succeeds Act," *Flypaper*, December 4, 2015, http://edexcellence.net/articles/states-v-districts-in-the-every-student-succeeds-act.

28. Marci Kanstoroom, Robert D. Muller, and Eric C. Osberg, "Foreword," in *A Byte at the Apple: Rethinking Education Data for the Post-NCLB Era*, eds. Marci Kanstoroom and Eric C. Osberg (Washington, DC: Thomas B. Fordham Institute, 2008), i–xix, xi; Kansas Department of

Education, "DQC DC Resource Navigation 2015–2016," August 31, 2015, http://community
.ksde.org/Portals/26/DQC%20DC%20Resource%20Navigation%202015-2016.pdf.

29. Kalil Deschamps, "2015 Pennsylvania Department of Education Data Summit: Moving
Beyond Compliance: Getting Value Out of Data," *REL Mid-Atlantic*, (December 19, 2014),
https://www.relmidatlantic.org/
content/2015-pennsylvania-department-education-data-summit-moving-beyond-compli-
ance-getting-value.

30. US Department of Education, "Dear Colleague Letter About Family Educational Rights and
Privacy Act (FERPA) Final Regulations," January 12, 2010, http://www2.ed.gov/policy/gen/
guid/fpco/hottopics/ht12-17-08.html.

31. Alyson Klein, "ESSA Committee Agrees on Special Education Testing Rules," *Education
Week*, April 19, 2016, http://blogs.edweek.org/edweek/speced/2016/04/essa_committee_
agrees_on_speci.html.

32. Manna, *Collision Course.*

33. Michael B. Henderson, Paul E. Peterson, and Martin R. West, "The 2015 EdNext Poll on
School Reform," *Education Next*, 2016, http://educationnext.
org/2015-ednext-poll-school-reform-opt-out-common-core-unions/.

34. Henderson, Peterson, and West, "The 2015 EdNext Poll on School Reform."

35. Sefe Emokpae, "Governor McAuliffe Talks SOL Reform with Local Students," *Newsplex*,
October 6, 2015, http://www.newsplex.com/home/headlines/Governor-Terry-McAuliffe-
Talks-SOL-Reform-with-Local-Students--330798942.html.

36. Interview with the author, April 20, 2016.

Chapter 8

1. Cheryl H. Lee et al., *State Government Finances Summary Report* (Washington, DC: US
Census Bureau, 2015).

2. National Center for Education Statistics, Digest of Education Statistics, "Table 162: Revenues
for Public Elementary and Secondary Schools, by Source of Funds: Selected Years, 1919–20
through 2004–05" and Mobile Digest of Education Statistics, "Table 32: Percentage Distribution of Revenues for Public Elementary and Secondary Schools, by Source of Funds: Select
Years, 1979–80 through 2010–11."

3. National Center for Policy Analysis (NCPA), "The Growth of Federal Involvement in
Education,"
NCPA.org, August 28, 2014, http://www.ncpa.org/sub/dpd/index.php?Article_ID=24794.

4. Government Accountability Office, *Federal Education Funding: Overview of K–12 and Early
Childhood Education Programs* (Washington, DC: US Government Accountability Office,
2010).

5. See Susan Welch and Kay Thompson, "The Impact of Federal Incentives on State Policy
Innovation," *American Journal of Political Science* 24, no. 4 (1980): 715–729. While federal
grants are designed to achieve national goals, Welch and Thompson point out that rarely is the
federal government "the inventor" of a policy; rather, the federal government seeks to get all
states to do what at least some states have already tried.

6. NCPA, "The Growth of Federal Involvement in Education."

7. See US Department of Education, "State and Local Implementation of the No Child Left
Behind Act, Volume VI—Targeting and Uses of Federal Education Funds," *Policy and Program
Studies Service Report Highlights* (Washington, DC: US Department of Education, 2010). See
also Jack Jennings, Caitlin Scott, and Nancy Kober, "Lessons Learned from Five States Over
Five Years," *Education Week* 28, no. 31 (2009): 30–36.

8. Washington Research Project and the National Association for the Advancement of Colored People, *Helping Poor Children? Title I of ESEA. A Report* (Washington, DC, and New York: WRP and NAACP, 1969).

9. Jon Fullerton and Dalia Hochman, *Title I Fiscal Requirements and School District Management: The Consequences of Intergovernmental Distrust* (Washington, DC: Center for American Progress and American Enterprise Institute, 2011).

10. Patrick Murphy, *Help Wanted: Flexibility for Innovative State Education Agencies* (Washington, DC: Center for American Progress, 2014).

11. Emmarie Huetteman and Motoko Rich, "House Restores Local Education Control in Revising No Child Left Behind," *New York Times*, December 2, 2015.

12. National Governors Association, "National Governors Association Issues First Bill Endorsement in Nearly 20 Years," November 30, 2015, http://www.nga.org/cms/home/news-room/news-releases/2015--news-releases/col2-content/nations-governors-endorse-esea.html.

13. Kelly McManus (Interim Director of Legislative Affairs, Education Trust) in discussion with the author, April 30, 2016.

14. Ashley Jochim and Patrick McGuinn, "The Politics of Common Core Assessments," *Education Next* (forthcoming, fall 2016). See also Ashley Jochim and Lesley Lavery, "The Evolving Politics of the Common Core: Policy Implementation and Conflict Expansion," *Publius* 45, no. 3 (2015): 380–404.

15. Anthony Cave, "Is Common Core No More?" *Politifact*, February 29, 2016, http://www.politifact.com/arizona/statements/2016/feb/29/john-mccain/common-core-no-more/.

16. Daarel Burnette II, "Here's an Early Look at Education Legislation Proposed This Year," *Education Week*, March 28, 2016, http://blogs.edweek.org/edweek/state_edwatch/2016/03/heres_an_early_look_at_education_legislation_passed_this_year.html.

17. Cindy Long, "Six Ways ESSA Will Improve Assessments," *NEA Today*, March 10, 2016, http://neatoday.org/2016/03/10/essa-assessments/.

18. Lorraine M. McDonnell, "No Child Left Behind and the Federal Role in Education: Evolution or Revolution?" *Peabody Journal of Education* 80, no. 2 (2005): 19.

19. Carmel Martin, Scott Sargrad, and Samantha Batel, *Making the Grade: A 50-State Analysis of School Accountability Systems* (Washington, DC: Center for American Progress, 2016).

20. Michael Petrilli, "ESSA Accountability: Don't Forget the High Achievers," *Flypaper*, March 28, 2016, https://edexcellence.net/articles/essa-accountability-dont-forget-the-high-achievers.

21. Michael J. Petrilli, "The Proposed ESSA Regulations: Return of the Bureaucrats," *Flypaper*, May 26, 2016, https://edexcellence.net/articles/the-proposed-essa-regulations-return-of-the-bureaucrats.

22. The law requires states to identify the lowest 5 percent of schools statewide based on the five indicators, high schools with graduations below 67 percent, and schools with consistently underperforming subgroups. Each of the required indicators must carry "substantial" weight and the academic indicators must be given a weight "much greater" than either the school quality or student success indicator. See Andrew Ujifusa, "Your Cheat Sheet for the Proposed ESSA Accountability Rules," *Education Week*, June 7, 2016.

23. National Council on Teacher Quality, *State of the States 2015: Evaluating Teaching, Leading, and Learning* (Washington, DC: NCTQ, 2015).

24. Stephen Sawchuk, "ESSA Loosens Reins on Teacher Evaluations, Qualifications," *Education Week*, January 5, 2016, http://www.edweek.org/ew/articles/2016/01/06/essa-loosens-reins-on-teacher-evaluations-qualifications.html.

25. Ibid.

26. Denise Juneau, Office of Public Instruction, State of Montana, Letter to US Department of Education, May 29, 2015, https://www2.ed.gov/programs/titleiparta/equitable/mtequityplan 102815.pdf.

27. Teach Plus, "Teach Plus Agenda for Teacher Preparation Reform," (Washington, DC: Teach Plus, 2014), http://www.teachplus.org/sites/default/files/downloads/Documents/teach_plus _teacher_prep_agenda_10.20.14.pdf.

28. Gail L. Sunderman, James S. Kim, and Gary Orfield, eds., *NCLB Meets School Realities: Lessons from the Field* (Los Angeles: Corwin Press, 2005).

29. Marguerite Roza et al., "How Within-District Spending Inequities Help Some Schools to Fail," *Brookings Papers on Education Policy* 7 (2004): 201–227.

30. Marguerite Roza, "The Sunlight Effect: More Equitable Spending on Its Way Regardless of Rulemaking," Brown Center Chalkboard, April 27, 2016, http://www.brookings.edu/blogs/ brown-center-chalkboard/posts/2016/04/27-sunlight-effect-equitable-spending-education- roza.

31. McManus, discussion with the author, April 30, 2016.

32. Michele McNeil, "Many States Left Key NCLB Flexibility on the Table," *Education Week*, April 10, 2014, http://www.edweek.org/ew/articles/2014/04/10/28multiple.h33.html.

Chapter 9

1. Richard Carranza, Council of the Great City Schools' executive committee meeting, July 18, 2015.

2. Discussion with Carl Thornblad, former executive director of the Council of the Great City Schools, June 10, 2015.

3. Unpublished analysis of federal funding to urban schools (Washington, DC: Council of the Great City Schools).

4. Letter to Congressman Boehner and Senator Kennedy on the Council of the Great City Schools' position on No Child Left Behind, December 13, 2001.

5. For further information, see Alisha Green, "It's Complicated: State and Local Government Relationships," *Sunlight Foundation Blog*, February 19, 2013, https://sunlightfoundation.com /blog/2013/02/19/its-complicated-state-and-local-government-relationships/.

6. Gabriela Uro and Alejandra Barrio, *English Language Learners in America's Great City Schools: Demographics, Achievement and Staffing* (Washington, DC: Council of the Great City Schools, 2013).

7. Gabriela Uro, unpublished survey results from the Council of the Great City Schools on the numbers of unaccompanied minors enrolling in urban schools, 2013.

8. Tom Ahart, testimony to the US Senate Committee on Health, Education, Labor and Pensions, Council of the Great City Schools, Washington, DC, May 18, 2016.

9. Stephen Goldsmith, "Mending the City-State Relationship," *Governing Magazine*, December 22, 2010, http://www.governing.com/blogs/bfc/mending-city-state-relationship.html.

10. Discussion with Airick West, president of the Kansas City (MO) Board of Education, January 23, 2016.

11. An example of a charter school law that applies only to the two biggest city school systems in the state is found in Missouri. Examples of state revenue caps on local governments and schools are found in Texas, Indiana, and New York.

12. Council of the Great City Schools, *Analysis of the Effect of the FY82 and FY83 Reagan Budget Proposals on Urban Schools* (Washington, DC: Council of the Great City Schools, 1982); Jonathon Lachlan-Haché, Manish Naik, and Michael Casserly, *The School Improvement Grant*

Rollout in America's Great City Schools (Washington, DC: Council of the Great City Schools, 2012).

13. http://www2.ed.gov/policy/elsec/leg/essa/session.html.
14. Barbara Jenkins, Council of the Great City Schools' legislative meeting, March 2015.
15. Michael Casserly, proposal to the National Assessment Governing Board (NAGB) to conduct trial NAEP assessment for large urban school districts, Council of the Great City Schools, Washington, DC, November 17, 2000.

Chapter 10

1. *Is It Helping Poor Children? ESEA Title I. A Report* (Washington, DC, and New York: Washington Research Project and NAACP Legal Defense Fund, Inc., 1969).
2. Ibid.
3. Commission on Chapter 1, *Making Schools Work for Children in Poverty* (Washington, DC: Council of Chief State School Officers, 1992).
4. Robert Gordon, "Democrats and the Future of Education Reform," *New Republic*, May 26, 2005.

Chapter 11

1. David Cohen and Susan Moffitt, *The Ordeal of Equality: Did Federal Regulation Fix the Schools?* (Cambridge, MA: Harvard University Press, 2009), 16.
2. Ibid., 20–24.
3. James S. Coleman, *Equality of Educational Opportunity* (Washington, DC: National Center of Educational Statistics, 1966), http://files.eric.ed.gov/fulltext/ED012275.pdf.
4. http://govinfo.library.unt.edu/negp/page3-7.htm.
5. Clinton's luck with Congress ran out fast, as the 1994 election brought a GOP majority in the House and several efforts to roll back sundry federal education programs, even to abolish the Department of Education. These mostly got nowhere but did manage to stymie the president's plan to create "voluntary national tests." The "voluntary national academic standards" that were launched under Bush—by Lynne Cheney and Diane Ravitch, of all people—and completed under Clinton mostly fell of their own weight.

Afterword

1. Patricia Albjerg Graham, *Schooling America: How the Public Schools Meet the Nation's Changing Needs* (New York: Oxford University Press, 2005).
2. National Commission on Excellence in Education, *A Nation at Risk: The Imperative for Educational Reform* (Washington, DC: The Commission, 1983).
3. Andrew C. Porter, Mitchell D. Chester, and Michael D. Schlesinger, "Framework for an Effective Assessment and Accountability Program: The Philadelphia Example," *Teachers College Press* 106, no. 6 (June 2004): 1358–1400.

Acknowledgments

O ver the years, we've been deeply involved in conversations about federal K–12 education policy. We've opined about what makes for good policy in essays, in op-eds, and behind the scenes. Our understanding of federal policy has been enormously influenced by the generous insights of fellow policy scholars, advocates, practitioners, and Capitol Hill staff.

But this book isn't about our opinions; it's an effort to provide you with insights from a diverse cast of expert academics and analysts in order to help you make sense of the federal education landscape and what the Every Student Succeeds Act means for America's schools. We are deeply indebted to this volume's contributors, who have been a pleasure to work with and learn from.

We are also indebted to the American Enterprise Institute (AEI) and its president, Arthur Brooks, as well as to the Manhattan Institute and its president, Lawrence Mone, for their steadfast support. We'd like to thank the terrific staff at AEI, especially Jenn Hatfield and Sarah DuPre, who provided key assistance during the editing process. Finally, we express our gratitude to the Harvard Education Press team, especially our editor, Caroline Chauncey, who offered skillful and timely guidance throughout the course of this project.

About the Editors

Frederick M. Hess is director of education policy studies at the American Enterprise Institute (AEI). An educator, political scientist, and author, he studies K–12 and higher education issues. His books include *The Cage-Busting Teacher*, *Cage-Busting Leadership*, *Breakthrough Leadership in the Digital Age*, *The Same Thing Over and Over*, *Education Unbound*, *Common Sense School Reform*, *Revolution at the Margins*, and *Spinning Wheels*. He is also the author of the popular *Education Week* blog *Rick Hess Straight Up*, and is a regular contributor to *The Hill* and to *National Review Online*.

Hess's work has appeared in scholarly and popular outlets such as *Teachers College Record*, *Harvard Education Review*, *Social Sciences Quarterly*, *Urban Affairs Review*, *American Politics Quarterly*, *Chronicle of Higher Education*, *Phi Delta Kappan*, *Educational Leadership*, *U.S. News & World Report*, *USA Today*, *Washington Post*, *New York Times*, *Wall Street Journal*, *The Atlantic*, and *National Affairs*. He has edited widely cited volumes on the Common Core, the role of for-profits in education, education philanthropy, school costs and productivity, the impact of education research, and No Child Left Behind.

Hess serves as executive editor of *Education Next*, as lead faculty member for the Rice Educational Entrepreneurship Program, and on the review board for the Broad Prize for Public Charter Schools. He also serves on the board of directors of the National Association of Charter School Authorizers and 4.0 SCHOOLS.

A former high school social studies teacher, Hess teaches or has taught at the University of Virginia, the University of Pennsylvania, Georgetown University, Rice University, and Harvard University. He holds an MA and PhD in government, as well as an MEd in teaching and curriculum from Harvard University.

Max Eden is a senior fellow at the Manhattan Institute (MI). Before joining MI, he was program manager of the education policy studies department at the American Enterprise Institute. His research interests include early education, school choice, and higher education reform.

Eden's work has appeared in scholarly and popular outlets such as the *Journal of School Choice, Encyclopedia of Education Economics and Finance, Washington Post, U.S. News & World Report, National Review, Claremont Review of Books*, and the *Weekly Standard*. He holds a BA in history from Yale University.

About the Contributors

Chad Aldeman is an associate partner at Bellwether Education Partners and served at high levels in the Obama administration's Department of Education, where he worked on ESEA waivers, teacher preparation, and the Teacher Incentive Fund. He penned several of the most cutting critiques of ESSA in major outlets including the *Washington Post* and the *Wall Street Journal*. His work has also been featured in the *New York Times*, *Inside HigherEd*, *Newsday*, and the *Des Moines Register*.

Charles Barone is the director of policy at Democrats for Education Reform (DFER) and Education Reform Now (ERN). He has led DFER's and ERN's efforts on reauthorizing the Every Student Succeeds Act, advising President Obama's 2008 transition team, advocating for state reforms under Obama's Race to the Top initiative, and setting DFER's policy agenda at the state and federal level in areas including accountability and testing, teacher preparation, and charter schools. Barone's work on education and children's issues over the past three decades has emphasized equity and excellence and spanned direct service, research, policy, and advocacy. He has authored numerous articles and book chapters on both policy and politics in peer-reviewed scholarly journals, trade publications, and mainstream media. A Capitol Hill veteran, Barone went to DC as an American Association for the Advancement of Science Congressional Fellow and became a top education advisor to the late Senator Paul Simon (D-IL) and to Congressman George Miller (D-CA). Under Miller, he acted as lead negotiator for House Democrats on the No Child Left Behind Act of 2001. Before his entry into Washington politics, Barone was a postdoctoral fellow in children's mental health at the Department of Psychology at Yale University, where he conducted basic and applied research in the New Haven Public School District. He has a doctorate in clinical/community psychology from the University of Maryland, College Park, and a bachelor's degree from the University of California, Santa Barbara.

Cynthia G. Brown is a senior fellow at the Center for American Progress. She was previously the vice president for education policy at American Progress through January 2014. Brown has spent more than forty-five years working in a variety of professional positions addressing high-quality, equitable public education. Prior to joining American Progress in 2004, she was an independent education consultant who advised and wrote for local and state school systems, education associations, foundations, and nonprofit organizations. From 1986 through September 2001, Brown served as director of the Resource Center on Educational Equity of the Council of Chief State School Officers. In 1980, she was appointed by President Carter as the first assistant secretary for civil rights in the US Department of Education. Prior to that position, she served as principal deputy of the Department of Health, Education and Welfare's Office for Civil Rights. Subsequent to this government service, she was codirector of the nonprofit Equality Center. Before the Carter administration, she worked for the Lawyers' Committee for Civil Rights Under Law and the Children's Defense Fund, and she began her career in the HEW Office for Civil Rights as an investigator. Brown has a master's degree in public administration from the Maxwell School at Syracuse University and a BA from Oberlin College. She serves on the board of directors of the American Youth Policy Forum, Perry Street Preparatory Public Charter School, and the Policy Innovators in Education Network.

Michael Casserly is the executive director of the Council of the Great City Schools, the nation's primary coalition of urban public school systems. Casserly has been in the middle of most federal education policy debates for nearly forty years, and has participated in six complete reauthorizations of the Elementary and Secondary Education Act. As head of the Council, Casserly has unified the nation's urban schools around a vision of education reform and initiated numerous national and local initiatives that have helped spur higher academic achievement among urban school students.

Mitchell D. Chester has served as Massachusetts Commissioner of Elementary and Secondary Education since May 2008. Chester began his career as an elementary school teacher in Connecticut, and later served as a middle school assistant principal and district curriculum coordinator. From there he moved to the Connecticut State Department of Education, where he oversaw curriculum and instructional programs. In 1997 he was named the Executive Director for Accountability and Assessment for the School District of Philadelphia, where he headed the offices of Assessment, Research and Evaluation, Student and School Progress, and Pupil Information Services. In 2001 Chester moved to Ohio, where he served as the Senior Associate Superintendent for Policy and Accountability for the Ohio Department of Education, where he oversaw standards, assessments, accountability, policy development, and strategic planning. He was responsible for Ohio's implementation of the No Child Left Behind Act. Chester participates in a number of national and international education policy initiatives, including as a member of the National Assessment Governing Board. He holds a doctorate in administration, planning, and social policy from Harvard University, as well as advanced degrees from the University of Connecticut and the University of Hartford.

Chester E. Finn, Jr. is a scholar, educator, and public servant who has been at the forefront of the national education debate for forty years. He is currently a senior fellow at Stanford's Hoover Institution and president emeritus of the Thomas B. Fordham Institute, where he is also a distinguished senior fellow. Finn is the author of a dozen books and more than four hundred articles, and his work has appeared in publications including *National Affairs*, *Commentary*, the *Public Interest*, the *Wall Street Journal*, *Education Next*, the *New York Times*, and *Education Week*. He has previously served as a professor at Vanderbilt University, counsel to the US ambassador to India, legislative director for Senator Daniel Patrick Moynihan, and assistant US Secretary of Education for research and improvement.

Jeffrey R. Henig is a professor of political science and education at Teachers College and professor of political science at Columbia University. He is the author, coauthor, or coeditor of ten books, the most recent being *The New Education Philanthropy: Politics, Policy, and Reform*. His book *Spin Cycle: How Research Gets Used in Policy Debates: The Case of Charter Schools* won the American Educational Research Association's Outstanding Book Award in 2010. Henig's scholarly work on urban politics, racial politics, privatization, and school reform has appeared in journals including the *American Journal of Education* and *Educational Evaluation and Policy Analysis*, and his more popular writing has appeared in outlets including *Education Week*, the *Chronicle of Higher Education,* the *Boston Globe,* the *Los Angeles Times,* the *Washington Post,* and the *New York Times.*

David M. Houston is a PhD candidate at Teachers College, Columbia University. His research interests include public opinion and education policy. He is currently studying education policy preferences and the political conditions under which various social and economic groups are more likely to get what they want from their school districts, cities, and states.

Alyson Klein is a reporter for *Education Week.* She covers federal policy and Congress and reported on the ESEA reauthorization process at length. She is coauthor of *Education Week's Politics K–12* blog, where she pens several posts a week, and often several posts a day, on the ins and outs of DC education politics. She's widely acknowledged as the go-to reporter for breaking education news and insights into how key players in DC are thinking and what they are doing.

Ashley Jochim is a research analyst at the Center on Reinventing Public Education. Her work there focuses on policy analysis and implementation, including work on state education agencies, Common Core standards, school choice, and district reform. Her research can be found in the *Policy Studies Journal, Politics and Governance,* and *Political Research Quarterly,* as well as in numerous edited volumes including the *Handbook of School Choice* and the *Oxford Handbook of American Bureaucracy.* Jochim is coauthor of *A Democratic Constitution for Public Education.* She holds a BA in political science and psychology and an MA and PhD in political science, all from the University of Washington.

Melissa Arnold Lyon is a PhD student in politics and education at Teachers College, Columbia University. Her research interests include urban education politics and policy regarding race, class, and neighborhoods. Prior to attending Teachers College, Lyon studied political science at Rice University, taught sixth grade, and supported beginning teachers.

Patrick McGuinn is a professor of political science and education and chair of the political science department at Drew University, and a senior research specialist at the Consortium for Policy Research in Education. He focuses on American politics and public policy and is the author of three books on education: *No Child Left Behind and the Transformation of Federal Education Policy, 1965–2005*; *Education Governance for the 21st Century: Overcoming the Structural Barriers to School Reform*; and *The Convergence of K–12 and Higher Education: Policies and Programs in a Changing Era*. McGuinn is a former member of the Institute for Advanced Study in Princeton and has produced a number of policy reports for the Brookings Institution, the American Enterprise Institute, the Center for American Progress, the New America Foundation, and the Thomas B. Fordham Institute.

Arnold F. Shober is an associate professor of government at Lawrence University. An expert in education politics, policy shifts, and state accountability, he is the author of *In Common No More: The Politics of the Common Core State Standards*; *Out of Many, One? The Democratic Dilemma of American Education*; and *Splintered Accountability: State Governance and Education Reform*. His work focuses on governance and education policy, and he teaches courses on public policy, parties and elections, public opinion, and American federalism. His work on state education policy has appeared in journals such as the *Peabody Journal of Education* and *Policy Studies Journal*.

Martin West is an associate professor of education at the Harvard Graduate School of Education and a faculty research fellow at the National Bureau of Economic Research. He is also deputy director of the Harvard Kennedy School's Program on Education Policy and Governance and editor-in-chief of *Education Next*. West studies the politics of K–12 education in the United States and how education policies affect student learning and noncognitive development. In 2013–2014, West worked as senior education policy advisor to the ranking member of the US Senate Committee on Health, Education, Labor, and Pensions. He previously taught at Brown University and was a research fellow at the Brookings Institution, where he is now a nonresident senior fellow.

Index